A Swedish Kitchen

RECIPES AND REMINISCENCES

The Hippocrene Cookbook Library

Afghan Food & Cookery
African Cooking, Best of Regional
Albanian Cooking, Best of
Alps, Cuisines of The
Aprovecho: A Mexican-American Border Cookbook
Argentina Cooks!, Exp. Ed.
Austrian Cuisine, Best of, Exp. Ed.
Belgian Cookbook, A
Bolivian Kitchen, My Mother's
Brazilian Cookery, The Art of
Bulgarian Cooking, Traditional
Burma, Flavors of
Cajun Women, Cooking with
Calabria, Cucina di
Caucasus Mountains, Cuisines of The
Chile, Tasting
Colombian, Secrets of Cooking
Croatian Cooking, Best of, Exp. Ed.
Czech Cooking, Best of, Exp. Ed.
Danube, All Along The, Exp. Ed.
Dutch Cooking, Art of, Exp. Ed.
Egyptian Cooking
Eritrea, Taste of
Filipino Food, Fine
Finnish Cooking, Best of
French Caribbean Cuisine
French Fashion, Cooking in the (Bilingual)
Germany, Spoonfuls of
Greek Cuisine, The Best of, Exp. Ed.
Gypsy Feast
Haiti, Taste of
Havana Cookbook, Old (Bilingual)
Hungarian Cookbook
Hungarian Cooking, Art of, Rev. Ed.
Icelandic Food & Cookery
India, Flavorful
Indian Spice Kitchen
International Dictionary of Gastronomy
Irish-Style, Feasting Galore
Italian Cuisine, Treasury of (Bilingual)
Japanese Home Cooking
Korean Cuisine, Best of
Laotian Cooking, Simple

Latvia, Taste of
Lithuanian Cooking, Art of
Macau, Taste of
Mayan Cooking
Mexican Culinary Treasures
Middle Eastern Kitchen, The
Mongolian Cooking, Imperial
New Hampshire: from Farm to Kitchen
Norway, Tastes and Tales of
Persian Cooking, Art of
Poland's Gourmet Cuisine
Polish Cooking, Best of, Exp. Ed.
Polish Country Kitchen Cookbook
Polish Cuisine, Treasury of (Bilingual)
Polish Heritage Cookery, Ill. Ed.
Polish Traditions, Old
Portuguese Encounters, Cuisines of
Pyrenees, Tastes of
Quebec, Taste of
Rhine, All Along The
Romania, Taste of, Exp. Ed.
Russian Cooking, Best of, Exp. Ed.
Scandinavian Cooking, Best of
Scotland, Traditional Food from
Scottish-Irish Pub and Hearth Cookbook
Sephardic Israeli Cuisine
Sicilian Feasts
Slovak Cooking, Best of
Smorgasbord Cooking, Best of
South African Cookery, Traditional
South American Cookery, Art of
South Indian Cooking, Healthy
Spanish Family Cookbook, Rev. Ed.
Sri Lanka, Exotic Tastes of
Swiss Cookbook, The
Syria, Taste of
Taiwanese Cuisine, Best of
Thai Cuisine, Best of, Regional
Turkish Cuisine, Taste of
Ukrainian Cuisine, Best of, Exp. Ed.
Uzbek Cooking, Art of
Warsaw Cookbook, Old

A Swedish Kitchen

RECIPES AND REMINISCENCES

Judith Pierce Rosenberg

HIPPOCRENE BOOKS
NEW YORK

The author gratefully acknowledges the permission of publishers to reprint excerpts from the following copyrighted material:

Excerpts from *Kondisboken: Klassika Svenska Kaféer och Knditorier.* pp. 7 and 67. Stockholm, Sweden: Albert Bonniers Förlag, 1996. Used by permission of Albert Bonniers Förlag.

From "Rånoch Våfflor," *Gastronomisk Kalender.* p. 97. Stockholm, Sweden: Gastronomiska Akademien, 1964. Used by permission of Gastronomiska Akademien.

From *Smörgåsbord: A Swedish Classic.* p. 6. Stockholm, Sweden: Svenska Institutet, 1996. Used by permission of Svenska Institutet.

From *Sveriges Historia i Fickformat.* p. 58. Stockholm, Sweden: LTs Förlag, 1995. Used by permission of LTs Förlag.

Book and jacket design by Acme Klong Design, Inc.
Cover art © Bonnier Holding AB, *Christmas Eve* by Carl Larsson, 1904

For more information, address:
HIPPOCRENE BOOKS, INC.
171 Madison Avenue
New York, NY 10016

ISBN 0-7818-1059-0
Cataloging-in-Publication Data available from the Library of Congress.
Printed in the United States of America.

Acknowledgements

This book would not have been possible without the help of many people. I want to particularly thank the following:

My family and friends in Sweden, especially Thomas, Kerstin, Frida, Carl and Elin Rosenberg; Anne-Marie Malmstedt; Margareta Rosenberg; Gunilla Gard; David and Birgitta Bartal; Ylva Egger; Peter and Ingeborg Gieguld; and Kalle and Riitta Norstedt.

My family in the States, especially Margaret Waterhouse; Thresia Korte Pierce, Duane and Lois Pierce, John and Cyndi Pierce, and Mark and Fen Pierce.

My editors Anne E. McBride and Rebecca Cole for their faith and their vision.

My colleagues in the culinary and writing fields, especially, Alice Arndt, Christina Fjellström, Lisa Forare Winbladh, Liselotte Forslin, Stefan Hällberg, Rachel Laudan, Ingmarie Lundh, Victoria Abbott Riccardi, Anne Robert, Kersti Wikström, Jennifer Wolcott.

My fellow teachers, students, and the administrators at Language Pacifica.

My mentor, Gail Pool, and the members of The Class who suggested this book and read and critiqued many versions.

My friends, Shelley Buck, Caryn Kupferman, Peggy Nemec-Groth, Elaine Sausotte, Rachel Travers, Elena Zhitnikov for their encouragement and support.

My husband, Carl, and my children, Michael and Christina, for everything.

Table of Contents

Preface

What is Swedish food? While some Americans may have heard the word "smorgas-bord," or even eaten meatballs with lingonberry jam at an IKEA furniture store, to most, Swedish cuisine is a mystery.

Sweden is vast. Looking out the window as the plane descends toward this coun-try that is roughly the size and shape of California, one sees lakes, woods, and fields. These, together with the country's extensive coastline, are the geographic fea-tures that have shaped the development of Swedish cuisine. From the Baltic Sea, the 100,000 lakes, and various rivers comes the wealth of fish and shellfish, such as herring, salmon, crayfish, and shrimp, which dominate the Swedish table. Forests cover 70 percent of the land mass, providing not only such game as moose, elk, reindeer, and wild birds, but also an abundance of mushrooms and berries. The fields are sown with wheat, barley, oats, and rye as well as fodder crops for pigs, sheep, and dairy cows.

Sweden is also a land where extremes in daylight are more pronounced than the seasonal differences in temperature. Although Stockholm shares the same latitude as Anchorage (59 degrees north), the former has milder weather, thanks to the Gulf Stream, with average temperatures ranging from about 27 degrees Fahrenheit in January to nearly 70 degrees in July. At the winter solstice, Stockholm has about six hours of daylight, while at Midsummer, there are eighteen, augmented by several hours of twilight. In the long summer days, root vegetables, particularly potatoes, carrots, and turnips, as well as other hardy produce, such as cabbages and apples, thrive.

The view from the airplane also reveals how sparsely populated this nation of 9 million people is. Until the mid-twentieth century, Sweden was a predominately rural society where people lived according to the rhythms of the seasons and the

Shaped like a giant snowball, Globen stadium is a distinctive feature of the Stockholm skyline.

church calendar. The court enjoyed a sophisticated cuisine that featured imported delicacies and followed French fashions; after all, the royal family is descended from Bernadotte, one of Napoleon's field marshals. Meanwhile, farmers made do with such staples as crispbread, salted and dried fish, cheese and other fermented dairy products, supplemented by wild berries, mushrooms, herbs and, for Christmas, pork. This simple, working class diet evolved into *husmanskost*, which loosely translates as "home cooking."

Today, Swedish cuisine is much closer to that of the court than of the peasant. Ordinary Swedes now have abundant access to imported foodstuffs, from Italian wines to cardamom and saffron, that were once reserved for the upper classes.

The timing and pattern of meals in modern Sweden is similar to that in the U.S. The day begins with breakfast between 6:00 and 8:00 A.M., often consisting of a sandwich of cheese and/or meat on a buttered roll. During the week, a substantial noon meal is usually eaten away from home, at company cafeterias or nearby restaurants. Most families eat their evening meal between 6:00 and 8:00 P.M., sometimes with a snack, such as sandwiches, before bed. For adults, coffee is the most popular beverage while children drink milk.

Not only the timing of meals but also the contents are similar in the two countries due in part to the commercial food industry. A growing percentage of Swedes begin the day with a bowl of American cornflakes and end it at McDonald's, snacking on soft drinks and chips in between.

In fact, the biggest change in the Swedish kitchen is its increasing internationalization, which reflects the country's changing demographics. Over the past twenty-five years, not only have more people immigrated to Sweden, thanks to generous asylum policies, but also more Swedes have traveled abroad. The result is that whereas pizza and pasta were once exotic, today they are so ordinary as to be considered part of *husmanskost*, while sushi, frozen yogurt, and pad thai are the latest trends.

As is true elsewhere in the world, some of the more time-consuming traditional dishes, such as *lutfisk*, or gelatinous cod, are either disappearing entirely or being replaced by factory-made products. And yet, some of the classics of *husmanskost*, dishes like Jansson's temptation, split pea soup with ham, apple cake with vanilla sauce, Lucia buns, and gingersnaps continue to be popular as comfort food. Adapted to the American kitchen, the recipes in this book celebrate these enduring classics.

Introduction

Summer mornings in Sweden, I often slip down to the kitchen for an hour of peace and quiet before my husband, Carl, and our two children, Michael and Tina, awaken. I sit at the pine table with my journal and a pile of recipe clippings, drinking coffee from a turquoise mug made by a local potter at Värmdö Krukmakeri. I watch the play of sunlight on the walls, papered in an indefinable mottled shade somewhere between pale yellow, apple green, and tan. From the glass door, partially open to catch the breeze, I can see the strip of unenclosed backyard, the oak tree, and beyond that, a meadow of tall grasses, some with heads the color of wheat, others tinged a soft violet. In the early morning silence, I often hear the soughing of the wind moving across this field, the air permeated with the damp, salty scent of the Baltic Sea.

On the far side of the field lies a footpath leading to Strömma Market, the grocery store that I eagerly return to each year, and the pier where the boat selling fresh salmon docks on summer Wednesdays and Saturdays. The main road that runs past the market leads from Fågelbrolandet, the land of the bird bridge, the island where we have our summer home, across three concrete bridges, to the city of Stockholm, where my husband spent much of his childhood.

For the past nine years, whenever we can get away from the demands of school and work in the U.S., my family and I come here to this forest-green house in the Stockholm archipelago. Here, we renew our ties with Sweden and with each other. We visit and host family and friends, explore the countryside by car or sailboat, attend museum exhibits and concerts, and indulge our taste for princess cake and reindeer stew.

More than two decades have passed since Carl and I first traveled to Stockholm together. We met at a commune in San Francisco in February, 1976. I was nineteen years old; Carl was nine months younger. On our first and only formal date, Carl took me out for a fondue dinner at a Swiss restaurant that reminded him of traveling through Europe with his Swedish father.

I had just received a small inheritance from my godmother and was eager to travel. Intrigued by Carl's dual nationality, I invited him to come with me to Sweden, a proposition he readily accepted. By the time we embarked on our journey, we had known each other only seven weeks.

On this, my first trip overseas, I was young, wildly in love, living intensely in the present, completely open to new experiences. Although I was sometimes overwhelmed by jet lag and the sheer newness of my surroundings, I clearly remember being awed by Stockholm's grandeur. The confluent waters of Lake Mälaren and the

Baltic Sea seemed to lace the city's islands together like so many blue ribbons. The sun glinted off the golden spires that towered above the green copper roofs in medieval Gamla Stan, the oldest part of the city, while the contemporary glass and steel structures downtown shone like polished mirrors. Everywhere, the crisp sea breezes carried the soft, lilting tones of the Swedish language.

Naturally, we stayed with Carl's father at his Stockholm apartment. Considerably older than my own father, Arne was a kindly, well-educated, cosmopolitan European, a gourmet who took me to all his favorite markets and restaurants, introducing me to the dishes he loved, from yellow split pea soup with smoked ham to fine-grained Swedish caviar on toast to clabbered milk with gingersnaps.

But my curiosity about other cultures and their cuisines had been awakened a decade earlier at a Christmas bazaar at Sacred Heart College, my mother's alma mater. I can still recall the long table, decorated with little paper flags and laden with platters of cookies: Austrian linzer bars, Greek baklava, Mexican wedding cookies, and delicate Swedish dreams. In the early 1960s, this was a truly exotic experience for a young middle-class girl growing up in Wichita, Kansas, in a family so assimilated and Americanized that all of the Old World recipes, customs, and traditions of our ancestors had been lost, save my mother's German Catholic faith. The sight of those flags, the taste of those sweets, opened a window to the wide world beyond the Kansas plains. I hungered for something more.

In the months following the bazaar, I checked out every international cookbook that I could find at the public library. My mother still teases me about the African recipe for bananas boiled in milk that seemed so unappetizing to her but that I insisted we try. I read dozens of foreign fairy tales, from stories of Irish leprechauns to Swedish trolls to Arabian genies. Later, I was drawn to books on the history and cultures of ancient Egypt, Aztec and Mayan Mexico, medieval England, and Heian-era Japan.

I not only read books about other places, I collected dolls dressed in foreign costumes: a Spanish flamenco dancer, a Mexican girl, an Indian boy in a Nehru jacket. I was likewise fascinated by languages, learning Pig Latin and how to count to ten in German, all that my mother had learned of her father's native tongue; I even tried to make up my own language.

As a child, I became curious about other cultures through cookies; as a young woman, I was immersed in Swedish culture by sharing meals with Carl's family and friends. A summer supper of tiny Swedish meatballs, boiled new potatoes, and a warm *kräm* of stewed gooseberries, cooked by Carl's brother Thomas and his wife Kerstin. A breakfast of just-baked waffles topped with cloudberries and whipped cream, at the home of our au pair Jenny's parents. An outdoor dinner of *tjälknul*, slow-roasted moose, thinly sliced like roast beef, with warm potato salad and, for dessert, *kolatårta*, a rich flourless chocolate and almond cake, prepared by our friends Peter and Ingeborg.

Years passed before I could hold a conversation in Swedish but to express my appreciation for the care lavished on me, I needed only three simple words, "*Tack för maten*," "Thanks for the food," the same phrase Swedish children are taught to say to their parents. Learning to cook in Swedish deepened my understanding of the language, just as traveling around Sweden and researching the history of foodstuffs and holidays has enriched my understanding of the culture.

Here in the Stockholm archipelago, I begin and end my day in the kitchen. As the shadows lengthen in the lavender twilight, I turn on the turquoise bell-shaped ceramic lamp from Värmdö Krukmakeri. Although we have no need for artificial light on these summer evenings, this lamp shining in the kitchen window is a Swedish custom observed year-round. Especially welcome during the months of winter darkness, such lamps warm not only those within but also

A view of the waterfront that runs along the Stockholm street Strandgatan.

passersby. As an outsider looking in on another culture, I see these lamps as symbolizing the warmth and comfort embodied in the Swedish ideal of home and my desire to be included at the kitchen table. Having a kitchen of my own in Sweden has allowed me to complete the circle and feed those who fed me.

Apprentice Cook

When I first travelled to Sweden in 1976, I had no idea that I was embarking on a fifteen-year apprenticeship in Swedish cooking. My goals were much simpler: I wanted to see Viking runestones and sample the local cuisine. A single tour through the Viking artifact collection at Stockholm's Historiska Museet satisfied my archaeological curiosity. But each taste of rosehip soup, gravlax with mustard-dill sauce, and warm cloudberry preserves over vanilla ice cream, only whetted my appetite and my desire to know more.

My future father-in-law, Arne Rosenberg, was the first bon vivant I had ever met. A tall, large but rather frail man, with thick glasses, a shock of dark brown hair, and an engaging manner, he immediately welcomed me into his family, even though I had known his eighteen-year-old son, Carl, only a few weeks. Arne had lived in the United States for fifteen years and had written two English-language books, *Air Travel Across the North Atlantic* and *Air Travel in Europe*, in which he eloquently argued for deregulation of international flights to facilitate the exchange of people and ideas. Generous with his time and knowledge, he clearly loved food, especially dining out.

I still have the menu from the first restaurant we visited, Gondolen. From the outside, this landmark actually looked like a gondola suspended seven stories above the streets of Stockholm, supported on one side by the headquarters of the restaurant's parent company and on the other by an elevator tower. The cover of the fold-out menu featured a full-color photograph of the restaurant's daytime panoramic view. But on that spring night, the three of us saw only twinkling lights and dark expanses of water through the triple-paned picture windows that lined both sides of the narrow room.

So many of the dishes listed inside the menu were totally new to me—roast pheasant, crepes filled with bay shrimps in a dill cream sauce, tournedos with béarnaise sauce, a broiled fish called brill, five varieties of herring. Encouraged by Arne, I eagerly chose the most exotic items. My dinner began with an appetizer of *löjromstoast*, fine-grained orange bleak roe served on toasted triangles of white bread, garnished with chopped red onion, sour cream, and a slice of lemon topped with a dill feather. I enjoyed the strange sensation of the tiny beads of caviar popping on my tongue. This was followed by a reindeer chop with stewed morel mushrooms. I did not think of Rudolf. For dessert, I chose a poached peach half filled with whipped cream flavored with *punsch*, a sweet anise liqueur, and topped with roasted almonds. I was captivated by the unusual flavors, so different from anything I had encountered in my previous nineteen years.

The second time Carl and I visited Arne, in 1978, we had a magnificent French dinner at Operakällaren, the city's most sumptuous restaurant. Arne had worked for a time in Paris, where he developed an appreciation for classical French cooking, the basis for Swedish court cuisine.

As a naive twenty-one-year-old, I was awed, and a little intimidated, by the efficient coterie of waiters, who seemed to anticipate my every move. I was also overwhelmed by the opulent dining room with its 1895 decor: carved oak-panelled walls, enormous chandeliers, and Oscar Björk's paintings of nubile young women cavorting by the water. These last caused such a scandal when first installed that King Oscar II was asked to intervene; he suggested that the painter could "allow the reeds to grow a little higher," which Björk did. The food was equally rich: salmon in puff pastry, creamy shrimp bisque, broiled lobster flavored with mustard and herbs—but what I remember most vividly was my disappointment that the Grand Marnier soufflé tasted not sweet but eggy.

Arne also introduced me to *husmanskost*, good home cooking. One dark December afternoon, we had the hearty traditional Thursday meal of *ärter med fläsk och plättor*, pea soup with ham followed by pancakes for dessert, at a downtown café. The peas in this thick, wintry soup were yellow split peas, cooked with cubes of ham that imparted a smoky flavor. Afterwards, we ate *plättor*, silver-dollar-size pancakes as light as crepes, their buttery richness offset by tart red lingonberry preserves.

On another occasion, Arne took us to the tearoom in the exclusive downtown department store NK (Nordiska Kompaniet), for what he called "the city's best *filbunke*," clabbered milk. In this now-vanished formal restaurant, with heavy, willow-green damask curtains and starched white tablecloths, we sampled one of the simplest Swedish dishes, clabbered milk, served in a clear glass bowl with a blue rim, accompanied by sugar to sprinkle on top and a side of gingersnap cookies. Eaten with a spoon, *filbunke* had the consistency of yogurt but tasted more like buttermilk. I'm not crazy about buttermilk but I certainly enjoyed that bowl of *filbunke*.

During these initial visits, I had very little exposure to Swedish home cooking. Not that we ate out every meal, but the simple dinners of boiled potatoes and fried hamburgers or Wiener schnitzel that we prepared in Arne's apartment were less adventuresome, and much less memorable, than our restaurant forays.

Two summers later, we returned to Sweden, for what would be our last visit with Arne. To say that 1980 was a year of tremendous change and stress would be an understatement. In April, Carl's paternal grandmother, Ingrid, died; in July, we wed; and in late August, we came to Sweden to visit family and friends. Although Carl's father was in failing health, his death that October was still a shock. And then on New Year's Eve, at thirteen minutes to midnight, our son, Michael Arne—big, healthy, and with a full head of hair—was born.

For the first time that summer, I met Arne's elder son Thomas, and Thomas' wife Kerstin, who lived with their children on the west coast of Sweden. Over the years since that first meeting, my relationship with Kerstin has become one of my most cherished friendships. Among the many, many things I have learned from her is the art of feeding a family. Just as my father-in-law shared his passion for Swedish restaurant fare, my sister-in-law introduced me to Swedish home cooking.

From the moment I walked through the pine door of Thomas and Kerstin's yellow wooden house, I felt welcomed. Kerstin immediately invited us to sit down at the kitchen table, as she has many times since. Within a few minutes the table was laden with fresh bread, rye crackers, butter, sliced tomatoes, cucumbers, liver pâté, salami, cheese, and orange marmalade, and she was asking "Would you like tea or coffee?"

Five months pregnant and continually ravenous, I was thrilled with the sandwiches. But these turned out to be only a prelude, a snack. In a short time, we were sitting down for a delicious dinner of small, juicy, browned Swedish meatballs, served in a thin pan gravy, with the traditional accompaniment, lingonberry jam; a salad of thinly sliced cucumbers from Kerstin's garden, marinated in white vinegar and a little sugar; and potatoes, also from the garden, mashed until silky smooth. For dessert, we had *äppelkaka med vaniljsås*, or warm apple cake with a hint of cinnamon, served with a pitcher of cold, creamy vanilla sauce.

While the four adults ate, six-year-old Frida and four-year-old Carl quietly nibbled their food and played on the long bench at the far end of the table. "Once you have children, mealtimes won't ever be the same—at least not for many years, " Thomas commented wryly.

Eight years older than Carl and I, Thomas and Kerstin seemed calm and confident as parents. No one else in our circles of friends, colleagues, or siblings had even thought about starting a family so, naturally, we looked to Thomas and Kerstin as role models, guides on the path ahead. Tall and willowy, Kerstin seemed warm and reserved, creative and correct. I admired her energy, her organizational skills, and her artistic talent expressed both in her oil paintings and on the larger canvas of her home. What surprised me was that Kerstin clearly derived pleasure from homemaking but she did not seem trapped by the domestic, as I feared that I would be. Sweden's comprehensive program of daycare and sick leave, generous maternity benefits and ample vacations, allowed her to have both a career as an elementary

Kerstin Rosenberg making a pie crust in her country kitchen.

school teacher and time at home with her children—and she clearly enjoyed both.

I was particularly amazed at how effortlessly Kerstin cooked, efficiently moving between the four-burner gas range, American-size refrigerator, stainless steel sink, and butcher-block counter, with occasional trips to the root cellar or the garden. Using fresh ingredients, she created simple, unpretentious dinners, arranged with an artistic flair. One night, for example, we feasted on succulent, baked whole salmon, edged on both sides with peas topped with slices of crisp cucumber and lemon—a feast for the eyes as well as the stomach. Kerstin had prepared her own mayonnaise to go with the fish, as well as a cool pineapple cream tart for dessert.

Kerstin not only cooked but she also baked, several times a week, loaves of what the French would call country bread, and each August bottled her own *saft*, or fruit syrup, from the red currant bush in her garden.

I happily spent hours in her kitchen, where Kerstin and I often had our best talks. Although I helped by scrubbing potatoes or peeling carrots, I was often too caught up in the conversation to pay adequate attention to how Kerstin boned a mackerel or stuffed a cabbage. What I learned from her had little to do with technique and a great deal to do with attitude, especially my attitude toward the essential task of feeding a family. Standing in Kerstin's kitchen, watching her whip up a sauce or turn out a cake, deftly and with a light heart, I realized that cooking could be a source of joy.

Three Red Spoons

In the summer of 1990, my relationship with Swedish food changed dramatically when I met Ingmarie Lundh. I had traveled to Sweden for a two-week intensive language course, under the auspices of Uppsala University. While the language teachers seemed bored, the cooking teacher, a jovial woman with a raspy smoker's voice and a ready laugh, expressed a contagious enthusiasm for her subject.

I knew that I had chosen the right elective from the very first evening when I sat down with Ingmarie and the dozen other students in the cooking class to feast on *skånsk äggkaka,* a puffy, golden-brown egg cake that tasted like a cross between a soufflé and a pancake, topped with crisp, lean bacon. Following this supper dish from the province of Skåne, we had *rabarberkräm*, a light rhubarb pudding sweetened with just enough sugar to balance the fruit's acidity, served warm with a splash of milk. All in all, a far cry from the previous evening's school cafeteria dinner of fried pork chops tasting of uncooked flour, mealy boiled potatoes, limp coleslaw, and insipid dried fruit soup.

Each afternoon, Ingmarie began class by reviewing the menu and recipes, all in Swedish. We then divided the work, each of us volunteering to help with a particular dish. After years of being limited to recipes translated into English and converted into American standard measurements, I was finally learning to cook both in Swedish and in metric.

Halfway through the course, I bought a set of three bright red metric measuring spoons to use with my growing file of metric recipes. These included a *matsked* and a *tesked*—the equivalent of a heaping American tablespoon and teaspoon—as well as a tiny spoon called a *kryddmått,* a spice measure, equivalent to one eighth of an American teaspoon.

Certain dishes from those marvelous classes stand out in my mind. One afternoon, we made my favorite Swedish pastry, *mazarin,* an almond tart with a white sugar icing. I was surprised to learn that the secret ingredient in the spongy filling of these moist tarts was mashed potatoes!

In Ingmarie's class, I had my first taste of *isterband*, a tangy pork, potato and barley sausage, served with *stuvad potatis,* or chunks of potato in a creamy white sauce garnished with bright green dill. A specialty from Ingmarie's home province of Småland, *isterband* was the sort of deliciously rich dish that I would indulge in only once a year.

Another night we made *ärter med fläsk och plättor*, pea soup with ham and pancakes, the same traditional Thursday supper I had shared with Arne so many years earlier.

Although the class was scheduled for 3:30 to 6:00 P.M., we invariably ran over-time. But no one seemed to mind; the time we spent cooking, eating and convers-ing in Ingmarie's company was so much more delightful than the meals or the evening activities provided by the school. Some nights we didn't finish washing the dishes until eight o'clock, and then we headed to the sauna for an hour before try-ing to cram in a little vocabulary review—not nearly as much fun as cramming in another pancake.

Toward the end of the course, Ingmarie gave even more generously of her time. She shared not only her cooking techniques but also showed us some of her *smul-tronställen,* her special places. For our next-to-last class, we met early, at 2:30 p.m., and didn't return until nine thirty that night. We drove first to Nyköping, where Ingmarie lived, for a tour of that coastal town. At the nearby nature preserve, Stendörren, we carried our lunch across a suspension bridge to a granite outcrop-ping overlooking a calm silvery sea. The view was glorious, *härligt,* as the Swedes say. In this magical setting, we picnicked on classic Swedish summer food: boiled new potatoes; *matjessill,* or spiced pickled herring, accompanied by sour cream and chives; rhubarb pie; vanilla ice cream; and *citrondricka,* a refreshing lemon drink not nearly as sweet as American lemonade.

For the last class, we again met early, this time driving to a pick-your-own straw-berry patch. On our return, we prepared a simple dinner of *Janssons frestelse,* or Jansson's temptation, a savory casserole of sliced potatoes, onions, and anchovies baked in cream, followed by the quintessential Midsummer dessert, strawberry torte.

Although I had not planned on taking the elective cooking course when I first enrolled in the intensive language program, the timing turned out to be perfect. Carl and I both yearned to spend more time in Sweden in a place of our own. However, neither of us was ready to take the plunge and move overseas. That sum-mer, we found the perfect solution, a vacation home on an island in the Stockholm archipelago. Six months after the course ended—and nearly fifteen years after my first visit to Sweden—I was ensconced in my own Swedish kitchen, cooking for family and friends, without the barrier of translations or conversions, using my three bright red metric measuring spoons.

Arrival

After the long journey from the States, my heart always lifts as I catch sight of the red wooden market building, with its white lettering on the side that reads, "Strömma Handel, estab. 1861."

Here, at Strömma Market, I reconnect with Sweden by stocking up on my family's favorite foods. The simple act of buying groceries forces me to shift my thinking from English to Swedish, dollars to kronor, pounds to kilos. Walking into Strömma Market, I step over the threshold into my Swedish life.

The scale of everything inside this grocery store, from the size of the carts to the width of the aisles to the height of the shelves, is smaller than an American supermarket. Although the business has been here for more than 130 years, the design of the store is contemporary. The aisle closest to the entrance is stocked with paper towels, potato chips, soda, and beer—a convenient layout for the many boaters who

Strömma Market offers not only traditonal Swedish staples such as rye crisps, smoked mackerel, and rose hip soup, but also more exotic fare like Italian proscuitto and American taco shells.

come into the market to grab a few essentials while waiting for the nearby Strömma Canal drawbridge to open. The market is also well-stocked with all of the basics for meal preparation and quite a few of the frills, even a deli section with grilled chicken and smoked fish.

Carl and the kids remind me to get reindeer meat and muesli, but they usually prefer to wait in the car, dozing after the long flight. Although I promise to be quick, I invariably become so absorbed that I forget to hurry.

For my husband, I buy the ingredients for the meat and potato hash called *pytt i panna*, "bits in the pan," which he makes with *falukorv*, a mild-flavored, smooth-textured, precooked beef sausage. Now considered the most Swedish of sausages, *falukorv* was ironically invented several hundred years ago by German mountain men working in the copper mines near Falun, in central Sweden, as a way to make palatable the tough meat of the oxen that powered the mine elevators. In addition to the potatoes and onions traditionally used in *pytt i panna*, Carl likes to include chopped carrots, which I put in my shopping cart along with eggs to serve over easy on top of each portion. For a side dish, I get a jar of sliced, pickled beets—

which taste far better and much fresher than the canned beets of my Midwestern childhood.

For my daughter, I pick up the ingredients for her favorite stew, which I prepare with green apples, onion, chanterelle mushrooms, crème fraîche—and frozen *renskav*, or thinly sliced reindeer meat. Reindeer stew may seem like an unusual choice for an American child. But Tina knows that in Scandinavia, reindeer are raised by the indigenous Saami people not for pulling Santa's sleigh—the Swedish Santa Claus is accompanied only by the occasional goat—but rather as an essential source of food, clothing, shelter, and tools.

For my son, I get a bag of "summer" muesli. This cereal includes not only dried apple, raisins, and flakes of oats and rye, but also tropical fruits whose very names—papaya, coconut, and pineapple—conjure images of sunshine, an effective marketing concept in this country of midwinter darkness.

Over his muesli, Michael likes to pour *filmjölk*, a kind of sour milk, which is thicker than American buttermilk and less acidic than plain yogurt. *Filmjölk* and other cultured milk products were first developed as an alternative to fresh milk, until recently a seasonal luxury in the harsh Scandinavian climate.

While my children are content to eat cereal for breakfast in Sweden, I adopt the native custom of beginning the morning with a cup of coffee and a sandwich. Not the fancy, open-faced sandwiches with elaborate garnishes served in restaurants that are designed to be eaten with a knife and fork, but a *macka*, a piece of bread with cheese, meat, or fish, topped with a slice of tomato, cucumber, or bell pepper and eaten out of hand.

So for myself, I buy a package of sliced, smoked reindeer meat and a piece of cheese from the deli section, either the mild *herrgårdsost*, or the stronger *prästost*, priest cheese, whose name is a reminder of the days when church taxes were paid in foodstuffs.

I add a tube of *Kalles kaviar*, made from the roe of Icelandic cod, which is cured in a sugar and salt solution for four to six months and then mixed with oil and spices. This "caviar" is so popular that each Swede consumes approximately one pound per year on average. Affordability is only part of the appeal. In fact, *kaviar* didn't become popular until 1935 when a new type of packaging was introduced: the aluminum tube.

Embellishing a cracker with dots and dashes of salmon-color *kaviar* is fun—like decorating a cake with a pastry tube but without the mess. The best canvas for this art form is *knäckebröd*, crispbread or hard bread, which I also buy at Strömma Market. For centuries, Scandinavians have baked large circles of unleavened rye bread with a hole in the middle. They would then dry the bread on rods suspended near the ceiling to preserve it for the coming winter. Today, *knäckebröd* is still a staple of the Swedish diet. Seldom baked at home, crispbread is sold in both the circular and in the more modern rectangular shapes. Besides rye, there are graham, sesame, cinnamon, and even a Christmas *knäckebröd* made from wheat flour and flavored with anise, fennel, and coriander. For Carl, I get the hearty rye and, for myself, the wheat "breakfast" *knäckebröd*.

Before I finish shopping, one of the children usually comes into the store to hurry me along—"It's already been twenty minutes!"—and to plead for an ice-cream sandwich or a "Banana Joe," a chocolate-coated, banana-flavored Popsicle that, despite its name, does not seem to be an American import.

"Don't forget the chips and dip," my child is sure to remind me. At least once each visit to Sweden, our family has a ritual meal of potato chips and sour cream dip. This tradition dates back to the first time Carl and I traveled together to Stockholm; we were teenagers then and quite addicted to junk food. Now, our kids are the ones who keep this custom alive; indeed, Carl and I can hardly get a single handful before Michael and Tina have inhaled the entire bag.

I maneuver my cart into the checkout line, paying while my child bags the groceries. Ten minutes after leaving Strömma Market, we pull into the gravel drive in front of our home-away-from-home. Now that there's food in the house, we can start settling in.

While my husband unloads the car and the mailbox, I carry the groceries upstairs to the galley kitchen. I close the door, to muffle the sound of tired children bickering as they unpack their bags, and set a pot of water on to boil. I make my favorite sandwich: crispbread with an artful squiggle of coral-color, dill-flavored *kaviar*, topped with two thin slices of seedless cucumber. I sit down at the pine table where I can see the young oak tree and the meadow beyond. I bite into the crunchy *knäckebröd* and sip my black currant tea.

At last, I have arrived.

Wild Strawberry Patch

The Swedish language has a word, *smultronställe,* which literally translated means a place where wild strawberries grow. But *smultronställe* also describes a serendipitous place, discovered by chance, which draws one back time and again for reasons of atmosphere or memory. For my cooking teacher Ingmarie, the nature preserve Stendörren was such a place. For me, it is Stavsnäs.

I found the harbor at Stavsnäs during our first summer in the Stockholm archipelago. I was alone when I made this fortuitous discovery and each summer I return alone to this port at the edge of our island, Fågelbrolandet. On my own, I feel a sense of possibility. In my solitude, with no one addressing me in the English that reveals my foreign status, I can even imagine myself a Swede.

Driving down to this harbor has become one of my summer rituals. I wait for a bright morning, when I know the sun will cast silver glitter on the water and warm the brisk sea breeze.

Undistracted by conversation, I am free to concentrate on the rhythms of the landscape as I drive. The sinuous curves of the main road follow the jagged coastline. I pass stands of pine and birch and then on my right, a lake appears.

Didriksdalsgård (Didrik's Valley Farm), reads the sign painted in white letters on the side of a weathered, dark red building. What else is there? I wonder as I drive past the road leading to the farm, an adventure for another day.

The woods on my left disappear as the view opens to the sea. Sailboats ply the waters and, in the distance, I can see the great span of the Djurö bridge, leading to the island of the same name.

The road forks and I take the right branch, dipping downhill toward Stavsnäs. For a few minutes, the sea vanishes from sight as I pass the gas station, grocery shop, and post office along the tree-lined road. Continuing past the narrow street that leads to the sailboats' summer harbor, I park in the large outdoor lot across from the winter harbor where the ferry boats dock. The Baltic stretches out to the horizon like a sheet of silver gossamer. Gulls shriek, a bell clangs, and I hear the clunk-clunk-clunk of a diesel motor. At this tiny port on the

Djurö Bridge in the Stockholm archipelago. Even though it is only August, the leaves on the deciduous trees are already beginning to turn.

edge of the Baltic, where no bridges connect the islands visible in the distance, I have the sense of being at land's end.

The adventure I seek in Stavsnäs is elusive. With its mix of locals, summer people, and tourists, almost all of whom are Swedish, Stavsnäs offers me the possibility of blending in. In my striped Swedish dress, I can slip on another persona, leaving my American identity back at the house with my husband and children. Alone, I can skirt the invisible edge between insider and outsider.

The harbor at Stavsnäs was one of the first places I discovered on the island and returning here anchors me. Each time I return, I reassure myself that, although the details may change, this corner of the world has not altered irrevocably in the intervening months.

Between the parking lot and the pier, several sky-blue wooden commercial buildings cluster around a courtyard. The island handicrafts store sells wooden baskets painted with the hot pink clover blossoms so prevalent here. There is an ice-cream parlor that offers a cornucopia of flavors: blueberry, chocolate, elderflower, almond praline, strawberry, and a "heavenly mix" of vanilla ice cream, caramel, marshmallows, and chocolate sauce.

An open-air plant and produce stand presides at the center of the courtyard. Potted plants cover one side, most of them flowering: daisies, forget-me-nots, begonias, and bleeding hearts, but the salty smell of the sea masks their light perfume. On the other side, bunches of feathery dill, giant zucchini, green peppers, and lettuce augment the staple Swedish root vegetables: beets, potatoes, carrots. There are eggs and smoked eel, kiwis imported from New Zealand and oranges from Spain, alongside baskets of *smultron*, wild strawberries found in the Swedish woods.

The bakery tantalizes with the scents of sweet almond, spicy cinnamon, and freshly baked rye bread. Invariably, I stop to treat myself to a cup of coffee and one of the pastries that I can find only in Sweden. I choose between a *smörbulle*, a spiral yeast bun flavored with butter and sugar and topped with *pärlsocker*, white sugar pearls, or perhaps a slice of *skogspaj*, "forest pie," filled with blackberries and raspberries under a lattice crust and served with vanilla sauce.

I like to sit at one of the tables outside the bakery, where I can write in my journal and still see the water. Every half hour or so, a long red bus from the city pulls up to the curb, braking with a whoosh. From my sheltered vantage point, I watch the disembarking passengers, laden with duffel bags, backpacks, picnic baskets, and baby strollers. For a moment, as these Stockholmers look around, getting their bearings, I feel the superiority of the local who knows the lay of the land. I could join these Swedish tourists, catch the ferry for a day trip to one of the archipelago's outer islands. But this port on the island of Fågelbrolandet is the place I have made my own. Each visit to Stavsnäs secures my connection to this place of serendipity, and ultimately, to Sweden itself. So I leave my *smultronställe* and return to my family, with a braided length of cinnamon bread in one hand and a basket of wild strawberries in the other.

Fast Food

In the United States, fast food and franchises have become so intertwined in the past few decades that hamburgers have almost become synonymous with McDonald's and Burger King. In Sweden, however, I associate fast food with the mom-and-pop places that attract me, perhaps because they resonate with dim memories of the hamburger stand my parents owned for a brief time when I was a preschooler.

Several times a week, I find myself pulling into the local *korvkiosk* or hot-dog stand situated on the main road into Stockholm. For some inexplicable reason, I always seem to be heading into the city shortly before lunchtime. If my children are along, they invariably announce that they are so hungry and, no, they can not possibly wait until we arrive at our destination.

Älgstakets Grill is located in Sweden's version of a strip mall: a few separate buildings facing a gravel parking lot. The teal-green building to the right houses two businesses: Siggesta Meat and Game, which carries such items as fresh eggs, rowanberry jelly, and reindeer salami, and a bakery called Delselius Bread Boutique. Another building to the left shelters a seasonal store selling patio furniture. And in the center, sits the hot-dog stand in a small, gray wooden structure with a takeout window and two tables under an awning.

One of the ubiquitous institutions of Swedish life, the *korvkiosk* can be found in the smallest town and the largest city. But the attraction of Älgstakets Grill rests as much on the careful attention lavished on each order as on the convenience of its location.

The kids debate: should they order a thick or thin wiener, or maybe they should try one of the dozen spicy sausages with such names as Currywurst, Arizona Hot, or El Toro? Should the frankfurter be boiled or grilled? They could have the hot dog in a small, round bun (the size and shape of an American dinner roll) or with no bun on a plate with French fries or mashed potatoes. In the end, they always order a thick, grilled dog in a *tunnbrödsrulle*, the most elaborate option on the menu.

To make one of these, the friendly woman who runs Älgstakets Grill warms a circle of *tunnbröd*, a thin flatbread similar to Armenian lavash or a flour tortilla, on the griddle for a couple of minutes while grilling the hot dog. She places three large scoops of mashed potatoes onto the buttered bread, and lays the thick wiener precisely in the center. A squirt of ketchup and a spoonful of roasted dried onions follow. "No salad?" she says, her voice rising. Of course, the child turns down her offer of cole slaw on top of the mashed potatoes. She then folds the bread like a burrito, wraps the bottom in foil and places the fork into the mashed potatoes before handing the neat package across the counter to Michael or Tina. The warm, substantial snack looks so enticing that sometimes I even order one for myself.

While Älgstakets Grill is open year-round, Nystekt Strömming, the fried–Baltic herring stand, situated at the entrance to the city's Slussen subway station, has a more erratic schedule. So erratic that one summer the portable trailer never appeared at all. Despite the sporadic hours, this is the perfect destination for a sunny afternoon. I usually order *strömmingsrulle*, Baltic herring roll-up: thin bread, with mashed potatoes and a salad of shredded cabbage, carrots and lettuce, topped

by a piece of crisp fried Baltic herring. The sweet taste of the fresh white fish and the warm softness of the mashed potatoes and bread make up for the slightly prickly texture of the harmless, threadlike bones.

This herring stand has not only delicious food but also a panoramic view of the city. From here I can see the island of Södermalm, where my father-in-law, Arne, lived, and the landmark elevator, Katarinahissen, leading to

From the plaza at Slussen in central Stockholm, one can see, to the left, the Nystekt Strömming, or Fresh-Fried Baltic Herring stand, and, to the right, Gondolen restaurant.

the rooftop restaurant Gondolen, where he introduced me to Swedish restaurant cooking. Across the water is the island of Djurgården, with the folk museum Skansen, Prince Eugene's palace Waldermarsudde, and the amusement park Tivoli Gröna Lund. In the other direction, I can spot the three golden crowns, symbol of Stockholm, glittering on top of the city hall tower.

Despite these pleasurable eating experiences, I have not become a convert to chain-owned, fast food "restaurants." Indeed, I have come to realize that fast food and chain ownership, so linked in the U.S., are not as synonymous as I had perceived. The difference lies not in the type of food but in the freshness of the ingredients and the carefulness of the preparation. For me, these attributes of the mom-and-pop places impart an irresistible subtle flavor that the chains, with their factory-like sameness, cannot hope to match.

Cloudberries

As the train hurtled through the light summer night toward the Arctic Circle, I tried not to fall out of the narrow berth. Beside me lay my six-year-old daughter, Tina; above us, slept ten-year-old Michael and, above him, our au pair, Jenny. We were on our way to visit Jenny's parents in her home village, nearly six hundred miles north of Stockholm. What I didn't yet know was that we were also heading into the heart of cloudberry country.

At 6:00 A.M., eight hours after leaving the capital city, we climbed down from the train, bleary-eyed but excited. Jenny's father, Helge, ushered us into his car for the two-hour drive to the Bäcklund family home in the sparsely populated village of Lillholmträsk, where we would spend the night.

With the exception of the coastal cities, northern Sweden is primarily wilderness. Here in the *fjäll*, as the mountainous landscape of the interior is called, the weather can change abruptly from sun to blizzard even in the middle of summer. In the area we traveled through, the forest seemed endless, broken only by occasional quiet lakes and patches of marshland.

This is the home of the *hjortron*, or cloudberry, the most delectable of Scandinavia's many berries. This delicate, slightly tangy fruit looks like an amber version of its cousin, the raspberry, but with larger drupelets. Growing only in the wild, the cloudberry thrives in the boggy areas of the far north.

Several mighty rivers cross northern Sweden, including the Vindelälven. We stopped at a point where a suspension bridge spanned the river. Even on this mild day, the Vindelälven was running fast, whitecaps dancing on the water's surface. No way was I going across that, I thought to myself, even before I saw the weight limit sign. No more than two people were allowed on the bridge at one time. Jenny's father took Michael's hand and led him across, followed by Jenny leading Tina, just as Helge had surely led her. Born and raised in this wild terrain, father and daughter moved with an easy grace while I stood on the bank near the car, holding my breath until the kids returned, flush with triumph.

We continued driving through spruce and birch forests, some heavily logged, following the same well-maintained narrow asphalt roads that Jenny's mother, Rosemarie, traveled daily in her job as a rural letter carrier.

By the time we arrived at the house, we were all famished. Rosemarie met us with hugs and then invited us out to the veranda. In a corner of the backyard, Helge started a fire in the rock-lined pit and put a pot of coffee on to boil, campfire style. Meanwhile, Rosemarie carried out a breakfast of hot, crisp waffles topped with whipped cream and cloudberries.

We had just missed the cloudberry's brief harvest season, which falls between mid-July and early August, but fortunately Jenny's parents are both avid berry pickers. Recounting her childhood quests for the elusive orange fruit, Jenny said, "Usually it's very hot when you pick them and there are a lot of mosquitoes out. You'd like to wear shorts but you can't because of the mosquitoes, so you have to wear pants and a long-sleeved shirt and mosquito-repellent oil. You get very warm and sweaty. You have to pick them one at a time and they're so wet, they have a lot of juice if they're completely ripe, so they sink to the bottom and you have to pick more and more just to fill a basket."

Jenny explained that harvesting the berries is not only messy but somewhat risky if you happen to get lost in the wilderness. "My mother and I were out picking, going from spot to spot. We were so sure that we were on the right track—the car on one hand, the mountain on the other side. Then after we'd been circling, we saw a TV antennae, but it was pointed the wrong direction. We weren't sure which way we were going!" Eventually, however, they found their way home.

Although botanists know them by the Latin *Rubus chamaemorus* and Canadians and Mainers call them bake-apple berries, I prefer the *hjortron's* more poetic English name, cloudberries. For me, this appellation evokes their heavenly taste. The *Oxford English Dictionary* suggests another explanation, that the berries grew so high up the slopes of two British mountains that the clouds were lower than the tops of the berry bushes.

Containing nearly as much vitamin C as strawberries, more vitamin A than any other Swedish berry, and a high concentration of benzoic acid, a natural preservative, the tangy *hjortron* is usually preserved either as jam or as frozen *mylta*, sweetened mashed cloudberries. At least as far back as the 1700s, long before vitamins were discovered and classified, Swedes knew that cloudberries protected sailors from scurvy.

Before this visit to the north, I had tasted cloudberries, but never in such abundance. Growing in bogs and on mountains, one berry to a stem, too fragile to be picked by machines during the brief harvest season, cloudberries are one of Sweden's most prized—and expensive—delicacies. Although *hjortron* can be found in all of the country's provinces, except the Baltic islands of Gotland and Öland, the farther north one goes, the better and more abundant the berries.

After the waffle brunch, we left the Bäcklund house to take a ride on what claimed to be the world's longest *linbana*, or cableway. I am not one for roller coasters and other fast amusement park rides but I do like the slow-moving trams at Disneyland. Still, the thought of traveling in a small cabin along a steel cable for two hours gave me pause—especially when the kids joked about jumping around to make the cabin really sway. If I had realized that we would be traveling twenty to sixty feet above the forest floor for more than eight miles, nearly a quarter of which was over water, I probably would have had a much harder time climbing aboard. Fortunately I learned these facts after the tram began to move.

As we glided along the steel cable, our voices were the only sounds audible—except for a "thunk" as we passed by each of the concrete supporting towers. At times, we seemed close enough to almost touch the nearest evergreen treetop. We were actually traversing only one-eighth of the sixty-mile-long cable route, built by the Swedish mining company Boliden AB during World War II as an alternative means of transporting mineral ore. From 1943 to 1987, 12 million tons of gold, copper, lead, zinc, sulfur, and silver ore were carried in buckets along this same steel rope.

Rosemarie had packed two thermoses, one filled with coffee and other with raspberry *saft*, a fruit drink, as well as sandwiches and pastries that we arranged on the tables between each pair of seats. The sandwiches were *tekakor*, or tea cakes, raised circles of wheat bread, spread with butter and topped with slices of mild cheese, while the pastries were homemade *mazariner*, buttery tarts filled with soft almond paste, the tops glazed with white sugar icing. Jenny must have told her mother that this was my favorite Swedish pastry.

Jenny and I chatted while the kids kept busy with the coloring pages and puzzles provided by the tour operator. In vain, we scanned the forest floor for deer, moose, fox, or other wildlife as the cable route passed over a portion of the national park Kronoskogen. Jenny told us that we should be able to see fish swimming in the lake as the cable car went over but we glimpsed not as much as a flash of a tail.

Michael was so disappointed about the lack of wildlife that on the way back to the house, Jenny's father drove us to a clearing where a herd of reindeer were foraging. These animals were undoubtedly owned by the Lapps, or Saami as the indigenous Scandinavians call themselves. Unlike wild deer, which bolt at the sight of humans, these semitame reindeer ignored us as we quietly approached close enough to see the velvet molt still attached to their antlers.

We continued on our way, stopping once to pick wildflowers. When Tina announced that she was thirsty, Jenny's father stopped the car again and led us into the surrounding woods. Helge took out his pocket knife and cut a piece of bark from the nearest birch tree, then folded the bark into a cup, which he filled at a tiny spring coming out of the rocks at the base of the tree, offering a drink to each of us in turn. I felt as though we were deep in the woods, but to my surprise we were less than five minutes from the Bäcklund home, complete with all the modern conveniences, including the essential deep freezer.

Rosemarie was already at the house, preparing a stew with potatoes, carrots, and other vegetables from her garden and meat from a moose that Helge had bagged the previous autumn. Although I am quite fond of the taste of game, the meal's crowning touch for me was the dessert of vanilla ice cream and cloudberries.

The next morning, the kids and I headed back to Stockholm, riding the bus for four hours and the train for six, while Jenny took a week's vacation with her family. When she returned to finish her year with us in Boston, she brought along a gift from her parents, two bottles of sweet cloudberry wine, a memento of our time together in the far north.

Edible Jewels

It was one of those rare, late spring days in Boston when the sky is bright blue and filled with puffy white clouds, the warm sun moderated by a cool breeze. In other words, perfect Swedish summer weather, the kind of weather that stirs my longing to return and makes me acutely wistful for all things Swedish, especially food.

That morning, I was talking with an American friend, Rachel, when I happened to mention that I had never seen currants for sale in this country.

"But I see them all the time; they're right beside the raisins," she replied.

Our misunderstanding had a simple explanation: in American English, the word "currant" describes two unrelated fruits. Rachel was referring to the tiny raisins used in scones and other tea breads; these dried seedless dwarf grapes are called currants after the Greek city of Corinth, where they have been grown since ancient times. I was talking about the fresh berries of the genus *Ribes*, grown in the northern latitudes of Europe, Asia, and North America, including Alaska, but seldom seen in the lower forty-eight except in the form of red or black currant jam and cassis, the black currant liqueur imported from France.

Rachel and I were not the only people to have been confused by the word "currant." When these northern berries were first cultivated in England, sometime before 1578, they were mistakenly believed to be grapes, the same grapes that produced the raisins of Corinth, and were called "bastarde currants." One early writer protested that this was too confusing and that the new berries shouldn't be called currants at all. Today, the British refer to the raisins of Corinth as "grocers' currants" or "shop currants" to distinguish them from the fresh currants widely grown in English gardens.

No such confusion exists in the Swedish language. The dried grapes from Corinth are called *korint* while the other currants, introduced to Scandinavia in the thirteenth century by traveling monks, are *vinbär*, wine berries.

I was first introduced to the fragile *vinbär* by my sister-in-law Kerstin, who grows both *röd vinbär*, red currants, and *svart vinbär*, black currants, in her country garden. Clustered on stems like champagne grapes, these berries are as large and round as prized pearls, with tiny seeds visible through their translucent skin. The red currant glows like a ruby bead, while the black currant has a dusky appearance, shadowy as a December afternoon. The ivory-color white currant, an albino variant of the red currant, is more difficult to find; rarer still is the green currant, which is a mutation of the black.

As nutritious as they are lovely, currants are loaded with vitamin C. In fact, black currants have so much ascorbic acid that they are nearly as sour as lemons. The less acidic red currants have an intense tartness that I find intriguing but which other people might describe as an acquired taste. White currants are sweet enough for anyone to eat out of hand.

Whenever I'm in Sweden during the late summer currant season, I bake a large meringue, fill the cooled shell with vanilla ice cream, and top it with red currants. This festive dessert nicely balances crunchy and smooth, sweet and tart. Red currants can also be cooked with other red fruits, such as cherries, strawberries, or raspberries, and then thickened with potato starch to make *kräm*, a summery fruit pudding.

Like many things of beauty, currants are ephemeral; they not only have a short growing season but are also highly perishable. Fortunately, these fruits are rich in pectin and marry well with sugar, making excellent jams, jellies, and beverages. I particularly like currant jam with game dishes, such as reindeer stew.

For centuries, Swedes have used *vinbär* to flavor grain alcohol, a tradition that Absolut Vodka has capitalized on. Red or black currant cordial is easy to make in late summer, requiring nothing more than a clean flask, enough ripe berries to halfway fill the bottle, and a sufficient quantity of unflavored aquavit or vodka to cover the berries. (So as not to overpower the berry flavor, I dilute the alcohol with an equal amount of water.) When making cordial, I usually add a few tablespoons of sugar to expedite the process, so that the berries need only steep for a couple of months.

Even better is *svartvinbärssaft*, a nonalcoholic black currant beverage. In a country that seems to love carbonation, this is one of the few soft drinks that is bubblefree. I like the tart taste, similar to cranberry juice, which for me is so distinctively Nordic.

However, none of these compare with the *rödvinbärssaft*, a sweetened red currant juice, that my sister-in-law Kerstin makes. After harvesting the currants from her garden in August, Kerstin cooks the fruit with sugar and water, then strains out the pulp and seeds. She bottles the resulting syrup and stores the sealed containers in the root cellar for the coming winter. Diluted in a pitcher with water, this pomegranate-color syrup is transformed into a transparent geranium-pink beverage with a refreshing sweetness, like a draught of the elusive Swedish summer.

Living Culinary History

Sitting on the kitchen windowsill, the off-white cups, hand painted in blue with my son and daughter's names, remind me of the cumulus clouds of a Swedish summer sky, the clear blue waters of Stockholm's inland sea, and the memories I have gathered at Skansen.

Skansen is the world's oldest open-air museum. Unlike Sturbridge Village, Plimoth Plantation, and other living history museums in the United States, which present life in a particular time and place, Skansen was designed as a microcosm of Sweden, with buildings gathered from every province, dating from the 1300s to the 1940s.

But this park is far more than just a collection of old buildings. Skansen's founder, Nordic languages scholar Arthur Hazelius (1833–1901), envisioned a living history museum in which heirloom flora and fauna, costumed folk dancers and musicians, seasonal markets and festivals would give visitors a glimpse of the traditional, agrarian way of life already fast disappearing as Sweden industrialized in the late nineteenth century.

Skansen provides a setting in which Swedes, and those of Swedish descent, can imagine the lives of their ancestors. This was Hazelius' intention—and it works. My son, Michael, was fascinated by the two room apothecary, not unlike the one his great-grandfather, Axel Rosenberg, owned. Our guide, a young man in knee breeches and tricorn hat, pointed out the small stuffed crocodile hanging as decoration and talisman over the pharmacist's desk; the iron stove cluttered with glass beakers; and even the locked cabinets where poisons such as arsenic were kept, a macabre detail thrilling to an eight-year-old boy.

In earlier years, my kids and I spent a lot of time at Skansen's playground, with its tunnels and sandbox, and at the zoo where they could pet goats and watch polar bears from a safe distance. But as they have grown older, they prefer the rides and concerts at the nearby amusement park, Gröna Lund, leaving me to Skansen's quieter pleasures.

Although my own ancestors are not Swedish, this living history museum fires my imagination just as it did my young son's. For me, Skansen is the place where Sweden's culinary history comes alive, engaging all my senses. Returning for what I think of as my annual food history tour, I head for my favorite exhibit, the *fäbod*, a rough-hewn cabin-*cum*-dairy, once common throughout central and northern Sweden.

In the harsh Scandinavian climate, fresh milk was a seasonal luxury until the twentieth century. During the long winters, when food supplies often ran short, the cows became so emaciated from hunger that they could barely stand, let alone produce milk. Once the snow melted in the late spring, they grazed on grass near the farm. By early summer, the cows were strong enough for the *valkullor*, or milk-maids, to lead them to higher pastures so that the land around the farm could recover. In the autumn, these unmarried or widowed women returned, hopefully with enough cheese and butter to last through the winter.

Stepping over the threshold into the low-ceilinged, one-room cabin at Skansen, where two women lived each summer from 1659 to 1920, I imagine both their

The main building at a *fäbod*, a summer dairy, in Dalarna, where cheese and other traditional dairy products are produced and sold.

hard work and their solitary freedom. The scent of freshly cut pine boughs strewn on the dirt floor mixes with the pungent smell of woodsmoke. A young woman guide, clad in a linen blouse and long skirt, stirs a blackened iron kettle over the open fire. She is cooking down whey, a by-product of cheese-making. When the water evaporates and the remaining milk sugars caramelize, the whey turns into a soft, thick paste called *messmör* (pronounced "may-smur"). She passes out samples of the iron-rich whey butter, its nutty caramel flavor complementing the

slightly sour rye bread. In the old days, the *vallkulor* also made *messmörkakor*, cakes made from whey butter, sugar, eggs, cinnamon, cardamom, and wheat flour. After forming the cakes into small, round discs, she decorated the tops by pressing them with a *kakstämpel*, an engraved wooden stamp. A milkmaid gave these treats to her male admirers, one of whom might have given her the hand-carved stamp.

The next stop on my culinary tour is quite a contrast to the rural sparseness of the *fäbod*. At Krogen Tre Bytor, the Three Barrels Restaurant, waiters in velvet knee breeches and striped vests move through candlelit rooms embellished with portraits hanging in gilded frames.

From the eighteenth-century menu, I usually order *nässelsoppa*, nettle soup, a creamy purée of light and dark green, which tastes like a blend of asparagus and spinach, and is topped with half of a hard-boiled egg. This soup originated among the landless farm laborers, whose children gathered the wild, and therefore free, nettle shoots, according to Marianne Sandberg, author of *Våra Svenska Matrötter* (Our Swedish Food Roots). One of Sweden's most nutritious wild plants, the nettle loses its sting when dried or cooked. Today, the fresh shoots are still prized by gourmets as one of the first edible signs of spring.

A number of other intriguing dishes are listed on the menu, such as *viltroulader i cider sås*, thin slices of elk meat baked in cider sauce; and *röding på Norrländskt vis*, alpine char cooked the northern Swedish way, that is, braised with cream and dill. The dish with the most unusual title is Cajsa Warg's *kalvöronor*, or "calf ears."

Attributed to the famous eighteenth-century Swedish cookbook writer Cajsa Warg, these are actually veal burgers, served with chanterelle mushrooms and mashed potatoes.

At the same time that Cajsa Warg was collecting recipes, coffee was becoming an increasingly popular beverage. By the nineteenth century, cafés serving coffee, tea, chocolate, pastries, and sandwiches were springing up in towns and cities throughout the country. One such café, Petissan, popular with engineering students at Stockholm's Technical University in the 1870s, is now permanently ensconced at Skansen.

Decorated with period blue-gray stenciled wallpaper, lace curtains, damask-covered tables, and dark wooden chairs, this small café is a snug haven, especially on drizzly days. At one end of the room, a buffet table beckons with platters of open-faced sandwiches and sweet-smelling blueberry muffins and *mazariner*, or almond tarts, baked at Skansen, along with pitchers of milk and *saft*, a noncarbonated fruit drink. The aromatic coffee in the copper kettles is the strong Swedish version; as elsewhere in Sweden, no one seems to have heard of brewed decaf.

One of my favorite seasonal desserts here is warm *rabarberpaj*, rhubarb pie, served with cold *vaniljsås*, or vanilla sauce. Baked in a buttery crust, this tart has a very light cheesecake filling embedded with chunks of rhubarb and topped with *pärlsocker*, crunchy bits of white pearl sugar. The pool of vanilla sauce intensifies the hint of vanilla in the pie filling.

Down the street in Skansen's nineteenth-century town quarter is the bakery, marked by a golden pretzel suspended above the doorway. The irresistible smell of freshly baked bread draws me into the front sales room, illuminated by hanging kerosene lamps. Buns and pastries are stacked onto the wooden display shelves and counters as they emerge from the large wall oven in the adjacent "flour room."

This bakery specializes in the pastries popular in Stockholm a hundred years ago. Many of these are quite similar to the treats with which I am familiar, such as *råg-bullar*, a slightly sweet rye roll, and *solbullar*, a vanilla custard–filled doughnut.

A few doors down from the bakery is the *kryddboden*, or general store. Teas and spices subtly perfume this tiny shop. From the dozen items displayed on the wooden counter, I might buy a spoon carved from fragrant juniper; a bag of old-fashioned hard candies, such as the red, licorice-flavored King of Denmark; or Skansen tea, a blend of black tea, dried black currants, and elderflowers. I am particularly intrigued by the bottles of *enbärsmust*, a noncarbonated soft drink made from water, lemon juice, sugar, and juniper berries. It tastes remarkably like Dr. Pepper without the fizz.

Produced by Majvor and Peter Asshof, these off-white and cobalt blue matte-finish ceramics from the Skansen series are examples of the Scandinavian aesthetic of combining function and beauty.

Before leaving Skansen, I usually stop at the *krukmakeri*. In this working ceramics studio, potters Majvor and Peter Asshof follow the Scandinavian modern aesthetic of beautiful *and* functional, creating pieces with a timeless simplicity. The shiny brown bowls and plant pots, embellished with yellow-green bands and swirled edges, also known as slip-decorated redware, are similar to the pottery at another living history museum, Plimoth Plantation in Massachusetts. And then there is the "archipelago" series of dishes in grayed blue, pink, and lavender, clearly inspired by the subtle hues of granite outcroppings.

But I prefer the Skansen series, with its off-white matte glaze and cobalt-blue edges, formed into shapes that range from a traditional mold for *sockerkaka*, sponge cake, to spice jars labeled "curry" and "chili"—ingredients that have only recently found their way into Swedish cooking. I look up at the shelf by the window, at the row of round cups, each decorated with a hand-painted name, just like those in my own kitchen, and feel the connection between past and present, between Sweden and home, between this place and me.

Temple of Gastronomy

The illustrated recipe for *messmörspäckad renstek* looked intriguing: a boneless joint of reindeer meat, rubbed with *messmör*, or caramelized whey butter, placed in a baking pan partially filled with black currant juice, then roasted. Scanning the list of ingredients, all of which I liked, I thought that these flavors of the far north would marry well. We were having friends for dinner and, although I wasn't consciously trying to impress them, I was in the mood to prepare something new, something exotic. Little did I know that this would be my biggest cooking fiasco.

Having friends and family over for dinner is our primary form of socializing in Sweden. For the first dozen years, we had nowhere to entertain and, therefore, no way to reciprocate the invitations we received from family and friends. Inviting them out for dinner would have been too extravagant as Stockholm lacks family oriented, moderately priced restaurants. Swedes do eat out, but for lunch or on celebratory occasions, when they are willing to splurge on a fine meal (and often a babysitter; children are seldom seen in most restaurants).

With its red brick facade and clerestory windows, Östermalm's Saluhallen is a landmark building in downtown Stockholm.

Not that cooking at home is cheap. Many foodstuffs are imported and until recently there was also a hefty 23.46 percent (now 12 percent) sales tax figured into the price. So when we are invited to visit, we do not assume that a meal will be included. By the same token, when we are invited to dinner, we feel honored, and express our gratitude by saying, "*Tack för maten*," literally, "Thanks for the food," just as Swedish children are taught to say to their parents.

I usually cook Swedish food to make my guests feel more at home. If time is short, I stick with dishes I'm adept at, using ingredients from the nearby grocery store. But occasionally, I am tempted to experiment with something more unusual, which may or may not work but at least gives me a good excuse to visit my favorite market, Östermalms Saluhallen, Stockholm's answer to London's Harrods' food hall.

With its massive red brick facade, clerestory windows, turrets, and cupola, this gastronomic temple looks every inch the grand dame it is on the Stockholm culinary scene. The inside is equally impressive. The ceiling, several stories high, is supported by an iron framework that dates from the Eiffel Tower era, the spacious interior divided into twenty-two independently owned stalls, each crowned by an elaborate wooden fretwork canopy with the proprietor's name in large white letters on a black background. Of the city's three food halls, this is the most prestigious and the most Swedish, in terms of both goods and customers. As an official purveyor to the Royal Family, the hall's merchants have stocked the pantries of all of Sweden's kings since opening in 1888. In addition to such luxury fare as snow grouse and live lobsters, there are also more humble items like cod pudding and stuffed cabbage rolls.

In fact, the food that I most associate with this market is the peasant dish *kroppkakor*, large potato dumplings filled with salt pork and onion. When my father-in-law, Arne, was still alive, he loved to visit Saluhallen and often purchased *kroppkakor*, which we ate boiled, with a pat of butter and freshly ground black pepper. I can still recall these simple dinners; we dipped each forkful of the dumplings, light as well-made gnocchi, into the rapidly melting pat of butter; the soft blandness of the potato mitigated by the bite of the cracked peppercorns, the salty pork and crunchy onion flavored with a hint of clove.

That day, my first stop at Saluhallen was Robert's Coffee, one of the newest vendors. I breathed in the aroma of fresh roasted coffee and ordered an Oriental Latte: double espresso, steamed milk, cinnamon, and cardamom. Located at the entrance to Saluhallen, this is always a great spot for people-watching. Most of the customers seem to be elderly couples or well-dressed, coifed middle-aged matrons who live in the neighborhood. Although tourists also wander in, they often walk out empty-handed, perhaps because nearly every sign is in Swedish, the weights in grams and kilos—or simply because they are staying in hotels with nowhere to cook.

At Melanders Vilt stall in Östermalm's Saluhallen, game cooks can purchase wild duck, pheasant, boar, bear, reindeer, and even kangaroo.

Before I buy anything, I like to walk around the hall scouting out the possibilities.

The wooden canopy at B. Anderssons is adorned with a stuffed moose head, announcing this stall's dedication to game. Smoked duck, elk salami, and wild boar can be found here, along with *rensadel*, reindeer saddle, a boneless cut of meat that I thought would be perfect for my recipe. Perhaps I should have taken the easier way out and bought pheasant burgers and a sauce made from Karl Johan (porcini) mushrooms to reheat at home.

At the other end of the hall, I stopped at Melanders Vilt och Fisk, which sells both game and fish, raw and cooked, including bear sausage and juniper smoked reindeer heart. Here, I could have purchased shrimp crepes or a *Västerbotten paj*, quiche made from Västerbotten cheese, for the main course. This strong, aged Swedish cheese is similar to Parmesan but not as dry; to be authentic, it must come from the village of Burträsk in the northern province of Västerbotten.

At S. A. H. Delikatesser, I found *kroppkakor* like we used to buy with Arne. *Sillbullar med korintsås*, or herring patties with dried currant sauce; *kalops*, or spicy beef stew; and *biff à la Lindström*, or beef and beet burgers, are a few of the *husmanskost*, traditional home-cooked dishes, sold here these are the comfort foods that many Swedes grew up eating but may no longer have the time, energy, or know-how to prepare it. But I was after something more elaborate.

I wandered over to Lisbeth Jansson's to check out the amazing variety of imported and domestic produce— depending on the season, fresh lychees from Asia, clementines from Spain, dill fronds from Sweden. I decided on chanterelles cooked in butter with diced shallots and a touch of cream as a side dish for the reindeer. In addition to raw fruits and vegetables, Lisbeth Jansson sells jars of preserves, bottled fruit drinks, and cartons of organic ice cream. Cloudberry ice cream topped with cloudberry jam would have complemented my Arctic entrée, but unfortunately, the ice cream would surely have melted before I got home.

The author's niece, Elin Rosenberg, selling cheese at the food hall in the city of Gothenberg.

At Tysta Mari's, I had trouble deciding between rhubarb with cream tea or Hedvig Eleonora tea, named for a nearby church. Choosing from among the more than sixty types of cheese was easier since I invariably go for my favorite *Blå Gotland* (Blue Gotland). Wrapped in dark blue wax, this mild, easy-to-slice cheese from the island of Gotland is particularly delicious on the *brytbröd* from Amandas Brödbutik bakery. This circular white loaf is actually a dozen rolls joined together; one can break off as many sandwich buns as needed—great for sailing excursions and picnics. The bakery also carries *jämtländskt korn tunnbröd*, a barley flatbread from the northwestern province of Jämtland, perfect for my reindeer dinner.

By now, I was starving. Whenever possible, I time my visits to the Saluhallen for mid-to-late morning, so that I can grab a quick lunch. I sat at the counter at Lisa Elmqvist, a restaurant and fishmonger that's been run by the same family for four generations, and ordered from the daily specials. In the summer, I like their *rimmad lax*, or thin slices of salt-cured salmon, similar in appearance and texture to gravlax but with less sugar and no dill. Served cold, the fish is usually accompanied by a warm side dish of *stuvad potatis*, or chunks of potatoes simmered in milk.

After lunch, I purchased everything I thought I could possibly need: black currant juice; a tube of caramelized whey butter; and a five-inch-thick boneless reindeer saddle, along with *Blå Gotland* cheese; two kinds of bread, *brytbröd* and *tunnbröd*; potatoes; chanterelles; raspberries; and Valrhona cocoa.

Not until I got back home and read through the entire recipe did I realize that both the oven temperature and the roasting time were a little vague. "Begin with the oven set to 150 degrees Celsius, after one hour, turn the oven down to 100 degrees." The recipe didn't say how many more minutes or hours were required, only that the meat would be done when its internal temperature reached between 75 and 80 degrees. I didn't have a meat thermometer, nor had I thought to buy one, since I had only read the list of ingredients. Oh well, I naively thought, how long can it take anyway? The recipe mentioned turning down the oven after the first hour; if I added another hour for good measure, that should be more than enough, I reasoned.

By then, I was a little concerned about how this dinner would actually turn out, so I quickly baked my reliable chocolate cake with the Valrhona cocoa. When our friends, Kalle and Riitta, arrived two hours after I'd put the reindeer in the oven, the meat still didn't look done. Nor did they seem to be salivating at the thought of this unusual dish; I suspect they would have been happier with ready-made pheasant burgers or Västerbotten quiche or even spaghetti. But dinner was in the oven, so Carl opened a bottle of wine, put out the cheese and breads, and everyone sat down to wait. Meanwhile, I chopped the potatoes and got the chanterelles ready to sauté.

After the roast had been in the oven for two and a half hours, I sliced into it but the meat still looked too bloody, so I returned the reindeer to the oven and turned the heat back up to 150 degrees. Perhaps I should have marinated the meat for twenty-four hours first, as most game recipes I've subsequently read suggest. More likely, my mistake was simply that I overcooked it, misjudging what the French call *à point*, perfectly done, for too rare. When I finally removed the saddle, which had roasted three and a half hours in total, it was, like its namesake, a little tough. "It tastes like liver," my son, Michael, astutely observed. Our friends were too polite to say anything more than "*Tack för maten.*"

Carl opened another bottle of red wine and I silently resolved that next time, I would read the recipe all the way through, not once but twice, before heading for the store. Happily, the chocolate cake, topped with raspberries and a dollop of crème fraîche, vanished to appreciative murmurs, with nary a crumb left over.

Medieval Repast

Even in broad daylight, Visby is full of ghosts. Strolling along the cobblestone streets, my ten-year-old daughter and I found it easy to imagine how this island capital might have looked in its glory days. A blond knight, sword rattling at his side, bends to kiss the hand of his cloaked lady. In the distance, the sound of monks chanting vespers and the smell of roasting mutton waft toward us.

Tina and I were walking in the shadow of the massive wall that still encircles the oldest portion of this "city of ruins and roses" on the island of Gotland in the Baltic Sea. Punctuated by towers that rise as high as sixty feet, this two-mile-long limestone wall was begun in the 1200s, when Visby was one of the wealthiest cities in northern Europe. Today, the area within the wall is a vibrant historic district with craft shops, cafés, and cottages. But each ruined medieval church reminded us of the turbulent past of this former Viking stronghold and Hanseatic League city-state.

Located just inside the medieval stone wall that surrounds the city of Visby, this outdoor cafe is one place to enjoy the local delicacy, *saffranspannkaka*, baked saffron rice pudding.

One of the most comfortable vantage points for soaking up Visby's medieval atmosphere is Sankt Hans Café. Companionably sitting in the café garden, which abuts the ruins of St. Hans' and St. Peter's churches, my daughter and I sketched the weathered columns, the crumbling archway, and the clumps of yellow wildflowers growing in the cracks between the stones. In between sketches, we nibbled on the local specialty, a saffron-flavored baked rice pudding called *saffranspannkaka*, served warm with a dollop of jam. Made from the indigenous blue raspberries called *salmbär* (*Rubus caesius* in Latin), this purplish jam tasted neither like blueberry nor raspberry but, rather, was similar to blackberry preserves.

Gotland is home to 58,000 people and at least as many curly sheep. Although the only live sheep we spotted during our weekend in the capital were penned across from the airport terminal, we saw ample evidence of their existence. There were hand-knit wool sweaters and sheepskin bicycle saddle covers, concrete rams blocking cars from entering pedestrian-only streets, and the white lamb at the center of the island's flag. Not surprisingly, while pork dominates cooking on the Swedish mainland, lamb has pride of place on Gotland tables.

This was certainly the case at the restaurant Wärdshuset Lindgården, or Linden Garden, where Tina and I sat in the rose garden under the linden tree for which this establishment was named. Accordionist Anders Schelling serenaded us while a fountain quietly bubbled in the background. Tina ordered steak and *saffranspannkaka* while I chose the dark local beer, *Gotlandsdricku*, and the Gotland menu, which began with an appetizer plate of island delicacies. These included slices of *gravad lamm*, or salted lamb; *fårfiol*, or smoked leg of mutton; and lamb salami, along with smoked salmon, pickled herring, and *Blå Gotland* cheese. Following this was the most unusual lamb dish I've ever tasted, the crunchy but tender *glödhoppa*.

This Gotland specialty is traditionally prepared by first marinating lamb ribs for a few days in a solution of water, salt, and sugar, then boiling the ribs with leeks and peppercorns. Removed from the bone, the meat is chopped, formed into patties, and coated with a mixture of bread crumbs and powdered mustard. Traditionally, the patties were cooked over live coals, hence the name *glödhoppa*, which can be translated as "hopping embers."

But for me, the finale of that meal was the mulberry ice cream with a sauce of homemade mulberry jam from Lindgården's own trees. Suddenly, I had a flash of memory. In my mind's eye, I saw the mulberry tree in the backyard of my childhood home in Wichita, Kansas. I recalled the sour taste of the underripe berries that my best friend Rashelle and I picked before the birds could get to them, and the purple stains their juice left on my fingers when I was my daughter's age—details that I had not thought about in decades.

Later, I wondered about the origin of these mulberries, which are not commonly found in Sweden. My friends Peter and Ingeborg explained that in the 1700s, Sweden dreamed of becoming the silk capital of Europe and an incredible sum of money was spent planting mulberry trees to feed imported silkworms. Initially, the trees did well but, after several hard winters, they died. A second attempt at planting mulberry trees also failed, although a few trees from that time survived around some of the castles in southern Sweden and also in the vicinity of Visby.

As Tina and I strolled down the main street after dinner, we heard recorder music coming from the basement of a whitewashed building nearby. Peering into the dimly lit restaurant, we caught a glimpse of an *eldslukare*, fire-eater, breathing out a gust of flames—just like in the masquerade scene in the movie *Much Ado About Nothing*. "Let's go there for dinner tomorrow night," Tina excitedly exclaimed.

The medieval-themed Medeltidskrogen Clematis is open only during the height of Visby's tourist season, from the beginning of July to the middle of August. As Tina and I stepped down into this cellar restaurant, lit entirely by candlelight, we entered another world. Clad in a leather apron and breeches, the waiter brought us ceramic flagons of *fläderdryck*, or elderflower drink, which had a piquant taste somewhere between apple juice and lemonade. He also gave each of us one utensil, a buck knife, and instructed us to slice the round loaves of bread crosswise so that we could use the bottom half as a plate.

"I wonder when they're going to breathe fire," Tina whispered to me in a voice filled with wonder.

My daughter and I shared an "affluent medieval platter," which began with a wooden bowl filled with slices of apple and sausage, chunks of cheese and smoked leg of mutton, shelled hazelnuts, and Tina's favorite, candied rose petals. The entrée arrived in another wooden dish: lamb cutlets, spareribs, and chopped cabbage braised in honey. My child's enjoyment of the food was no doubt heightened by the opportunity to eat an entire meal with her hands.

Although musicians serenaded us with recorder, drum, and tambourine, we kept wondering about the fire stunt. Had we missed it or were we too early? By the time we finished dinner at 10:00 P.M., my sleepy girl was reluctantly resigned to missing the spectacle. Then just as we left the restaurant, a waiter stepped out saying, in Swedish, "We're going to breathe fire now and your daughter might like to see it."

Although I had attended medieval fairs back home, I could never quite forget, for even a second, that the costumed players and I were standing on the brink of the twenty-first century. But this time was different.

We quickly reseated ourselves and waited in anticipation. The tension rose as the musicians began chanting a dirge in time to the beat of a handheld drum. Holding a lighted torch aloft, our waiter took a swig from a green bottle and then blew on the torch, causing a rush of flames to shoot upward.

The medieval-themed restaurant, Medeltidskrogn Clematis, in Visby is the site of fire-breathing performances every night during the brief summer tourist season.

In that illuminating flash of roaring flame, in the cellar of a centuries-old house, embraced by Visby's mighty stone wall, on an island in the Baltic Sea, I was able to suspend my disbelief and for the briefest moment feel the touch of the past, like the brush of a velvet gown.

Medieval Markets

Enchanted by that first trip to Visby and eager to sample more period food in an authentic atmosphere, we returned the following August for the city's annual Medieval Week, a festival that has become a high point of our Swedish summers.

Walking into the meadow where a medieval market was set up under the shade of ancient oak trees, I felt as though I had stepped back in time. In the distance, I could see Visby's towering twelfth-century North Gate and hear the roar of the crowd as they cheered and jeered the knights on silk-caparisoned horses jousting in a nearby field. Among the tournament-goers were Carl, Michael, and Tina, but I stayed behind to wander around the marketplace. Strolling among the several dozen wooden booths, I fingered bronze brooches and sheepskin caps; breathed in the intoxicating smell of freshly baked rye bread; and sipped a cup of *dragöl*, a honey-flavored beer available only here on the island of Gotland.

The scent of barbecue drew me to the far end of the meadow. As I came closer and noticed the spread-eagled boar roasting on a spit over a campfire, I was taken aback. Confronting my dinner not in the form of grilled hot dogs or plastic-wrapped pork chops but as a whole pig, minus only the skin, unnerved me— even as it strengthened the illusion of having entered another time. And yet, I was as fascinated as I was repulsed by this primeval sight. My carnivore instincts intact, I couldn't resist the opportunity to taste wild boar. A pale blond woman in a green linen gown sliced off some morsels of roast meat. She stuffed these into a pocket of flatbread, adding raw shredded rutabaga, cabbage, yellow onions, and an herbal dressing. The rutabaga's peppery, slightly bitter taste took a little getting used to, but the meat had an agreeable wild flavor, quite unlike that of domestic pork.

While the festival's merchants and performers were required to wear medieval garb, many of the island's residents and mainland tourists didn't bother. Tina and I, however, eagerly embraced the opportunity to dress up. Unsure of what to wear that first year, we both improvised costumes of ankle-length white cotton night-dresses and long linen aprons, hair covered with linen dishtowels tied at the nape of the neck like a modern nun's headdress. My husband and son both wore contemporary shorts and shirts, but Carl donned his green leather mask with Pinocchio-style nose, while Michael painted his face half white and half black, with a star of the opposite color on each cheek. Dressed like escapees from a Renaissance fair, we looked as foreign as we, in fact, were. But that didn't matter. Although we got a few curious looks, we also got nods of approval for our participation from those in more authentic clothing.

As soon as we checked into our hotel and changed, we set off in search of medieval food. Following a group of robed islanders, we came to Kapitelhusgården, a thirteenth-century chapter house or religious center with several buildings facing a central courtyard. Here, a medieval market with a dozen artisans displaying their handicrafts was arranged around the courtyard's perimeter. While I admired the intricately worked belt buckles and pewter goblets, I was disappointed that this market had almost nothing in the way of food. The sole exception was a woman selling crackers made from an ancient grain called *dinkel* (*Triticum speltum* in Latin,

Members of the juggling group, Pax, performing in the woods outside Visby's city walls.

and spelt in English). She claimed the recipe came from the German mystic writer and musical composer Saint Hildegard of Bingen. From the taste of those crackers, I hope that Hildegard was a far better writer than a cook.

Fortunately, the food at the chapter house tavern was much better. We indulged in period delicacies, such as dense, sweet almond pie, slices of cold smoked sausage, mugs of herbal tea, and flagons of *fläderdryck*, an elderflower drink, which tasted like a cross between apple juice and white wine. We also had *ungstrull*, translated literally as "oven enchantment," a rye roll filled with diced ham and onion that seemed to magically puff up as it steamed.

The biggest market was held on the festival's final Sunday. Festival officials led the procession through the city's East Gate and up the cobblestone main street followed by their wimpled wives, robed priests, and velvet-garbed noble lords and ladies. Next came the musicians and a troupe of young jesters, children clad in red and green with tinkling bells hanging from their pointed hats, some walking on stilts, others riding in a clattering wagon. Jugglers and beggars, fishwives and farmers jostled with hundreds of camera-toting tourists, making their way slowly from one wooden stall to the next.

The market catered to all ages and tastes, with goods ranging from comic jester caps to gruesome fox head pouches, from beeswax lip balm to chain-mail coats, from delicate silver ankle bracelets to waterproof leather canteens. All of the market's wares, including the food, were expected to be, if not authentic, at least historically plausible.

At one stall, I tried on an extravagant but fragile gold thread robe and a blue pillbox hat with a white silk veil and burnt orange ribbons, the type of dress a prosperous merchant's wife might have worn in the fourteenth century. Such a woman would have enjoyed not only fine clothes but also such delicacies as French wine, German beer, spiced candy, and perhaps the services of a professional cook.

One of my favorite stands was run by an older woman dressed in a gray nun's habit, accompanied by her plump pug. The silver-haired dog waited patiently as his mistress did a brisk business selling glass candleholders and exotic crystallized incense, including frankincense and myrrh, which reminded me of my Roman Catholic childhood.

Fortunately, the festival organizers did not insist on olfactory authenticity, sparing us the overpowering and probably nauseating odors of the Middle Ages. Instead, floating on the salty sea breezes was the enticing perfume of cinnamon and roasting nuts, the yeasty aroma of juniper beer, the comforting smell of woodsmoke, and the sweet scent of straw used to wrap fragile purchases.

We began our explorations at one end and slowly worked our way down the main street, doubling back from time to time for a second taste of our favorite treats. Gradually we noticed that although there was a wide variety of edibles, all of them were snack foods, presumably so that the market did not directly compete with the city's many restaurants.

While restaurants as we know them did not exist in the Middle Ages, bakeries, breweries, and butcher shops could be found in the larger towns. Only the wealthy could afford white bread so most of the bakers' wares were made from barley, oats, or perhaps rye, which arrived from the East around 1200 C.E.

Lina Kramp of Copenhagen selling taffy apples coated with nuts or oats at the open-air market during Visby's annual Medieval Week.

Just as bread was the staff of life in medieval times, so it was at the festival. The breads ranged from puffy yeast rolls to paper-thin crackers made from a blend of barley, rye, and wheat flours. While the latter were rather bland alone, they would have been the perfect foil for a salty spread like anchovy butter.

The best-tasting and most authentic-looking bread was baked on a hot stone over a wood fire, the heat of which was so intense that the leather-aproned baker worked shirtless—and should have worn a mask to prevent smoke inhalation. The thick circles of grilled flatbread had a pleasantly chewy texture and a delicious smoky flavor, complemented by the spread that the baker applied as soon as the bread left the fire, a delicious mixture of butter, chopped olives, garlic—and sun-dried tomatoes. Given how popular Italian food has become in Sweden these past two decades, perhaps it's not so surprising that the vendor didn't realize that tomatoes came not from ancient Rome but from the New World—and that they did not arrive in Europe until after the Middle Ages.

In medieval times, the Mediterranean was the source of the world's most expensive spice, saffron. Despite its cost, this spice was extensively used in aristocratic cooking as a food coloring agent. One booth at the fair specialized in saffron yeast rolls and Gotland's ubiquitous dessert, *saffranspannkaka*. This baked saffron rice pudding was topped, as usual, with whipped cream and jam made from *salmbär*, the island's indigenous blue raspberries. Believed to have aphrodisiacal powers, saffron was one of many seasonings imported by Gotland's wealthy merchants.

The use of flowers in medieval cookery appeared at the fair as well in the guise of cookies delicately flavored with dried rose petals or lavender blossoms. Flanking the cookies were brown paper bags of rose sugar and lavender sugar, complete with recipes. At another booth, a brown-robed monk stirred a copper cauldron filled with hazelnuts coated with sticky syrup; periodically, he called out to potential customers to buy some nuts and "Save the abbey!"

Not all of the food offerings were so exotic. One of Michael's favorites was the stall selling large, raw carrots for about twenty-five cents each; another booth featured green apples.

Needless to say, there were no carbonated raspberry sodas or colas at this market. Instead, we quenched our thirst with elderflower juice and *gotlandsdricku*, a home-brewed juniper-flavored dark beer. Even more unusual were the health elixirs made from the juices of *älgört*, or meadowsweet, and *björklöv*, or birch leaf—the latter full of carotene, the wise saleswoman assured me. In earlier times, meadowsweet was strewn on floors as a primitive room freshener and added to beer and mead as a flavoring agent. Her proffered sample of meadowsweet drink tasted vaguely like spicy, bitter apple juice. I preferred the *salmbäsrsaft*, blue raspberry juice, which tasted more like blackberry or boysenberry than raspberry.

These reproductions of twelfth century off-white ceramic mugs are from Szilasi Keramik store in Visby.

For those who wished to set their own medieval table, merchants sold off-white ceramic cups copied from twelfth-, fifteenth-, and sixteenth-century models, spoons carved from aromatic juniper, knives with antler handles, and golden-brown ceramic plates engraved with the message "Welcome to Our Table," spelled out not in English or Swedish but in ancient runic letters.

At that evening's outdoor banquet, rust-color ceramic flagons functioned as combination entry ticket, drinking cup, and souvenir. This closing event was first organized as a private dinner for the actors, merchants, musicians, and others who had worked at the festival, but was eventually opened to all. The banquet was scheduled to begin at 6:00 p.m. but, when we arrived a few minutes later, we found hundreds of visitors, most in modern dress, waiting in line, first to get into the cordoned-off main square and then to obtain their dinner from the several vendors set up around the perimeter. The festival's participants were already inside the square, which looked like a movie set with a couple of hundred men, women, and children in medieval dress sitting at rough wooden tables, eating roast chicken, wild boar sandwiches, and rolls stuffed with onions and ham.

We thought about joining the long queue, but decided instead to return to the restaurant Medeltidskrogen Clematis, for a dinner of spareribs and cabbage braised in honey and baked pear crisp served with a dollop of *lavendalkräm*, or sour cream flavored with a hint of lavender—and another spectacular fire-breathing performance. Next time, we would have to show up earlier for the medieval banquet—as if we needed a reason to return to this city of ruins and roses.

Café Society

In 1983, when I first walked into Vetekatten (The Wheat Cat) in downtown Stockholm, I was already a coffeehouse connoisseur. As an undergraduate at the University of California at Berkeley, I spent endless hours in the dark, smoky Café Med, where my friend Peggy and I shared almond horn cookies and discussed the difficulties of studying languages, while the young men at neighboring tables plotted their futures. If I was alone, I preferred the café on Bancroft Avenue housed in a glass conservatory surrounded by wooden decks crammed with tables. On a warm spring day, this was the ideal place to sit with a tall iced latte, listening to groups of students arguing in Italian, French, and Persian.

Naturally, when I visited Stockholm, I was drawn to the Swedish equivalent, the *konditori* [pronounced "con-di-to-ree"; plural, konditorier, "con-di-toe-rear"]. Open from early morning to early evening, the *konditori* is a meeting place where customers can enjoy a cup of coffee or tea, a sandwich or a pastry; they can even pick up a loaf of bread or a cake to take home.

I discovered Vetekatten by chance on a shopping expedition. I was exhausted, and as I walked out of a handicrafts store, I was intrigued by the cat sign hanging from the adjacent building. I walked through the first set of glass doors, past a hallway painted lavender with green speckles and through another set of glass doors to enter the old-fashioned café. Later, I learned that this *konditori*, opened in 1928, is one of Stockholm's largest and best known.

Using the original owner's recipes, the staff bakes almost everything from scratch on the premises with minimal reliance on modern technology—even the egg whites for the meringue desserts are beaten by hand rather than by machine.

Vetekatten's interior exhibits this old-fashioned quality as well. At the glass counter near the entrance, I usually order something sweet, perhaps a *mazarin*, an oval tart with a firm crust and a soft almond filling, topped with a slick of white icing. I carry my plate to whichever of the three rooms suits my mood: the proper tearoom with worn, velvet-upholstered rococo sofas; the square-shaped nautical room lit by brass hurricane lamps; or the airy back room painted white and flooded with light. The coffee, kept warm in a thermos as is the Swedish custom, waits on a separate self-service table laid with bone china cups in the famous "Blå Blom" pattern, white with embossed blue hyacinths. At frequent intervals, waitresses wearing ruffled, blue-striped smocks refill the thermoses.

Through the years, I have serendipitously stumbled upon a few cafés, such as Vetekatten, which combine quality baked goods and historic atmosphere; now I can turn to Maria and Johan Kindblom's book *Kondisboken: Klassika svenska kaféer och konditorier* (The Konditori Book: Classic Swedish Cafés and Konditori), which profiles fifty-seven coffeehouses that have retained their period charm.

The Kindbloms hope to encourage the preservation of this "unpretentious little cultural heritage." For the *konditori* is more than just a pastry shop with a few tables. As the authors write in their introduction, "The *konditori* changed Sweden. It was the first respectable gathering place where all—men and women, wealthy and workers—could meet and socialize outside the home. The more leisure time we gained, the more *konditorier* there were and at one time every small town had at least two or three to choose from. Each with its own specialties and clientele." [Italics added.]

Elderly couples, young mothers with toddlers, vacationing summer people, and construction workers make up the bulk of the customers at my neighborhood café, Munkens Konditori, the Monk's Café, on the neighboring island of Djurö. As many mornings as possible, I head for Munkens, which I like for its casual atmosphere, its geographical proximity, and its fabulous baked goods. Now that our children are older, Carl and I often duck out to the *konditori* for an hour, first thing in the morning, while they sleep in.

The twenty-minute drive from our home is part of the pleasure. The road winds along the edge of the island, past birch trees and ponds, then rises as it takes us across the dramatic Djurö bridge, a steel ribbon arcing above the cobalt-blue water. On the other side of the sound, Djurö is much like our own island, flat with low hillocks, granite outcroppings, and summer cottages obscured behind stands of trees—plus a

Located on the island of Djurö, Munkens Konditori is a pleasant place to while away an hour on a summer morning over a cup of black currant tea and a cardemom bun.

miniature golf course overlooking the tranquil tideless sea. A grocery store set alongside the main road partially obscures the pine-green, A-frame structure that is our destination.

Established in 1926, Munkens was located in Stockholm until the early 1990s when the owners moved their *konditori* business out to the archipelago. An example of modern Swedish design at its best, the interior features a multitude of windows, white walls, and a cathedral ceiling of slatted pine, brightening this one-room café on even the grayest days. The space is never overwhelming, thanks to the begonias and ficus trees, and the handmade vases and watercolor paintings by local artists, all of which enliven the indoor seating area furnished with butcher-block tables and rush-seated wooden chairs. The room feels warm and cozy, like a friend's sun porch.

Stepping up to the glass counter, I scan the shelves, deciding on the day's indulgence while remembering what everyone else wants. When my turn comes, I give my order to the young brunette woman who places the food on plain white stoneware and hands me my chosen loaf of bread in a brown paper bag printed with the words "Munkens Konditori" and the image of a monk.

One of Munkens' fresh yeast buns provides the perfect foil for a cup of strong Swedish coffee, a brew more akin to espresso than to Folger's. For years, I almost always ordered a *kanelbulle*, a Swedish cinnamon bun that has little in common with its fluffy American counterpart. Instead of oozing with frosting, the *kanelbulle* is only lightly sprinkled with crunchy bits of pearl sugar so that cinnamon remains the dominant flavor. Perhaps the *kanelbulle* also appealed to me because its spiral shape and wonderfully dense texture reminds me of the pecan rolls I loved to unwind as a child, a Swedish twist on a familiar theme.

Lately, however, I have developed a taste for Munkens' *kardemummabulle*, a knot-shaped yeast bun with the subtle peppery flavor of ground cardamom. Sometimes, I indulge in something sweeter, such as a *mazarin*, a pastry French in origin, named after the Italian-born French statesman and church leader, Cardinal Jules Mazarin. Or I might have a *katalan*, a similar pastry named after the ancient region of Catalonia bordering France and Spain. This small pastry has a round buttery crust and almond-paste filling, spread with raspberry jam and the sheerest layer of icing. A softer version of the *mazarin*, the *katalan* seems to melt in the mouth.

Or if we're in Sweden over the holidays, I might choose a seasonal treat, such as the gingerbread cookies shaped like hearts or pigs, or *semla* (plural, *semlor*), a raised bun with a hint of cardamom, filled with almond paste and whipped cream. Traditionally semlor were served in a bowl of hot milk or cream only on Tuesdays during Lent, the forty days preceding Easter, but now these popular pastries are available every day of the week during this period and, at some bakeries—but not Munkens—as early as New Year's Day.

For our daily bread, we alternate between the white French bread that Carl and the kids favor and the rye breads, such as *Djurölimpa* and *ölimpa*, which I crave. Named after the island of Djurö, where Munkens is now located, *Djurölimpa* is made from a mixture of rye and wheat flours; sweetened with *sirap*, or sugar beet syrup; and delicately flavored with anise, fennel seeds, and the zest of Seville or bitter oranges. While *Djurölimpa* has a rectangular shape, *ölimpa*, or island loaf, is round and contains graham as well as rye and wheat flours, sugar beet syrup and caraway seeds. Neither as sweet as, say, zucchini bread nor as sour as the pumpernickels back home, these rye breads are particularly delicious slathered with creamy Swedish honey and accompanied by a cup of tea.

For Michael, I bring back a *mazarin* and, for Tina, a *kokosboll*, or coconut cocoa ball, made from softened butter, sugar, cocoa, and fine-grained oatmeal, rolled in coconut. We might add a small bag of Carl's favorite cookie, *drömmar*, or dreams. The butteriness of these aptly named morsels is tempered by *hjorthornssalt*, or ammonium bicarbonate, a forerunner to baking powder, which gives these cookies a light and tingling taste. Sometimes I'll buy a flaky, semicircular pastry filled with custard, that looks like a giant Danish but is actually called a *Wienerbröd*, or Vienna bread. Also found in Denmark, this pastry tastes much lighter and fresher than the American version, probably because it is made with plenty of real butter.

Although Starbucks has not yet arrived in Stockholm, there are a growing number of "coffee shops" serving cappuccinos and lattes, flavored with spices and syrups, Swedish *bullar* (buns), and American-style carrot cake and brownies. According to one food writer, the difference between these coffee shops and the *konditorier* is that, in the latter, you are expected to buy a pastry or sandwich to accompany your coffee, whereas, in the former, the emphasis is on the beverage.

The Kindbloms point to the development of another Stockholm café, Oscars Konditoriet, as a hopeful sign of the times. When two sisters, Renée and Lotta Voltaire, took over this café on the edge of the tony Östermalm district several years ago, they maintained the simple 1930s interior but revised the menu to include not only enlarged Swedish cinnamon buns but also such exotica as Italian *panini* sandwiches and American brownies. Noting that this combination of old-fashioned milieu and exciting, new sandwiches and baked goods has attracted customers from across town, the Kindbloms express the hope that many other period *konditorier* will also face such a "new future."

Preserving historic premises may be a worthy goal but I am concerned that, by broadening their menus to appeal to the latest trends, these *konditori* owners are abandoning that which makes their institution unique, namely, the delights of the Swedish pastry tradition.

To paraphrase one review of the Kindblom's book: Save our cultural heritage. Have another *mazarin* with that espresso.

Two of the author's favorite pastries at Munkens Konditori are *kokosbollar*, coconut cocoa balls, and a *mazarin*, or almond tart.

Prohibitions

The story of the development of the Swedish *konditori*, or bakery-café, is entwined not only with the history of coffee-drinking, but also with the consumption of alcohol, especially the hard liquor known as *brännvin*, or aquavit.

Brännvin came to Scandinavia from Russia in the 1400s. Although the word can be literally translated as "burnt wine," this beverage was initially distilled not from grapes but from grain, generally barley. At first, distilled alcohol was considered medicinal, a remedy for everything from indigestion to infertility to cancer. People believed that *brännvin* contained, in concentrated form, all of the nutrients found in the grain, and later potatoes, from which it was distilled. In addition, the alcohol was often flavored with herbs or spices to which various magical powers were attributed. Caraway *brännvin*, for example, was said not only to strengthen the appetite but also to influence the weather!

Three hundred years later, King Charles XII brought coffee to Sweden, having acquired a taste for the bitter drink during his five-year internment in Constantinople, following his defeat at the Battle of Poltava in 1709. As Lars Elgklou writes in *Kaffeboken* (The Coffee Book), the drink's popularity spread slowly, inhibited by the high price of the imported beans, a pound of which cost as much as a servant's cash wages for an entire year. Still, by 1728, Stockholm could boast fifteen coffeehouses with a limited clientele of upper class men.

While coffee was a novelty indulged in by the urban wealthy, *brännvin* had become the national beverage, especially in rural areas. As historian Alf Åberg writes of the situation in the 1700s, "Everyone drank—young and old, rich and poor." Agricultural workers were partially paid in alcohol, a shot of *brännvin* each morning; soldiers expected the same in cold weather. To meet this demand, every farm had its own distillery; consuming grain that would otherwise be turned into nourishing bread and porridge.

Responding to the grain shortage—which was also a result of the war that King Charles XII had lost to Russia and Turkey—the government forbade farmers from distilling alcohol. In 1756, the farmers in parliament retaliated with a law banning coffee, then consumed almost exclusively by city dwellers. Although prohibited from serving coffee, coffeehouse owners were allowed to continue selling *brännvin*.

This first coffee ban was lifted after thirteen years but three more prohibitions followed on the grounds that with increasing consumption and a still damaged economy, the cost of importing coffee beans was draining too much money from the national treasury. Between each of these bans, the last of which ended in 1822, the number of coffee devotees skyrocketed, fueling a black market that made each prohibition less effective than the last. Even the Queen Mother was said to have indulged.

Not only coffee but also sugar was an imported luxury item, available only to the well-to-do. The *sockerbagarna*, or confectioners, produced jams, ornamented cakes, ice cream, and candied rose petals that they initially sold through pharmacies and later in their own rather humble shops.

By the early 1800s, the temperate, decorous bourgeois were flocking to new establishments operated by Swiss bakers who had recently immigrated to Sweden. At these "Swisseries," decorated with brass detailing, marble counters, and fashionable furniture, customers could enjoy tea, hot chocolate, and coffee (when it wasn't banned), as well as dainty baked goods made with new types of dough enriched with butter and eggs.

However, these Swisseries were not universally appreciated. Seeing their livelihoods threatened, the native confectioners protested against the newcomers to the government, complaining that they used excessive amounts of imported sugar and almonds. When the government turned a deaf ear to their protests, the Swedish confectioners had no choice but to adopt the new pastries and serve them, along with *brännvin* and coffee, in their expanded premises. By 1849, the two rival baking contingents had joined forces to promote the *konditori* business.

Over the next few decades, the number of these cafés expanded rapidly, a boom fueled at least in part by women. Discouraged from patronizing restaurants except in the company of a man, women turned to the *konditori* as their public meeting place. And women *konditori* owners were among the first to cater to their increasingly female customers. For example, when Maria Kristina Lindström opened her Café Tysta Mari (Quiet Mary Café) in Stockholm in 1834, she provided a smoke-free environment to attract women patrons.

As Sweden industrialized, more women took jobs outside the home. By the 1920s, women working, for example, in the booming textile industry around the town of Ålingsås, were going to the *konditorier* to buy the bread they no longer had time to bake and enjoy a quick cup of coffee and a brief respite from their demanding workdays. Ålingsås still has one of the country's highest number of cafés per capita.

High levels of *brännvin* consumption also continued through the first half of the nineteenth century. In the 1820s, it was estimated at forty-six liters per person per year—compared to nine liters per person per year in the 1980s. But by the mid-1850s, public opinion was shifting as the temperance movement gained strength. The parliament restricted the right to distill *brännvin* and, eventually, the government set up a monopoly of state-owned liquor stores, which kept the price of alcohol artificially high.

By the early 1900s, coffee had surpassed *brännvin* to become Sweden's national drink, but the imported beans were still a luxury item and would remain so for several decades. Coffee-lovers carefully dried leftover grounds and reused them; fresh coffee was reserved for Sundays and holidays. Even then, real coffee was usually mixed with ersatz or "Swedish" coffee, such as roasted chicory, rye, or bran mixed with molasses. Numerous coffee substitutes were discovered during the prohibitions, some of them very inventive. In his 1748 essay on coffee, the botanist Linneaus wrote that he considered beechnuts to be the best-tasting substitute. During World War I, when coffee was rationed in neutral Sweden to roughly three and a half ounces per person per month, Elisa Adelsköld published a booklet with twenty-five coffee substitutes, including ripe asparagus seeds.

Traditionally, coffee was boiled with water in a pot, then strained through a "coffee skin," a square piece of dried fish skin, usually eel or burbot, to remove the grounds. Although an eighteenth-century Swedish parliamentarian tried to introduce his countrymen to the French-developed drip process of brewing coffee, this method did not become popular until the 1960s. Some contemporary Swedes, including my sister-in-law Kerstin—who only switched to the percolator in the early 1990s—seem to prefer the taste of coffee boiled in the pan, which was, after all, the original way coffee was prepared.

By the 1940s, Sweden surpassed the rest of the world in per capita coffee consumption. (Today it is second only to Finland.) From the 1920s to the 1960s, the number of konditorier continued to grow, patronized by men and women, young and old, the well-to-do and the working class. Indeed, my husband, Carl, fondly remembers the konditori near his Stockholm high school, Skanstull Gymnasium, where he and his friends drank coffee or tea, ate cinnamon buns, and chatted between classes in the early 1970s.

However, unbeknownst to Carl, another wave of imported customs was already threatening the konditori business. In the decade between 1960 and 1970, half of Sweden's five thousand konditorier closed. The Kindbloms attribute this nosedive to the "three big kondis killers": convenience stores, fast food, and television. Instead of dining and socializing in cafés, an increasing number of Swedes chose to stay home, watch television and eat convenience foods. By 1973, McDonald's had arrived in Stockholm. Many konditorier were converted into pizza parlors or takeout stands selling kebabs or hot dogs; others simply closed.

Although I missed the golden age of the konditori, fortunately Swedish café life has resurged since the late 1980s. Perhaps, this was spurred in part by the increase in both the number of retirees as the population ages and the number of women on maternity leave during baby boomlet in the 1990s. Even among young people, there has been a revival of café culture.

As for brännvin, another imported trend is succeeding where centuries of government intervention failed. Since the 1970s, wine has increasingly become the alcoholic drink of choice in Swedish restaurants and homes. Now that Sweden is a member of the European Union, wine from fellow member states, including France and Italy, has become both fashionable and affordable. Today, the state-owned liquor stores, known as systembolaget, carry such an assortment of high-quality wines, not only from major exporters but also from small vintners, that Swedish voters have seen no reason to abolish this government monopoly.

But no matter how popular wine becomes, I suspect that there will always be a place for *brännvin*, preferably flavored with berries or such herbs as Saint-John's-wort, especially at Midsummer.

Cake Party

Food is at the heart of many of life's celebrations, including even minor occasions such as the end of the school year. In my own American childhood, there was usually a party on the last day of class in elementary school and, even in high school, one or two teachers would bring doughnuts as a final gesture of goodwill.

In Sweden, the end of the school year is likewise celebrated with parties, as I discovered when my sister-in-law Kerstin invited me to attend the closing day at the elementary school where she taught. At her school, the festivities were not confined to individual classrooms but involved the entire school community in a grand finale, a *tårtkalas*, or cake party.

The day began with the children arriving at school, each carrying a gift for their teacher: a single summer blossom. Roses, lilacs, daisies, bluebells, and other flowers soon lined the classroom windows. Later, after the morning concert, Kerstin and her co-teacher gave each student a card and a lollipop, along with a paper bag filled with a selection of the year's work.

By the time Kerstin and I reached the cafeteria, the party was in full swing. Although built only five years ago, this school had already acquired traditions. Each school year begins with a *tipspromenad*, a contest in which students walk around searching for slips of paper, posted on trees and bushes, with questions to answer. A prize goes to the one who gets the most right answers. And each school year ends with a cake potluck.

At least fifty homemade cakes were laid on the long table in the cafeteria, with parents and children crowded along both sides. I took a couple of photos while Kerstin tracked down a pair of plates, forks, and cups for us from the faculty lounge. All of the parents had brought their own dishes and utensils, along with blankets to spread on the grass and thermoses of coffee or juice to share.

The parties at my children's schools always featured a mix of homemade and store-bought goodies. But at Kerstin's school, although a few of the cakes were more artistically decorated, not a single one of them looked as though it had been purchased from a bakery. While Americans tend to ice their cakes with buttercream or confectioners' sugar, Swedes prefer whipped cream, often with candies or fruit on top. Strawberries had just come into season so, naturally, there was a preponderance of strawberry tortes. These golden sponge cakes, or *sockerkakor*, were layered with strawberry jam, whipped cream, and sliced strawberries, then covered in more whipped cream and garnished with additional berries. There were also a number of *prinsesstårtor*, or princess cakes, made from the same sponge cake base but layered with vanilla custard and whipped cream, then topped with a sheet of marzipan, usually tinted green. Children who suffered from food allergies, as my own brothers had, were not totally left out; there was a separate table with two or three gluten-free cakes and a plate of strawberry-topped, dairy-free meringues.

For myself, I chose slices from three of the most unusual-looking desserts: a mocha brownie cake decorated with M&Ms; a vanilla cake covered with a marzipan Swedish flag, its deep blue field overlaid by a yellow cross; and a *mazarintårta*, a crumbly piecrust filled with ground almonds and covered with a thin layer of hard pink sugar icing, dusted with powdered sugar. This last, a larger version of my favorite pastry, the *mazarin*, was the only pielike offering.

Out in the schoolyard, Kerstin and I perched on a granite slab, eating cake, drinking coffee, and watching the children running around in the clear June light, free at last.

For Kerstin, this particular school ending seemed to have a bittersweet quality familiar to working parents everywhere. For as she said good-bye to her students, her own daughter, Elin, was graduating from *högstadiet*, the Swedish equivalent to middle school that ends at ninth grade, with her father and siblings in attendance.

On the way back to the house, Kerstin stopped at the bakery to pick up the special cake she had ordered for lunch. This was no ordinary cake but rather a *smörgåstårta*, or savory sandwich cake. I had never had a close-up look, let alone a taste, of one of these made-to-order cakes, so I was quite curious.

And yet the concept of a sandwich cake seemed vaguely familiar. Indeed, I later learned that back in the 1930s, Americans were enamored of something called a "surprise" sandwich loaf, a dish that, interestingly, had its own student connections. In her book, *Fashionable Food: Seven Decades of Food Fads*, Sylvia Lovegren describes this loaf served at ladies' club events. The name refers to the fact that the savory sandwich loaf was disguised as a cake. It was made from a loaf of white bread sliced horizontally, spread with fillings (such as egg salad, sardine butter, or chopped pimientos and mayonnaise), reassembled, and frosted in cream cheese. Eaten with a fork, the "surprise" sandwich loaf was so popular at college club meetings that it was sometimes called a "Betty Co-ed."

A decade later, the 1946 edition of *Stora Kokboken* (The Big Cookbook) had a recipe for *sandwichtårta*, a sandwich torte made from layers of white and dark rye bread spread with several flavored butters of parsley, cheese, and meat, and then covered with mayonnaise and garnished with bay shrimp and lettuce leaves. But whether Sweden imported the idea from the States—or vice versa—or whether the recipe originally came from England, home of the Earl of Sandwich, I never did find out.

Back at Kerstin's house, we gathered in the garden's enclosed gazebo to fete fifteen-year-old Elin with homemade *hallonsaft*, or raspberry drink, and *smörgåstårta*. From the outside, this cake, with its mayonnaise frosting, did indeed resemble the whipped cream cakes at the school potluck. But while the sweet cakes were simply decorated with fruit or candy, the top of this savory torte was elaborately garnished with rows of black olives, sliced tomatoes, cucumbers, pineapple pieces, and bay shrimp; then bordered with slices of cheese rolled up like flower petals; the whole crowned with parsley sprigs. On the inside, the sandwich cake consisted of white bread layered with lighter, Swedish mayonnaise, studded with bay shrimp, peas, grapes, mandarin oranges, mimosa salad, and bits of liver pâté and roast beef.

These combinations of toppings and fillings might give the impression of a salad bar run amok, but the simplicity of the two main ingredients, bread and mayonnaise, lent a consistency to the dish as a whole so that the experience was more like bites of different sandwiches. Since I'm not a mayonnaise fan, I wasn't sure if I would even like the sandwich cake, but this mayonnaise was creamy and slightly sweet, with a hint of pineapple.

In fact, I enjoyed it so much that the next time Carl and I celebrated our anniversary in Sweden, I ordered from nearby Munkens Konditori not only a princess torte similar to the one we had at our wedding, but also a sandwich cake, which we shared with our children on the deck outside the kitchen at Fågelbro.

Sexy Midsummer Strawberries

I was driving along the Värmdö Way, the road that links our home on the island of Fågelbrolandet to the city of Stockholm, when I first saw it. There, in a parking lot near the hotdog stand, was a bright red, seven-foot-tall strawberry. On closer inspection, the giant fruit turned out to be a fiberglass kiosk. From a window cut out in the front, a young woman was selling square paper boxes filled with the first sweet *jordgubbar*, or strawberries, of the season.

The strawberry harvest is a harbinger of Midsummer, the three-day summer solstice holiday—and of the monthlong July vacation. With its bright red color and succulent sweetness, the strawberry is the perfect symbol for Sweden's most sensuous season.

Swedes have long had a reputation abroad for sexiness. In the years when we had Swedish au pairs, I made a point of showing each new young woman the *Wall Street Journal* article on sex, suicides, and Swedes so that she would know what kind of stereotypes some Americans harbored about her country. One Swedish woman interviewed in the piece commented that American men were always expecting her to jump—either into their bed or out the window.

Having married into a Swedish family, I have found that, behind their reserved albeit often attractive facades, most Swedes are, well, reserved. Shy. Alcohol may loosen their tongues but seldom their libidos—at least not publicly. And topless beaches notwithstanding, only children swim nude in the presence of other people.

While I was raised in a society where the nude body is paradoxically seen as both inherently sinful and the ideal way to sell almost anything, my husband, Carl, grew up with the Swedish view that sees the body and its functions, including sexuality, as a natural part of being human. Information about reproduction, birth control, and sexually transmitted diseases are integrated into the school curriculum in a matter-of-fact way from kindergarten on. But knowing how the body works does not diminish the mysterious nature of sexuality or of sensuality.

When I think of Sweden and sex, what immediately comes to mind are images of summer, a fleeting season imbued with almost mystical reverence. Summers are brief but intense here in the Land of the Midnight Sun. The sky remains light for twenty-one hours a day in Stockholm in late June and early July. That doesn't translate into nonstop sunshine, as rainstorms are not uncommon this time of year. However, the entire country is organized so that virtually everyone has a chance to catch any available rays. Not only teachers like my sister-in-law Kerstin and friend

Ylva, but dentists, doctors, bureaucrats, factory workers, and executives—virtually everyone I know has several weeks of summer vacation. Every business that possibly can closes for the month of July, including some of Stockholm's best restaurants.

If the summer looks like it's going to be cold and rainy at home, our friends and relatives might book a charter trip to the Mediterranean. But when the weather promises to be sunny, many Swedes prefer to stay in their own country, enjoying the simple life in a cottage by the sea or beside one of the thousands of lakes that dot the land. In one of my favorite Swedish songs, "Öppna landskap" (Open landscapes), contemporary songwriter Ulf Lundell gives voice to this longing to live close to nature, if only for a few brief weeks.

Even in the city, I feel a palpable joie de vivre on those days when the sun shines and the breeze is mild. Bicyclists fill the streets and sunbathers, many of them topless, throng the beaches. Sailboats and motorboats ply the city's waterways. Ice-cream stands do a booming business. Young men and women, blond and well-groomed, sit in outdoor cafés, drinking cappuccinos and flirting. Even the most reserved Swedes smile more readily and strike up conversations with strangers.

The Swedish summer exerts a magical pull on me as well, luring me across an ocean. For there is something about this Nordic season, an indefinable, stirring, hedonistic quality that heightens my awareness of my own and other people's bodies. Is it the light, the sun rising at 2:00 A.M., and setting the last hour before midnight? Is it the brisk wind off the Baltic Sea swirling around my legs? Is it the scent of pine forests with their secret clearings? Or is it the sight of all those upright maypoles erected for the summer solstice?

In ancient Viking times, the summer solstice was sacred to Freya, the Norse fertility goddess, and celebrated with bonfires. Young women leapt over a small fire or danced around a larger one in the hope that they would soon be married and blessed with children. Today, bonfires are lit throughout the country on the last night of April, May Eve, also called *Walpurgisnacht*, to celebrate the coming of spring.

When Catholicism swept the land in the twelfth century, Midsummer's Eve was assigned a fixed date: June 24, John the Baptist's Day. Not only fire but also water, especially dew, were believed to be imbued with magical power on the summer solstice. Rolling naked in that morning's dew was said to increase a young woman's attractiveness. The solstice dew also had health-giving properties. Mothers bathed their small children in it to protect them from sickness. Wise women went out into the woods and fields early on Midsummer's Eve to pick herbs and other medicinal plants while the dew was still on them, when they were at their most potent. A housewife might also drag a dishtowel through the dew. She would then take the water collected from the towel and mix it with flour to form small cakes, one for each bread-baking session of the year, as a charm so that the baking would be successful.

Midsummer dreams had the power to foretell a young girl's future spouse, provided she followed certain ritual steps. She could cook a "dream porridge" with equal portions salt and flour. Or she could eat a salted herring, tail first, before going to bed—but she was to drink nothing whatsoever that evening, no matter how thirsty she became; the man who brought her a drink in her dream would be her future spouse. Or she could go out to the fields and gather, alone and in silence, nine different kinds of flowers to place under her pillow, a custom I first heard about from my Swedish cooking teacher, Ingmarie.

In some parts of central Sweden and on Gotland, young men called *lövgubbar*, or leaf men, were covered in birch leaves and flowers like walking maypoles—perhaps as a personification of the season or of a pre-Christian god of vegetation. In villages in Dalarna and southern Sweden, pretend weddings were staged until the early 1900s, with the prettiest girls crowned "Midsummer brides." Today, on Midsummer's Eve, vestiges of this custom linger as women and girls often wear white dresses and flower crowns woven with daisies, bluebells, and red clover, like the ones I make for my daughter, Tina. These same blossoms decorate the *majstång*, or maypole.

When we attended the Swedish Lutheran Church in Los Angeles, I wondered why the priest enthusiastically celebrated Sweden's Nationaldagen, or National Day, on June 6 but never said a word about Midsummer. With all of the pagan references, I can now see why.

Some five hundred years ago, the ancient bonfires were replaced by a German import, the maypole. Shaped like a cross with two wreaths hanging from the shorter horizontal pole, entirely wrapped in birch leaves, the *majstång* is erected in neighborhoods and villages throughout the country on Midsummer's Eve, now the Friday closest to June 24. When our family lived in Massachusetts, we attended the Boston Swedish School's annual Midsummer party and graduation. Along with other parents and children, we joined hands danced around the bedecked pole, singing odes to summer and childhood favorites like "*Små groddarna*" (The little frogs).

While folklorists and magazine writers occasionally comment on the symbolism of inserting a wooden pole into the ground, most Swedes seem to ignore this aspect. And yet, the connection between the summer solstice and sex is not too obscured. For example, the Midsummer's Eve edition of one national newspaper surveyed young men and women on whether and why—or why not—they planned to use a condom on this magical night. I cannot imagine a similar story running in, say, the *New York Times*.

Midsummer is a time not only for trysts but also for feasting. Like nearly everyone else in Sweden, we eat herring and potatoes, washed down with aquavit and/or beer, preferably outdoors. One type of aquavit particularly associated with this holiday is *Hirkum Pirkum*, flavored and tinted red with the buds of Saint-John's-wort (*Hypericum perforatum* in Latin). In "*Öppna landskap*," Ulf Lundell sings about the pleasures of distilling his own aquavit, spicing it with Saint-John's-wort, and drinking it with herring and home-baked rye bread in the wide-open spaces near the water. This medicinal flowering herb, often steeped in aquavit, has been used for centuries not only as a treatment for depression, migraines, menstrual difficulties, and flatulence, but also as a primitive truth serum and protection from the devil.

Sill, or herring, is the star of the Midsummer menu. My favorite type of pickled herring is the spicy, commercially produced *matjessill*, related to the Dutch herring dish *maatjesharing*. This delicacy is also called *jungfrusill*, or virgin herring, because the fish used are below the reproductive age of four or five years. Caught in the autumn off the coast of Iceland, these herring are rubbed with a mixture of salt, sugar, and mystery spices. They are stored in barrels for at least three months; when ripe, the fish are skinned and filleted, then canned in a mixture of salt, sugar, vinegar, and spices.

Matjessill has a buttery texture and a taste that combines the sharpness of vinegar and the smoothness of sugar, along with an elusive spiciness. Although the producers refuse to reveal which spices they use, the test kitchen director for the ICA publishing company, Birgitta Rasmussen, recalled that the homemade *matjessill* of her childhood included allspice; she also suggested that commercial canners might add sandalwood to give the fish a rosy color.

I buy *matjessill* at my neighborhood market, Strömma Handel, where the small tins are stacked on shelves in the cold section, next to jars of pickled herring in mustard, cream, or tomato sauces. We make open-faced sandwiches with small strips of herring on crispbread, topped with a dollop of sour cream and diced chives.

Looking as though they were freshly dug out of the garden, new potatoes are customarily sold with the dirt still clinging to their thin skins.

Midsummer is also the beginning of the local potato season, a crop that Swedes get very excited about. The potato was initially embraced as a substitute for grain in distilling alcohol—too much of the country's rye crop was going into making aquavit instead of bread—but in the early 1700s botanist Jonas Alströmer championed the root vegetable's potential as a food source.

I'm always surprised to see that, even in the largest supermarkets, new potatoes are sold unwashed, presumably to give the consumer the illusion that they have just been dug out of the field, which, of course, is when they're at their best. Swedish new potatoes have such thin skins that the peels can be removed merely by rubbing. Freshly dug from my sister-in-law Kerstin's country garden and simmered with bunches of dill until tender, the new potatoes taste both delicate and earthy.

Some years we have a simple meal of herring sandwiches, boiled potatoes, and aquavit at a picnic table on the back deck; other times we attend a party with a more elaborate menu.

One of our first summers in Sweden we spent Midsummer at the home of Conny and Rénee, friends of Carl's brother Thomas. Conny is a photographer while his wife, Rénee, is an equestrian rider and former model. We ate outside at long tables under a tarp rigged against the side of the house to keep off the rain. In addition to herring and potatoes, there was *grönsakspaté*, or vegetable terrine; *prinskorv*, or tiny smoked sausages; and *köttbullar*, or meatballs; mild cheese; French-style bread; and green salad. If the weather had been better, we would have sat outside for hours drinking and chatting, but the damp chill and steady rain eventually drove us indoors. We curled up on sofas and chairs in the cozy living room, the gray daylight warmed by the glow of candlelight, talking and drinking more wine, then coffee with the traditional finale, *jordgubbstårta*, or strawberry torte. Covered in whipped cream and decorated with a dozen whole strawberries, this lovely yellow sponge cake is layered with strawberry jam, whipped cream, and sliced strawberries. It is the quintessential Midsummer dessert.

While the wild strawberry, *smultron*, is native to Scandinavia, the larger, hybrid strawberry, *jordgubbe*, has only been cultivated on a large scale in Sweden since the mid-twentieth century. Despite its brief tenure on the Midsummer menu, for me, the strawberry—with its sun-kissed warmth, firm but yielding texture, juicy sweetness, heart shape, and bright red coloring evocative of the sun, sex, and life itself—is an apt symbol of the summer solstice and the joyfulness with which Swedes embrace the return of the light.

Wedding Feast

From the moment I saw the musicians, dressed in yellow knee breeches and striped vests, standing at the front of the church, I knew that this wedding was going to be different from any that I had witnessed in the States. We drove twelve hours north from Stockholm to attend the wedding of Carl's high school friend Peter and his bride, Ingeborg, in her home village, Kall—whose name means cold. Here, pastoral Sweden approaches mountainous Norway in the northwestern province of Jämtland (pronounced "Yemt-land").

Soon, two fiddlers struck up the tune of "Jämtland Bridal March" as Ingeborg walked down the aisle in a modern, full-skirted white wedding dress with roses and cornflowers adorning her hair. To my astonishment, she was accompanied not by her father but by her tuxedoed groom.

Peter and Ingeborg walked together through the *lövportal*, a leaf gate formed by a pair of potted birch saplings, to stand in front of the minister. Instead of huge bouquets of flowers at the altar, small bunches of wild purple pansies and golden buttercups graced the entrance to each pew of this stark, whitewashed Lutheran church.

Never having been to a Swedish wedding before, I hadn't known what to expect. The fact that our friends, who live in Stockholm, had decided to wed in the same country church where Ingeborg had been baptized and her parents married, indicated that this wedding might be traditional. But what did traditional mean in this context?

In Sweden, one of the last western European countries to industrialize, traditional is nearly synonymous with rural. Communities in this sparsely populated land developed regional variations in music, food, dance, dress, and even language. Many of these local distinctions have disappeared in the past century but some remain. In planning their wedding, Peter and Ingeborg drew upon both the national rural culture and specific surviving traditions from the bride's home province. Previously, I had seen glimpses of Sweden's rural heritage preserved and displayed in museums such as Skansen. But not until I attended this wedding did I understand its importance in the lives of contemporary Swedes.

After the ceremony, we walked back to the ski lodge where most of the guests were staying for the reception. The calendar said July 3, but the lilacs were just beginning to bloom and the temperature hovered around fifty degrees Fahrenheit, with overcast skies. Although we began with a champagne toast on the gorgeously green lawn, we soon headed inside to a pine-clad dining room whose picture windows offered a stunning view of snowcapped Åre Mountain. Facing their guests, the bride and groom sat beneath a tabletop archway entwined with fragile golden buttercups and tiny purple pansies, the same type of flowers that had graced the church.

Just as these wildflowers had been gathered from nearby fields, the dinner itself represented the bounty of the northern forests, lakes, and sea. This perfect Swedish summer meal began with *viltsallad*, a small salad of julienned *älg*, or moose, with a touch of horseradish sharpening the flavor of the binding mayonnaise. Flaky heart-shaped biscuits and a mound of bright orange *löjrom*, or bleak fish roe, delicately salty and so fine-grained that it tickled the tongue like champagne, rounded out the appetizer plate. Freshly caught from one of Jämtland's three thousand lakes, the chilled, poached salmon trout was succulently sweet with a silken texture and rosy hue. Slender green and thick white asparagus and a lettuce salad sprinkled with corn kernels provided a pleasing contrast in color and texture. Even the dessert, lingonberry parfait, a frozen swirl of sweetened whipped cream and tart red berries, was a Jämtland specialty. The parfait exemplified the region's tradition of pairing local berries and dairy products to create fabulous desserts—as did the bride's wedding cake.

The highlight of a Swedish wedding dinner is usually *prinsesstårta*, or princess torte, a vanilla cake layered with custard and whipped cream and covered with a sheet of marzipan. However, Ingeborg has never cared for almonds. She chose instead a strawberry-studded *gräddtårta*, a luscious, fluffy sponge cake filled and covered with whipped cream.

Throughout the evening of feasting, dancing, jokes, and games, we toasted the bride and groom, led by the toastmaster, who wore the same local costume as the church musicians had. We raised our glasses of champagne during the appetizer course, white wine with the entrée, liqueurs with coffee at dessert time. At midnight, the reception ended, as many Swedish parties do, with *Jansson's frestelse*, or Jansson's temptation, a hearty dish of julienned potatoes, onions, anchovies, and cream. This hot dish, served with cold beer, vodka, or aquavit, was traditionally meant to warm guests for the long sleigh ride back to their farms.

With this briny casserole, we had warm *tunnbröd* (pronounced "tune-brood"), a flatbread that the bride's mother had baked in the village oven. A specialty of northern and central Sweden, *tunnbröd* comes in two varieties. One is the soft bread we had at the wedding (and at our favorite fast food places in Stockholm), which can be folded and is usually eaten fresh; the other, a crisp version that lasts all winter and is similar to the hardtack found throughout Scandinavia. In the past, *tunnbröd* was made primarily with barley, the grain best suited to Jämtland's climate, or with a mixture of barley and oat meals. Today, however, this unleavened bread is usually produced from a combination of wheat and rye flours.

The day after the wedding, my family and I had the opportunity to tour Ingeborg's home village with Peter as our guide. Entering the cozy *bakstuga*, the community's baking hut, was like stepping into another, earlier era. We watched as several women worked at the flour-covered table, shaping, flattening, and piercing circles of dough with a spiked rolling pin. Using a narrow wooden stick, the women lifted each cross-hatch patterned round of dough off the table, onto a board with a long handle like a pizza paddle, which they used to slide the bread into the wood-fired, brick oven. The aroma of freshly baked bread nearly overpowered me with longing.

As we reluctantly backed out of the hut, one of the women thoughtfully offered us some of the flatbread, which had a chewy texture and a seductively smoky, wood-grilled taste. According to folk tradition, anyone entering the *bakstuga* must be offered a *smakbröd*, a taste of the bread; otherwise, the offended visitor would take the "baking luck" away with them. Perhaps our benefactress was influenced by this old belief. Nonetheless, I was touched by her hospitable gesture—belying the stereotype of "cold" Swedes—and revealing once again the traditional, rural culture that is industrial, urban Sweden's hidden heart.

A traditional baking hut at the castle Nääs Slott on Sweden's west coast.

Crayfish Madness

As soon as paper lanterns, round as harvest moons, with smiling faces, begin to appear in the shop windows, I know that the Swedes are on the brink of crayfish madness.

For over a hundred years, the opening of the crayfish season, on August 8, has marked the beginning of a round of outdoor parties to fete one of Sweden's most prized delicacies, the humble crawdad—and to bid farewell to cherished summer.

Only a few weeks after their wedding, Peter and Ingeborg invited Carl and me to a crayfish party—my first *kräftskiva*. We sat outside at long wooden tables under trees strung with paper moon lanterns. Ingeborg brought out platters of cold boiled crayfish, garnished with crowns of yellow dill flowers, along with Västerbotten cheese, a hard, sharp cheese from the province of the same name, and loaves of French bread shaped like crayfish.

Everyone wore a plastic bib and a paper party hat—both embellished with images of crayfish—the former to contain the mess, the latter to encourage guests to cut loose and act like children. Cracking shells, pulling off legs and heads, slurping the salty juices, and extracting the tiny bits of the sweet meat—eating food with one's fingers is both childish and intensely sensual. Playful flirting came easily in such a setting, especially since each guest was seated between two members of the opposite sex, neither of whom was his or her date. Throughout the evening, glasses were raised, but not clinked, as the group called out "*skål!*" (cheers!). Half of the guests—those of us who were designated drivers—sipped sodas or nonalcoholic beer while the other half freely partook of aquavit and strong beer. But everyone sang the traditional drinking songs. No wonder the *kräftskiva* has been called a children's party for adults.

The opening of crayfish season may be a uniquely Swedish holiday, but the custom of eating crayfish is not. Although the ancient Romans considered crayfish to be food fit only for slaves, medieval Christian monks and nuns found the crustaceans a tasty substitute for meat, particularly during the long Lenten fast. By the 1400s, their fondness for this shellfish had spread to the upper classes, particularly in Germany.

Of the five hundred varieties of freshwater crayfish worldwide, only five are indigenous to Europe, one being the *flödkräftor*, which has lived in the creeks and streams of southern and central Sweden as far back as the Stone Age. The earliest written Swedish references to crayfish date from the 1500s, including a circa-1522 prescription for a cholera preventive that called for crayfish dissolved in grain alcohol. Forty years later, King Erik XIV introduced the Swedish court to crayfish prepared by the cooks he imported from Germany in an attempt to keep up with continental trends. By the 1700s, the crawdad had caught on with the upper classes to the extent that Sweden's then foremost cooking expert, Cajsa Warg, included a dozen recipes for crayfish pâtés, puddings, soups, and buns (often flavored with parsley) in her famous cookbook, *Household Management Guide for Young Women*. In the nineteenth century, crayfish stuffings and stews became passé in Sweden. Instead, crayfish were boiled in the shell with bunches of dill flowers, and served whole, the way they still are today. Accompanied by bread, cheese, and aquavit, they were often consumed out of doors, as illustrated in Carl Larsson's idyllic painting, *Crayfish Catching*.

Crayfish became more popular among Swedes in part because of romantic portrayals by artists such as Larsson, and writers including the eighteenth-century balladeer Carl Michael Bellman and the nineteenth-century playwright August Strindberg. At the same time, the Swedish crayfish gained a reputation for sweetness among the Germans, who imported barrels of salted crayfish tails. Increasing scarcity spurred demand even higher. Finally, in the 1860s, the Swedish government limited fishing of these crustaceans to the period between August 8 and November 1 (later extended to January 1). Naturally, the opening of the season became an excuse for a party and the August *kräftskiva* was born.

However, not every Swede loved crayfish. In Norrland, the northern third of the country, Swedes of all classes were generally unfamiliar with this nonindigenous shellfish. (Norrlanders developed their own traditions connected with *surströmming*, herring caught in the late spring and fermented throughout the summer in barrels that are opened on August 15, the sour herring premier.)

In southern and central Sweden, the poorer classes viewed crayfish as a source of income but had no interest in actually eating them, not least because they looked like bugs. Even the great Swedish botanist Linneaus, who was allergic to shellfish, had classified the crayfish as insects. This aversion makes sense when one considers the fact that shellfish poisoning had serious consequences even in nineteenth-century Sweden.

In the twentieth-century postwar period, with improved living standards, sanitation, refrigeration, and transportation, the crayfish finally attained almost universal popularity in central and southern Sweden—just as the *flödkräftor* were on their way to extinction from decades of overfishing and a recent, rapidly spreading plague. The situation became so desperate for crayfish lovers that in 1969, the Swedish government imported sixty thousand live crayfish, packed in snow, from Lake Tahoe in California, to replace the vanishing indigenous species.

For a time, Swedes had to content themselves with frozen crawdads imported from Turkey, Spain, Australia, and Louisiana. Today, fresh Swedish crayfish are again available, descended from the remnants of the native *flödkraftor* interbred with the immigrant *signalkräftor* species. They are, however, more expensive than the frozen imports.

Throughout the 1970s and '80s, the government restricted the sale of crayfish, whether fresh or frozen, native or imported, to the period between August 8 and New Year's Day, in an attempt to maintain tradition, and perhaps to bolster the fresh crayfish industry. Eventually, the government repealed the restriction and, in 1995, the words "crayfish premier," which had marked the season's August 8 opening, were removed from official calendars.

Swedes may now have the government's permission to enjoy crayfish whenever they please, but my guess is that the August *kräftskiva* will continue. Although one could serve crayfish for a family supper on a rainy March night, this would strike most Swedes as rather strange, in part because crayfish are too expensive for a casual dinner. Crayfish might appear as an appetizer for a New Year's Eve gathering, but they are really too messy to eat indoors in any quantity. Summer is the only season where the weather is warm enough to spend hours sitting outdoors, and with June devoted to Midsummer, and July to the mandatory five-week vacation, mid-August is the ideal time for this end-of-summer rite.

For the enduring appeal of the *kräftskiva* lies not only in the Swedish love of crayfish, or of drinking parties, but in how this tradition also marks the change of seasons. By the second week in August,

An August delicacy, crayfish boiled with dill flowers is showcased at Lisa Elmqvist's fish stall at Östermalm's Saluhallen.

most families have returned from their summer holidays, the children to school and the adults to work. Friends, who may not have seen each other during the flurry of summer vacations, are eager to catch up. The evenings are still relatively light and warm. The opening of the crayfish season provides the perfect opportunity for friends and family to gather for one last riotous outdoor party to celebrate the briefest, sweetest season.

At Peter and Ingeborg's party, which fell only a few days before our return to the States, there came a moment—the brief, melancholy moment that perhaps defines every crayfish party—when the sun sank below the horizon, reminding us that the period of midnight sun was over and another summer had passed. But the moon lanterns still softly shone above us and the party continued into the night.

Cake on a Spit

The pale yellow cone with airy latticework sides and squiggly lines of pink icing towered over the other items on a shelf behind the bakery counter at Stockholm's exclusive department store NK. From my reading, I recognized that this hollow meringue confection was a *spettekaka* (pronounced "spet-a-ka-ka"), a cake baked on a spit, a specialty of Sweden's southernmost province, Skåne. But I didn't know that this ten-inch-high example was a rather small *spettekaka*, especially compared to those baked in the 1800s. Back then, this traditional rural wedding cake routinely reached a height of four feet.

Intrigued by this fanciful pastry, so different from any other in the Swedish dessert repertoire, I resolved to someday journey to Skåne, not only to sample *spettekaka* in its native setting but also to see for myself exactly how such a delicate-looking cake could be baked on a spit.

To learn more about *spettekaka*, I traveled first to the southern city of Malmö, to interview Carl-Bertil Widell, master confectioner and author of *En sockerbagare här bor i staden* (A Confection Baker Lives Here in the Town). Named after a line in a late nineteenth-century children's song, his book chronicles the history not only of Sweden's pastry tradition but also of many individual confections, including *spettekaka*.

Speaking Swedish with the broad accent of his native Skåne, Widell said that the first mention he found of *spettekaka* dated from 1646 in the city of Antwerp. This conical confection migrated northwards and, by the early 1800s, had reached Sweden's southernmost province, where it became the traditional wedding cake. For a rural wedding, there might be eight or ten cakes, each measuring four feet in height, brought by guests carrying large straw baskets. Neighbors would divide the ingredients' cost—a cake that used less than sixty eggs was considered proof of poverty—and the farm wife with the deftest touch would do the actual baking. Such cakes were status symbols not only for the bakers but also for the host. Having many large cakes at a wedding showed that the host had a number of wealthy friends and, correspondingly, a higher status in the community.

Over time, Widell explained, this meringue dessert became so popular that some women, known as *spettekaksgummor*, began to specialize in baking these difficult confections for weddings, birthdays, and other festive occasions. But by 1870, these women bakers faced increasing competition from the *konditorier*, or bakery-cafés, which included *spettekaka* in their daily specials.

Today, *spettekaka* has become an endangered art form. Only a dozen or so individuals and bakeries in Skåne make it. Widell suggested several reasons for this, including the tendency to smaller social gatherings and the fact that few home cooks have the required equipment, expertise, or time. Even with the motorized rotisserie, making *spettekaka* is too time-consuming not only for home cooks but even for most contemporary bakery-cafés.

And yet, the *spettekaka* lives on in Skåne for weddings and other special occasions. Widell poetically said, "During the late autumn, when the weather is gray, rainy, and cold, and the landscape is still, the mood is lightened with big festive parties, such as the eel parties and goose dinners, and at these, it is obligatory to have *spettekaka*, followed by ice cream and port wine."

By this time, I was more eager than ever to watch *spettekaka* being baked. Widell was not optimistic. He gave me the names of several specialty bakers from the phone book but cautioned that, unlike pastry makers who operated storefront bakeries or cafés, most of the remaining *spettekaksgummor* bake privately.

Indeed, my initial attempts to find a baker proved unsuccessful. The next day was Saturday and the nearest open bakery was in Helsingborg, thirty minutes away from the inn where I was staying. Unfortunately, I could not understand the broad accent of the man who tried to give me directions. I got utterly lost. Loathe to miss out on lunch at the inn, I decided to table my search until Monday morning. The inn's lunch menu promised *kuskaspis*, the Skåne term for *äggkaka*, literally, egg cake, a provincial specialty that is a cross between a pancake and an omelet, baked in a cast-iron pan and served with bacon and lingonberries. For me, this dish never fails to call up happy memories of the cooking class where I first learned to make *äggkaka* from Ingmarie.

The following night, at the inn's restaurant, I got my first taste of cake baked on a spit. To my surprise, this lightweight meringue pastry wasn't as achingly sweet as I would have predicted but rather had a delicious eggy flavor. The taste strengthened my resolve to track down a *spettekaka* bakery, for now I wanted not only to watch this cake being made but also bring one home to my family.

With only a few hours to accomplish my mission, I started calling *spettekaka* bakeries first thing Monday morning. This time, I was lucky. The first place I called was open. Naturally, I got lost on my way to Bröd och Spettekaksbagerit in Boarp, just outside the coastal resort town of Båstad, where the Swedish Open tennis tournaments are held. But my searching and waiting paid off; baker-owner Malena Nilsson turned out to be enthusiastic, knowledgeable, and willing to let me take all the photographs I wanted.

"Today, it takes four hours to bake a *spettekaka* with an electric rotisserie; you can imagine how long it took to bake by hand," she said. Although Nilsson keeps her recipe a secret, visitors can learn about the process from the illustrated chart posted on one wall of the café and by observing through the large window directly opposite the rotisseries.

When I arrived, Nilsson had several cakes in progress, each at a different stage. While bakers in previous generations had to beat the batter for two hours with a bundle of juniper twigs, Nilsson used an electric mixer. I watched as she loaded the thick batter—made from eggs, sugar, and potato starch—into a large pastry bag. She piped the first layer in concentric circles horizontally around the metal cone covered in a special paper. She then reloaded the pastry cone, stood in front of a second rotating spit, and piped another layer, this time vertically. Each layer must bake dry before the next can be added. There is no set baking time or temperature that must be reached; she does it "by eye and experience," Nilsson said. The third cake was in the final stage of baking. All she needed to do was pipe on the icing of confectioners' sugar and egg whites and let it dry for an hour. Then Nilsson would lift the cone off the heat, slip the cake off the cone, remove the paper, and set the newly baked *spettekaka* inside a plastic bag.

On her fliers, the baker listed her cakes' sizes by giving both the height in centimeters and the number of eggs used; these ranged from nearly ten inches high with five eggs, to thirty-nine inches tall with forty eggs. Her customers generally order the meringue confections for weddings, funerals, and baptisms. For weddings, she adds a smooth-edged "crown" piece on the top with the date and the couple's names in sugar icing; this piece is often kept as a memento. Stored in a dry place at room temperature, *spettekaka* will last months; from the wedding to the first christening, she joked.

Unfortunately, over the past fifteen years, the number of customers has declined and, correspondingly, fewer bakeries offer the confection. Nilsson estimates that twenty years ago, there were 50 to 60 *spettekaka* bakeries, compared to the 10 or 12 remaining today. The difficult and time-consuming nature of baking *spettekaka* seems to be one of the reasons; Nilsson has had older women bakers come into the store who tell her they've never even tried to make *spettekaka*. "The younger people don't want to learn and the older generation feels too old to keep going," she added.

At midlife, Nilsson seems to be going strong. This is good news for those fortunate enough to live within driving distance of Boarp. Since I don't, I couldn't leave without buying a cake to take home, although I had no idea how I was going to fit even the smallest one into my luggage.

Boarding the plane the next afternoon, I was in a quandary. Wrapped in a plastic bag, my cake was almost ten inches tall and nearly as wide at the base. I had no room left in my bags, already loaded with cookbooks. Nor had I thought to bring or buy a separate suitcase for my treasure. Since the *spettekaka* was too wide to fit under the seat in front of me, the overhead bin seemed to be the only option. But if I put the *spettekaka* up there, unprotected, it would almost certainly be pulverized by roll-on suitcases. I could carry the cake back on my lap—after all, it was only eight hours' flying time. But what if I dozed off and the cake fell out of my hands and wedged itself into the narrow aisle, where it would surely be crushed by a serving cart?

Just before takeoff, I came up with a possible solution. Wrapping the cake in my winter jacket just might provide enough padding to protect it in the overhead bin. Throughout the flight, I was tempted to check on my cake but didn't dare. When we finally landed, I carefully opened the compartment and unwrapped my coat, prepared for the sight of splintered meringue. But the magnificent *spettekaka* had arrived unscathed.

Martin Goose

My trip to Skåne to investigate *spettekaka*, cake baked on a spit, coincided with the provincial holiday St. Martin's Day. Once a holy day, St. Martin's Day, November 10, is now primarily celebrated with a unique menu: black soup, roast goose, and *spettekaka*. As I prepared for my journey, I wondered not only about *spettekaka* but about who Saint Martin was and how this saint's day survived the Reformation. What was black soup and would I have the temerity to try it or would I chicken out and order consommé? And what was the connection between this holiday, the goose, and the province of Skåne?

Born in 317 c.e. and named for Mars, the god of war, Martin served in the Roman army until he converted to Christianity and became a monk. According to legend, when the church authorities wanted to make him bishop of Tours, the humble Martin was so reluctant to assume this office that he hid in a goose-sty. However, the geese began honking so loudly that the hapless monk was soon discovered and the bishop's miter placed on his head. The story goes on to say that the annoyed Martin ordered the geese to be slaughtered. Two hundred and fifty years after his death on. November 11, 397 c.e., Martin was canonized, becoming the patron saint of horses, travelers, vintners, and France. Since early November was the time of year when Europeans slaughtered their geese, the French naturally celebrated their patron saint's day by feasting on roast goose.

During the Middle Ages, the custom of eating goose on November 11 gradually spread from France to Germany and eventually to Sweden, where geese had been domesticated for nearly four thousand years. Among the Vikings, the goose was associated with both the chief god Odin and the war god Thor.

Shortly after the custom of St. Martin's Day goose dinners arrived in Sweden, the country converted from Roman Catholicism to Swedish Lutheranism. Since Lutheranism does not believe in the intercession of saints, most saints' day celebrations gradually disappeared. However, a few of these, such as Lucia Day and Michaelmas, were so integrated into the agricultural calendar that they have been celebrated into modern times. In the case of St. Martin's Day, there was an additional reason that the holiday survived the Reformation—the father of the Reformation, Martin Luther, was born one day earlier, on November 10. Martin's Day, as the holiday was now called, was moved to the eve of the saint's day, and continued to be celebrated.

In Skåne, Martin's Day had a greater importance than elsewhere in Sweden. It marked not only the first day of winter but also the end of the fiscal year. Debts were settled, local aldermen appointed, and farmworkers' contracts renewed. With the harvest safely stored, people had the time and money to celebrate. Master craftsmen, in particular, feted their young apprentices and journeymen. This holiday meal, like that served on Christmas, included *lutfisk*, or dried ling cod soaked in slaked lime and soda; roast goose; and *risgrynsgröt*, a rice porridge cooked with milk. *Lutfisk* and rice porridge remain traditional Christmas dishes to this day but, on the Martin's Day menu, they were eventually replaced by black soup and *spettekaka*.

Since ancient times, Scandinavians have used iron-rich animal blood in soups, puddings, and dumplings, often flavored with such exotic spices as ginger, cardamom, cloves, and cinnamon. While the upper classes in Skåne ate blood soup frequently, the farmers considered this a luxury to be served on festive occasions such as Christmas and weddings—but evidently not on St. Martin's Day. Instead, the idea of serving black soup, roast goose, and *spettekaka* on St. Martin's Day seems to have been invented in the 1850s and '60s by Stockholm restaurateurs.

Today, blood soup has nearly vanished, save for its annual appearance on Martin's Day. While waiting for the goose dinner at my hotel to begin, I chatted with my Swedish tablemates, all of whom were at or near retirement age. They were almost as unfamiliar with black soup as I was. Although they had eaten blood pudding from childhood on, most had tasted blood soup only once, if at all. Like me, they were a little hesitant but still game to try.

The soup arrived with some ceremony in white bowls with pink floral rims, served with a slice of goose-liver pâté on the side. We blew on the hot, thick, chocolate-color purée. Meanwhile, the chef described how he made the soup, a recipe remarkably similar to a sixteenth-century recipe I later found.

He began by cooking veal stock, chicken stock, thyme, marjoram, cloves, allspice, apples, and figs together. Once the stock had absorbed the spices, he strained the soup and added the goose blood over low heat, being careful not to let the liquid boil lest it turn into porridge. At this stage, he added the alcohol: Madeira, port, and cognac, and seasoned the soup to taste with black pepper. The soup then rested in the refrigerator for two days. As he warmed the soup gently on the stove just prior to serving, the chef intensified the flavor with a final, unexpected ingredient, *glögg*, mulled Christmas wine.

I liked the soup's taste. It reminded me of gingersnap cookies or a Mexican chocolate mole sauce. But sipping blood still felt strange. I couldn't quite bring myself to accept a second helping.

Nobel Banquet

For nearly one hundred years, Sweden has hosted one of the world's most impressive public dinners, the Nobel banquet.

I have long wondered what would it be like to attend this celebration held each December 10, Nobel Day, at Stockholm's City Hall. In my mind's eye, I see the limousines pulling up beside the stately red brick building and the cameras flashing as photographers press to get a closer view of the invited celebrities. Thirteen hundred and forty-eight guests in evening gowns and tuxedos file into the enormous Blue Hall and find their places at the sixty-five tables. The warm air is scented with bouquets of red carnations and mimosa contributed by the mayor of San Remo, Italy, where inventor Alfred Nobel spent his last days.

Perpendicular to all of the other tables, the head table is illuminated by gold French candelabras and adorned with crystal obelisks representing the different prizes; here the families of the newest laureates sit waiting. The air fills with the chatter of introductions and speculations on the evening's menu. Then the orchestra strikes up the entrance march, voices quiet, and tension rises.

At precisely 7:00 P.M., the king, queen, and crown princess of Sweden descend the marble staircase, followed by the laureates wearing their eighteen-karat gold medallions engraved with Alfred Nobel's portrait. A handful of university students from among the two hundred in attendance, representing the prize winners of tomorrow, escort the honored guests to their places.

The head of the Nobel Foundation stands and salutes the king with a toast. His majesty rises and proposes a toast in honor of Alfred Nobel's memory. So begins the three-hour banquet.

Looking over one hundred years of Nobel menus, I can see how tastes and circumstances have changed over the course of the twentieth century, as Hélène Bodin and Stefan Torstensson point out in their book, *Nobelfesten* (The Nobel Banquet). For example, one of the most lavish Nobel menus was the 1913 seven-course dinner that began with turtle soup and included several vintage wines, an aged Madeira, and port. By contrast, the 1947 postwar menu was austere, with sandwiches, roast chicken, and apple tart with vanilla sauce, served with only generic red wine and sherry.

One of the most appealing menus detailed in *Nobelfesten* was the one for 1980, the year that Harvard professor Walter Gilbert, whose lab my husband later worked in, was co-winner of the chemistry prize. The entire dinner showcased Swedish ingredients, beginning with an appetizer of smoked salmon on a bed of spinach, accompanied by a poached egg, followed by a main course of reindeer filet with an aquavit and chanterelle sauce and potatoes Lyonnaise (sliced potatoes fried with onions). The grand finale was the traditional ice-cream bombe, with an outer layer of vanilla frozen custard and an inner layer of lingonberry sorbet, topped with spun sugar and a flaming sparkler.

While the menu may sound deceptively simple, the Swedes invest the same precision in organizing the Nobel banquet as they do in making Hasselblad cameras and ball bearings. Twenty cooks assist the head chef and the executive chef, while the waitstaff numbers 210, including extra personnel in case someone gets sick or is too nervous to do their job. Timing is crucial. Because the meal will be cooked and plated several stories above the dining room, the chosen dishes must be able to tolerate a brief delay before serving. The serving of each course is timed in advance down to the second, so that the temperature of the food will be as close to the ideal as possible: The appetizer and main course should each be served in two minutes, counting from the moment the first waitress appears at the door with a tray on her shoulder until the last waiter has walked down the staircase and reached his table. The famed ice-cream parade is allowed three minutes.

Just setting the table for the Nobel banquet requires one hundred man-hours: five hours and twenty people wearing white gloves to prevent fingerprints. The distance between each place setting has been measured so that all are equally wide, an example of the Swedes' characteristic diplomacy.

While City Hall may seem an unlikely venue for such a prestigious event, Stadshuset, with its brick tower topped by three gold crowns, is a stunning architectural monument, designed by Ragnar Östberg, one of the founder's of the Swedish Romantic Movement in the early twentieth century.

One summer, I toured Stadshuset, including the Blue Hall where the Nobel banquet is served. Built in the style of an Italian Renaissance piazza, complete with a colonnade, a grand staircase, and a balcony extending from one wall, the Blue Hall also has one of Europe's largest pipe organs. Curiously, the only blue is the blue-green veined marble floor. Although the architect had planned to cover the brick walls and paint them a shade of blue to complement the floor, he is said to have been so delighted with the look of the natural red brick that he insisted the walls remain unchanged. He had also proposed to deepen the blue impression by giving the hall a glass ceiling, but the logistics proved too difficult, so tall windows set high in the walls were substituted. However, Östberg liked the name "Blue Hall," which he thought sounded Swedish, reflecting as it did, the background color of the Swedish flag and the waters of Stockholm's Lake Mälaren, and so the name remained.

By contrast, the Golden Hall, where the Nobel ball is held, very much lives up to its title. I tried to imagine the room filled with a thousand of the world's brightest scholars, the company dwarfed by the twelve-meter-high (about thirty-six feet) walls. Inspired by Sicilian and Byzantine churches, the architect had the walls covered in a gorgeous mosaic incorporating 18 million pieces of gold and colored glass. At the center, the Queen of Lake Mälaren, a personification of the capital city, sits on her throne under the Midsummer sun, receiving homage from representatives of both Eastern and Western nations.

Although only companies and organizations can rent out the Golden Hall, we could in theory host a party at the Blue Hall for a mere four thousand dollars or so, depending on the exchange rate. However, for a fraction of that price, we enjoyed a three-course Nobel menu in the City Hall's restaurant. Opened in 1922, the interior decor of the City Hall restaurant is a monument to the raucous Stockholm of the late 1700s, when troubadour Carl Michael Bellman penned his songs in praise of wine and women. Carved into the stone archway are the words "Bacchus we worship. Here is our church." The walls are painted with faded scenes of bacchanalian landscapes and classical gods and goddesses—and a portrait of a Chinese emperor, a nod to the eighteenth-century Swedes' interest in China.

Groups of ten or more who reserve in advance can choose a menu from almost any of the Nobel dinners dating back to 1901, while smaller parties, such as our family of four, are limited to the most recent year's menu.

The dimly lit dining room, with its vaulted ceiling, has a rather worn look in contrast to the elegantly modern, gold-edged Nobel dinner service. Our 1996 Nobel banquet began with *homard à la daube*, a gelatin ring filled with chunks of sweet lobster, thin slices of leeks, and chopped dill fronds, topped with cauliflower cream sauce and garnished with *löjrom*, or bleak roe. This cold starter had a fresh seafood taste that I associate with Scandinavia. The main course of stuffed guinea fowl, accompanied by sautéed root vegetables and a *mandelpotatis* purée—a purée of almond potatoes from Lapland—also bore a Swedish stamp.

We watched as a Japanese tour group's ice-cream bombe arrived with the same type of sparkler used in the Nobel banquet. Ours was served in slices, each topped by a small candle and garnished with star fruit and berries. The outer layer of the bombe was vanilla ice cream, while the inner sorbet had a delicious but mysterious taste that the waitress said was *åkerbär*, or arctic raspberry.

Never having seen arctic raspberries before, I was curious about them. Related to the raspberry and the blackberry, *åkerbär* grows in northernmost Sweden. The plant looks similar to a wild strawberry but the reddish-brown, almost violet berry is shaped like a small raspberry. These aromatic berries are difficult to pick but worth the effort; no less an authority than the botanist Linneaus has described them as the finest of all of Sweden's berries. After twenty-five years of research, Dr. Gunny Larsson developed *allåkerbär*, a cross between the wild Alaskan and the wild Swedish arctic raspberries, which can be cultivated, although this too takes a great deal of effort, with a three-year wait between planting and first harvest.

One day, while perusing the shelves at Stockholm's celebrated food hall, Östermalms Saluhallen, I found a small jar of *åkerbär* jam. Unlike the ice-cream bombe, in which the creamy vanilla overpowered the more delicate berry, this jam had an intense flavor. It was "more raspberry than any raspberry you've ever tasted," as my friend Rachel put it, after sampling a jar of jam that I had brought back to Boston.

Too bad there isn't a Nobel prize for botany.

Saint Lucy's Day

As a young mother, I was obsessed with the idea of establishing family traditions, particularly around Christmastime. Having few rituals to pass on from my own childhood, I turned for inspiration to my husband's Swedish heritage. One of the customs that we adopted was Lucia Day.

Early in the morning each December 13, we enacted the ritual drama of the Lucia breakfast. I helped the children prepare, then climbed back into bed next to my still-sleeping husband and closed my eyes. The tape in the hall began playing, and I heard them singing along with the Swedish words. I opened my eyes as Tina entered our room, dressed as the Lucia bride, Santa Lucia, in a white gown with red ribbon sash. The crown of electric candles on her head twinkled in the dim room. In her hands, she carried a tray with a pot of tea, a pitcher of milk, four cups, a pile of gingersnap cookies, and *lussekatter*, or Lucia cats, saffron yeast buns studded with raisins. Her brother, Michael, followed, wearing his starboy costume, a long white gown and cone-shaped white paper hat, embellished with gold stars that gleamed like the star on the wand he held. As soon as they stopped singing, I grabbed my camera and snapped a quick picture before the kids threw off their headgear.

The author's daughter, Christina, as Santa Lucia.

In Sweden, the festivities of Lucia Day take place against a backdrop of black velvet, midwinter darkness. The holiday begins early in the morning there, too, with costumed children bringing their parents breakfast in bed. Older children might then walk through the still-dark streets to the home of a favorite teacher to awaken him or her with singing, coffee, and Lucia buns. Perhaps the sky will have lightened to a washed-out blue by the time they have settled in at school where the celebration continues with the Lucia bride; her *tärnor*, white-gowned female attendants; and the starboys parading around the school.

But Lucia Day is not only a holiday for children. Men and women working in offices and factories throughout the country also hold Lucia processions, bringing coffee and buns—and sometimes *glögg*, or mulled wine—to their co-workers. Young women vie to represent their community in Lucia competitions. Perhaps the most spectacular of these takes place in Stockholm, where the writer who was awarded the Nobel Prize in Literature on December 10 crowns the city's Lucia three days later.

There is something oddly moving, almost mystical, about the Lucia procession, the young people entering the darkened room with their candles, their high voices solemnly singing of the heavy silence of the winter night and the sudden arrival of the light-clad saint. Symbolizing the light of faith and the promise of the sun's return, Santa Lucia has become an icon of winter, nearly as popular as *jultomte*, the Swedish Santa Claus. Although Lucia Day, in its modern, secular incarnation, has only been celebrated on a national scale since the 1920s, variations of today's celebration can be traced throughout Swedish history to the Middle Ages and beyond.

Though I was raised Catholic, I only knew Saint Lucy as one of the many virgin martyrs. The daughter of a wealthy family, the fourth-century Sicilian girl used her dowry to feed the Christians hiding in the catacombs, wearing a crown of candles in her hair to light her way. Blinded after her arrest, she died in 303 C.E. and became the patron saint of eyesight. Her feast day was celebrated on December 13, then the winter solstice. Interestingly, the Romans had an early December holiday to the goddess Juno Luciana, who was associated with childbirth and, in particular, responsible for opening the eyes of newborns.

Meanwhile, the Vikings marked the longest night of the year with feasting, drinking, animal sacrifices, and offerings of golden loaves of bread representing the sun or perhaps the Norse grain goddess Freya's beloved animal, the cat. When the Swedes converted to Christianity in 1100 C.E., they adopted the church calendar with its plethora of saints' days, including Lucy's. Her feast day marked the beginning of the mandated fasting from meat, which lasted until Christmas Day. Even after the Reformation ended the fast and the adoption of the Gregorian calendar moved the solstice to December 21, Lucia Day remained an important deadline for Christmas brewing and baking.

The custom of dressing up and holding processions around the time of the winter solstice goes back centuries at least and may have come to Sweden from Germany. In the Middle Ages, young people living on farms held parties on the winter solstice with a Lucia bride and groom, dressed in straw, leading the dancing. (A similar custom was also observed at the summer solstice.) From the 1600s, young male scholars in western Sweden staged "starboy" plays on or around Lucia Day—which marked the end of the fall school term—to raise money for the next semester's tuition. Similarly, young laborers, also dressed in white nightshirts and paper cone hats and carrying star-tipped wands, traveled from farm to farm on Annandag Jul, the twenty-sixth of December, or on Twelfth Night, the sixth of January, singing in exchange for bread and beer.

At Skansen, this custom is kept alive, as we saw when we visited the outdoor folk museum on the day after Christmas. Looking around an eighteenth-century farmhouse, we were surprised to see a group of eight or nine teenaged boys enter, all clad in long white gowns. Pastel paper tassels hung from the peaks of their tall, white hats. Standing in front of the blazing hearth, these starboys began singing Swedish Christmas carols. The cabin was soon crowded with other tourists, drawn by the cheerful voices and the warmth emanating from the room. The only thing missing was the beer, sausages, and rye bread that the young stable hands would traditionally have received in exchange for their serenade.

The first known account of something resembling the modern Lucia breakfast was written in 1764 by a priest visiting a wealthy family in southwestern Sweden. He described being awakened by a vision of angels—a young serving woman in white gown and wings, carrying a candle, followed by a second young woman bearing a small table set with "all manner of choice edible and liquid goods." As this tradition continued to spread among the landed gentry in southern and western Sweden over the next century, the daughter eventually took over the role of Lucia wearing not wings but a crown of candles. The beer and sausages on her tray were replaced by the increasingly popular coffee, accompanied by *lussekatter*.

In the 1890s, Lucia Day began to be celebrated at Skansen, the Stockholm folk museum dedicated to preserving Sweden's rural culture amid increasing industrialization. When the newspaper *Stockholm Dagbladet* sponsored a beauty contest in 1927, in which readers chose the capital's first Lucia, the holiday was transformed from regional to national.

After tracing the twists and turns of Lucia's path from ancient Syracuse to present-day Sweden, I was left with the question of why Lucia is such a popular figure now. I thought about the contrasts evident in today's Lucia pageant—between dark and light, ancient and modern, religious and secular, children's solemn grace and naive gaiety— and about the historical symbolism. Lucia's crown of candles reflects the bonfires of the ancient pagans and the primeval attraction of firelight in the still-palpable Arctic darkness. The Lucia buns, nicknamed devil's cats, are reminders of the ancient grain goddess and of the miracle of the harvest. The Lucia tradition connects modern Swedes not only with their past but also with each other. In an era of increasing isolation and alienation, Lucia symbolizes the spirit of nurturing and generosity, the importance of good food, family, and friends. She represents the light of hope shining in the existential darkness, the warmth of compassion in the frozen void.

Swedes living abroad have carried the Lucia tradition with them, organizing performances at Christmas fairs and parties around the world, such as those in which my own children participated in at the Swedish Seaman's Church in southern California and at the Boston Swedish School.

I enjoy these public performances and yet, for me, the heart of the holiday is the Lucia breakfasts we have each year at home. The first time we celebrated Lucia, Michael was not quite one year old. Singing "Santa Lucia" in my halting Swedish, I carried a pot of tea and a plate of gingersnap cookies to my husband and son. By the time the next Lucia Day came, my almost two-year-old son walked with me, wearing a robe made from a white pillowcase and a starboy's paper cap. Once our daughter, Tina, was big enough to wear the plastic crown, she took over as Lucia, carrying the buns we baked the day before.

Now that my kids are older, they do most of the preparation themselves and I have the luxury of being served breakfast in bed. I love waking to my children's voices singing along in Swedish to the old tape, the glow of candles lighting up the dark room. Eleven-year-old Tina is still willing to plop down on the center of our bed, her crown askew, oblivious to the saffron bread crumbs falling all around her. In contrast, deep-voiced, fifteen-year-old Michael, who has long outgrown his starboy costume, sits perched on the edge of the bed, with a napkin fastidiously held under his Lucia bun. Next year, I realize, one or both of them may be unwilling to participate in this ritual breakfast that has come to mean so much to me. I raise my camera to capture this fleeting moment.

Almond Tarts

As a child growing up in the Midwestern United States, I looked forward to the weekend each December when my mother would make a batch of sugar cookies. Now I bake these same cookies with my own children, cutting the chilled dough in the shape of angels and bells, stockings and hearts, along with the odd cow, and spreading them with the same icing, made with a cup of confectioners' sugar and a few teaspoons of boiling water, tinted turquoise, rose, and grass green.

A winter view of Strömma Canal in the Stockholm archipelago.

We also bake *mandelmusslor*, the almond tarts that my husband's Swedish grandmother made each Christmas. These are golden, buttery cookies with fluted edges, thick but easily broken, suffused with a delicate almond flavor. While they can be eaten plain, they taste even better when the center depressions are filled with whipped cream and a dollop of amber-color cloudberry or ruby-red strawberry jam. I serve these on a special platter of translucent apricot glass, usually on Christmas Eve.

The first time I tasted these almond tarts was in December 1978, when my not-yet husband, Carl, and I were in Stockholm visiting his father, Arne. Few cars were on the road that Christmas Eve morning as the three of us drove across town to Reimersholm, one of the city's many islands, and parked on the quiet street where Arne's mother lived. Eighty-eight years old, Ingrid spoke no English although she may have understood a little. I had had only ten weeks of Swedish classes, so our conversation was limited. But the warm welcome she extended to me, her grandson's American girlfriend, did not require translation.

I have only a few snapshots from that morning. Eight of us sat around the dining room table: Arne, Carl and I, Ingrid and her younger son Bosse, his wife Ebba, and their two grown children, Margareta and Hans. Although that winter was the coldest in sixty years, the sun was streaming in the window. A small Christmas tree decorated with Swedish flags, woven straw hearts, and electric candles stood in the corner. Beside it was an antique, Karl Johan–period sofa with green striped upholstery on a curved wooden frame and armchairs covered in orange and beige plaid wool.

A thermos of coffee was on the table, along with delicate china cups and saucers. I'm sure there were other sweets, perhaps a braided length of saffron bread studded with raisins or heart-shaped gingersnaps, but the only dessert I remember from that day was the pièce de résistance, the almond tarts.

Ingrid offered me the recipe, which I copied down and took back to the States. Eagerly, I purchased a dozen fluted tart pans, some diamond-shape, others oval. But the first time I tried Ingrid's recipe, the proportions seemed off—I had to keep adding flour to make the dough stiff. And apparently I didn't grease the pans well enough because the tarts stuck, only to crumble when forcefully evicted.

My poor results might have been due to the difference between American and Swedish flours. (All-purpose American flours tend to be much higher in protein, which is good for bread but not for these tarts.) Or perhaps they would have turned out better if I had followed Ingrid's instructions more closely. In addition to the two hundred grams of peeled almonds, the recipe called for ten to twelve bitter almonds, the fruit of the pink-blossomed almond tree. "Do not leave out the bitter almonds," Ingrid had told me. But while bitter almonds are sold in small bags and as an extract in nearly every grocery store in Sweden, they're difficult to find in the U.S., so, eventually, I developed my own recipe.

For many Swedes, *pepparkakor*, gingersnaps, are the quintessential Christmas cookies, and sometimes we also bake or buy these. But for our family, almond tarts are the only Swedish cookies truly synonymous with Christmas, because that Christmas in Sweden was the first and last time that we were all together. About sixteen months later, Carl's grandmother died peacefully in her sleep at the age of ninety, followed six months later by my father-in-law, Arne.

Now the rococo sofa holds court in our living room, attended by the two armchairs and three side chairs that Carl inherited from his grandmother, and his father's mahogany secretary. Someday our two children, Michael Arne and Christina Ingrid, may come to own these tangible pieces of memory that once belonged to their namesakes, along with my collection of cookie cutters, fluted tart pans, and Christmas recipes.

Christmas Smorgasbord

The Christmas season in Sweden is a six-week-long extravaganza, beginning in late November with the first Sunday in Advent, and ending January 13, Knuts Day, when the Christmas tree is ceremoniously removed. But the culinary high point is December 24, when family and friends gather around the *julbord*, or Christmas smorgasbord, for the most lavish meal of the year.

Traveling across the Atlantic to spend the holiday in the Swedish countryside with Thomas and Kerstin, I imagined a modern version of the Christmas Eve scene in Ingmar Bergman's movie, *Fanny and Alexander*: the house festively decorated and illuminated by candlelight, the groaning smorgasbord, and young and old dancing through the rooms, singing the traditional carol, "Now It Is Christmas Again."

And indeed, from the moment we walked into Thomas and Kerstin's home, at dusk on the twenty-third, I kept thinking of the Swedish word *stämningsfull*, which means "full of feeling, atmospheric." The air was redolent with the scent of cloves, ginger, and cinnamon from the gingerbread house their fourteen-year-old daughter, Elin, was making.

Every room had a subtle touch of Christmas, from the ceramic figurines of mischievous *tomtes*, or gnomes, in the upstairs hallway to the twin gingerbread hearts, inscribed with the words *God Jul*, or Merry Christmas, hanging by ribbons from a kitchen curtain.

The most anticipated day of the year began with a breakfast of *risgrynsgröt*, thick, creamy rice pudding. My artistic sister-in-law had embellished the pudding's surface with ground cinnamon sprinkled in a cross-hatch pattern. Alongside it stood a pitcher of slightly sweet, blue-violet *blåbärssoppa*, or blueberry soup, a sauce to cut the richness of the pudding.

Risgrynsgröt has a history dating back more than six hundred years. In 1328 C.E., Birgitta, the wealthy noblewoman who became Sweden's first saint, introduced this porridge at her father's funeral feast. By the 1700s, this dish, made from expensive, imported grain, had trickled down from the nobility to prosperous farmers but remained a luxury reserved for major holidays. Even today, when Swedes consume more rice than ever before in their daily diet, *risgrynsgröt* is usually prepared only on Christmas Eve.

In keeping with tradition, Kerstin had hidden a single almond in the rice pudding; according to folk belief, the finder will be wed during the coming year. My eleven-year-old daughter, Tina, poked and prodded her portion with the tip of her spoon, searching, then burst out with, "I found it! I found it!" Her seventeen-year-old cousin teasingly asked, "Who are you going to marry, Tina?" Feigning annoyance, she shot back, "Oh, be quiet!"

Young Swedish children leave a small bowl of rice pudding outside on the doorstep to placate the *hus tomte*, a mythical gnome usually portrayed with a full white beard and red stocking cap. According to legend, each farm had a gnome who lived in the barn or under the house like a guardian spirit. If properly treated, the gnome would help the farmer look after the animals, but if neglected, he would leave the pasture gates open or play other tricks.

The remainder of the morning was spent putting the final touches on the *julbord*, or Christmas smorgasbord. In the past, Kerstin might have spent days preparing everything from scratch. But this year, she taught school until the twenty-third and therefore included several ready-made dishes in our dinner. By one in the afternoon, fourteen of us were gathered in the candlelit parlor with another ten relatives arriving later for dessert.

We toasted the holiday with a glass of *glögg*, or mulled wine, customarily made with red wine simmered with cinnamon, cloves, ginger, and cardamom. A relatively recent addition to the Christmas beverage menu, *glögg* arrived in Sweden from Germany in the 1800s. For this occasion, Carl's brother, Thomas, concocted a special version known as *vitglögg*, or mulled white wine, fortified with gin and pure alcohol. Rather than simmering the wine with the dried spices, which would evaporate some of the alcohol, Thomas flavored this potent drink with a liquid extract. The children joined in with a nonalcoholic *glögg* made from black currant syrup diluted with water. In keeping with tradition, everyone added a teaspoonful of whole blanched almonds and raisins to their drinks before toasting "*God Jul!*"

Like all smorgasbords, this one began with fish. We had two kinds of pickled herring, one in a mustard sauce and the other in a cream sauce, along with a whole smoked salmon. However, in the rush to prepare everything, Kerstin had forgotten all about the *lutfisk* stored in the freezer. No one seemed to miss the bland gelatinous cod customarily hidden under a blanket of white sauce.

The centerpiece of this *julbord*—and almost every other around the country—was the *julskinka*, or Christmas ham. While some Swedish families today choose turkey or goose instead, pork remains the most popular holiday entrée. Kerstin cooked the ham in the traditional way, first curing it with salt, then boiling it for several hours with *julkorv*, or Christmas potato sausage, then leaving the ham in the broth overnight to cool. The next day, she dried off the ham, covered the outside with a coating of egg and mustard, sprinkled it with bread crumbs, then baked the meat at a high temperature for fifteen minutes before serving. The ham emerged from the oven with a golden-brown crust, a complex, aromatic flavor, and a firm, meaty texture; in short, the best ham I'd ever tasted.

On the stove was a pot of water in which the Christmas ham and sausages had been boiled for *doppar i grytan*, the old peasant custom of dipping a slice of bread into this flavorful broth. Some Swedes still refer to Christmas Eve as *doppare da'n*, or dipping day. Once considered a treat, this dish seemed to attract few takers.

The smorgasbord included at least a dozen other de rigueur holiday dishes. There were meats such as *leverpastej*, or chopped chicken liver pâté, garnished with cornichons and Cumberland sauce; *revbensspjäll*, or ginger-flavored, oven-roasted pork ribs; *julkorv*, the Christmas potato sausage; and tiny smoked *prinskorv* sausages; as well as Kerstin's delicious meatballs.

Winter vegetables appeared in several guises: braised red cabbage and apples; *rödbetssallad*, a tart salad of chopped red beets blended with sour cream and horseradish; and *Janssons frestelse*, or Jansson's temptation, the same potato, onion, and anchovy casserole I enjoyed at Ingeborg and Peter's wedding reception. The Swedish staple, *kokt potatis*, or boiled, white potatoes—peeled but otherwise unadorned—acted as a foil for these complex dishes.

Rounding out the meal was a yellow cheese, six inches tall and nearly as wide, studded with caraway seeds, and decorated with a red-and-white band embroidered with the words *God Jul*. The selection of accompanying breads included Kerstin's homemade French-style loaves, hardtack, and *vörtlimpa*, a holiday rye bread flavored with orange zest and *vört*, an infusion of malt used in beer-making.

In the middle of the afternoon, more of Kerstin's relatives arrived for dessert and coffee. Almost all of her immediate family were now present: parents, two sisters, one brother, their spouses and children, even her older sister's ex-husband. Only Thomas and Kerstin's elder daughter, Frida, was absent; she was spending the year studying in the U.S., where Thomas was born and where his siblings still reside. With two dozen people, the house was too crowded for dancing around the Christmas tree, which was safely tucked into a corner.

In the past, Swedish housewives were expected to present their guests with at least seven kinds of Christmas baked goods. I was amazed that Kerstin and Elin had managed to turn out six different desserts. Elin had baked two cakes—an orange pound cake and a *mjuk pepparkaka*, or spice cake—while Kerstin had made four types of cookies. These included chewy, moist macaroons; *slytbollar*, or soft butter cookies with strawberry jam centers; *kringlor*, or butter cookies shaped like pretzels; and, of course, *pepparkakor*, or gingersnaps, topped with slivered almonds. Rolled very thin, the *pepparkakor* dough had been cut in the shape of tiny boys and girls, hearts and pigs (a reminder of the Christmas ham) and baked at a high temperature for a few minutes, giving them their characteristic crisp "snap."

Both the hard gingersnap cookies and the soft spice cake evolved from the spiced honey cakes imported in medieval times from Germany, where they were baked by monks and nuns for medicinal purposes. Flavored with exotic spices such as pepper, ginger, cinnamon, and cloves and sweetened with honey, these hard cakes were considered an aid to digestion, a remedy for diarrhea, poor eyesight, and melancholy—and a male aphrodisiac.

Darkness comes early this time of year. By three thirty in the afternoon, the light was so thin that the scene outside the kitchen window—the neighbor's light gray house with white trim, the dark bare trees, the cloud-covered sky—looked like a black-and-white photograph tinted with the palest blue wash. But inside, the kitchen glowed with warmth and color.

Sitting in the cozy room, I contemplated the wallhanging my sister-in-law had embroidered, its simple message illustrating the season's gustatory pleasures that Kerstin and her family had so generously shared with us. Three gnomes stitched in red each carried something for the Christmas feast—a three-pronged candle, steaming porridge, baked ham—while the fourth, smaller gnome sat with a basket of apples. Stitched above the figures were the words *Gröt och skinka, lilla äppelbiten, Tänk vad gott det smakar Nisse liten* (Porridge [rice pudding] and ham, the little apple bit, Think how good it tastes, little elf). And, indeed, it did.

Waffle Day

As soon as we moved into our home on Fågelbro Island, Michael and Tina insisted that we purchase a waffle iron as our very first appliance. Shaped like five golden hearts joined at their pointed ends, Swedish waffles get their light crisp texture from the whipped or sour cream folded into the batter. Topped with more whipped cream and jam (or in our family, maple syrup), these waffles are best eaten immediately, before their ephemeral crispness vanishes.

My children became fond of these waffles not only from trips to Sweden but also, ironically, from attending church in Los Angeles. At the Scandinavian Seaman's Church, I could often bribe them to keep quiet with the promise of waffles after the service. Each and every Sunday, the church coffee table featured homemade waffles, divided into individual hearts, accompanied by strawberry or raspberry jam.

In Sweden, waffles are so popular that there is even an official Waffle Day, March 25, perhaps the only such holiday in the world. For centuries, waffles have been an edible symbol of the return of the light and the beginning of the summer half of the year.

In the northern latitudes, the four seasons are overshadowed by the striking difference between winter's darkness and summer's brightness. The spring equinox marked not so much the still-frozen earth's reawakening as it did the beginning of longer days. The rapidly lengthening daylight meant that the hens would once again lay eggs, which they had ceased to do during the darkest months of the winter. To celebrate this gift of the new season, Swedes consumed eggs, and dishes rich in eggs, including waffles. When Sweden converted from paganism to Christianity, hard-boiled eggs became specifically associated with Easter and waffles with March 25, Marie Bebådelsedagen, the Virgin Mary's Annunciation Day.

I was curious about how March 25 went from being known as Annunciation Day to Waffle Day, but found little concrete information. Apparently, the holiday's name was first simplified from Marie Bebådelsedagen to Vårfrudagen, Our Lady's Day. Folklorists then conjecture that the name was further abbreviated in popular usage to *våfferdagen*. Since March 25 was already associated with waffles, it only required a slip of the tongue for *våfferdagen* to become Våffeldagen, Waffle Day, as it was known in the official Swedish Lutheran Church calendar until the 1950s.

Baking waffles used to be much more labor intensive, judging from the eighteenth-century sugar waffle recipe written by Cajsa Warg, one of the first Swedish cookbook authors to provide exact measurements and detailed directions. Her recipe calls for six eggs, one cup sugar, one and a half cups flour, and about four ounces of butter. Warg then instructs the cook to "lay the waffle iron on the fire and let it become very warm," spread the dough evenly, then clamp the heavy iron together, and hold it over the hot fire, turning so that it bakes evenly on both sides.

A century later, this same exhausting method would have been used by my friend Ingeborg's great-great-grandmother, who in the mid-1800s was well-known for her waffles. Whenever someone came during the summer to visit her small cottage in the northwestern province of Jämtland, she invited them to stay for waffles and coffee. Although she probably used much less, if any, sugar and likely substituted barley flour for the more expensive wheat flour, she would have baked the waffles with the same kind of iron, holding the long tonglike handles over an open fire out of doors.

The two halves of an old-fashioned waffle iron and several coffee grinders on display at Tant Brun konditori, which is named after the character "Auntie Brown" in a classic children's book.

As time passed, her children moved off the farm and after she died, the land was sold. Decades later, as a young bride, Ingeborg's mother, Eivor, wanted to see the place where her great-grandmother had lived. Hiking in the area, she found not only the site but even some of the foundation stones from the original cottage. Sitting on the ground nearby, resting and reflecting on her ancestors, Eivor set her hand down in the grass—and touched cold metal.

Looking down, Eivor discovered—to her utter astonishment—a waffle iron.

Judging from the location, she surmised that this must be the exact same waffle iron her great-grandmother had used. This extraordinary find, with its cast iron, rectangular shape, and deep pockets similar to that of Belgian waffles, now hangs on the wall in my friend Ingeborg's childhood home.

By the last decades of the 1800s, a new type of waffle iron was devised to be used with the increasingly common indoor cast-iron stove. This new waffle iron had shorter handles and an "eye" at one end, which fit into a hook protruding from the stove, so that the waffle iron could be more easily turned. Moreover, the shape changed. Instead of being rectangular, these waffle irons featured the round, scallop-edged, five-heart design still seen throughout Scandinavia today. There also seems to have been a change in waffle recipes, so that while the äggvåffla, or egg waffle, continued to be made with the season's bounty, another type of waffle, frasvåfflor, a crisp waffle made with whipped or sour cream, also became popular.

Around the turn of the century, waffles began to be served not only at home but also in special cafés; a number of these våffelbruk opened in Stockholm, offering waffles and coffee year-round.

One of these waffle stands is preserved at Skansen, Stockholm's outdoor folk museum. The waffle stand keeps erratic hours but whenever possible, my family and I order one or more plates of these hot, crispy waffles—baked in modern electric irons and then slathered with whipped cream and raspberry jam—which we eat at a nearby picnic table overlooking the duck pond.

In today's Sweden, these *våffelbruk* are few and far between. Nor are waffles on the menu at most *konditoris*. Unlike cinnamon buns and princess cake, which can be baked in advance and are staples at every bakery the length and breadth of Sweden, waffles must be prepared to order and presumably are too time- and labor-intensive for many busy cafés. However, I am always on the lookout for waffles and, over the years, have discovered a few places that offer these delicate griddle cakes.

Whenever our errands took us to Gamla Stan, Stockholm's Old Town, my young children used to plead, "Can't we please stop for waffles?" We walked down the pedestrian-only shopping street, looking for the waffle sign hanging above the doorway leading into Jack's Bar—which, despite its name, did not serve alcoholic beverages. The polished mahogany countertops and the emerald green Victorian wallpaper provided a cozy ambience in keeping with Jack's location in the city's oldest neighborhood.

Swedish five-heart waffle with cloudberry jam at Jack's Bar in Stockholm's Old Town, Gamla Stan.

Besides waffles, the menu included such standard grill fare as Swedish meatballs with mashed potatoes and American-style hamburgers with French fries. With only five stools and a steady stream of customers, this hole-in-the wall was no place to while away the afternoon but nonetheless offered a brief respite from the city's hustle and bustle. Sitting by the window with a cup of strong Swedish coffee and a hot crisp waffle, topped with whipped cream and tangy cloudberry jam, always revived me. Unfortunately, Jack's Bar is now an ordinary café featuring espresso.

We can still find waffles at the Ceramic Center's café in the town of Gustavsberg, between our home and Stockholm. One of Sweden's leading porcelain manufacturers, Gustavsberg is a fun destination, with its porcelain museum and seconds shop, where I add to my collection of dishes in the East Indian blue-on-blue pattern. There's also a notice board for people selling vintage porcelain where I look for the humorous fish plates in the Löja series that my husband's parents once collected. When my kids were younger, they would each paint a plate or cup as a memento of the summer. Of course, we always stopped for a waffle at the adjacent café with its whitewashed stucco walls stenciled with red flowers and grass green trim.

Further afield, my favorite waffle café is located in Dalarna, the province that many Swedes consider the most typically Swedish. Here the customs of the preindustrial peasant society are still somewhat preserved, albeit mostly for tourism's sake. Whenever we are traveling through this area, I steer us to the village of Tällberg and the Hotel Klockargården. Among the hotel's log cabins, there is a gift shop featuring

Swedish crafts, especially textiles, with a second-story café specializing in waffles. Almost as good as the waffles is the view of deep-blue Lake Siljan set in a circle of pine trees.

As for Waffle Day itself, I was surprised to learn that the custom of eating waffles on March 25 nearly disappeared in the 1950s, when *våffeldagen* was removed from the official church holiday calendar. My sister-in-law Kerstin, for example, didn't celebrate Waffle Day at all during her childhood. But in the past few decades, this holiday seems to be undergoing a revival, spurred by the media and modern technology. Newspapers and magazines remind people of the holiday through feature articles and recipes, and through advertisements paid for by grocery stores and kitchen appliance retailers. Thanks to packaged waffle mixes and electric waffle irons, today's busy parents can whip up a quick batch of waffles, even if March 25 falls on a weekday, thus passing the tradition on to the next generation.

In our family, I was for years the primary waffle baker but lately my teenage son has taken over. Several times a week, throughout the summer, Michael makes his favorite sour cream waffles, not from a packaged mix but from scratch. He doubles the recipe, sets the table with our sturdy black-and-white Stockholm plates, and serves the waffles one at a time, hot off the griddle. In our home away from home, waffles have become such an integral part of our Swedish summers that any day can be—and often is—a Waffle Day.

The early history of both waffles and wafers is shrouded in mystery. Perhaps the most well-documented theory about the origin of the waffle comes from Dutch researcher Janny De Moor, who has written that both the waffle and the wafer cookie evolved from the unleavened bread consecrated by Christian priests, who, in turn, had borrowed the idea of decorated unleavened wafers from the Jews. De Moor noted that, between 1200 and 1400 C.E., raised waffles were popular in Belgium and Austria, while wafers, flat or rolled, were preferred in Paris, the Netherlands, and western Germany. As for how they might have spread to Sweden, she suggested that these "treats were transported to the north by peddlers traveling from fair to fair."

The Disappearing Cookie

Researching the history of a dish or recipe is always intriguing, sometimes straight-forward, but other times not. For example, my inquiries into the history of waffles led me to a related pastry, which seemed to have nearly disappeared—until I met a young woman who bakes *rån*, or wafer cookies, every year for the holidays.

I was not the only one who assumed that these cookies were on the verge of extinction. In the 1930s, researchers at Nordiska Museet (the Nordic Museum) were collecting *rån* recipes and related information in order to preserve the memory of the Swedish wafer cookie. In a 1964 essay, Ann-Sofi Schotte-Lindsten declared, "The old *rån* iron has become a museum piece," even though a few heirloom irons might still be used on special occasions or by those who particularly value old-fash-ioned delicacies. In modern cookbooks, the only reference I had ever seen was the occasional mention in connection with Gotland, but I had never come across one on my visits to the island.

Culinary researcher Dr. Christina Fjellström of Uppsala University remembered her grandmother baked *rån* but neither her mother nor she had continued the tra-dition. However, when she mentioned my research, her young colleague Hanne Sepp said, "We do that at home!" and offered to demonstrate the technique.

I arrived in Uppsala on June 22, the day before the university closed for the sum-mer holidays. Christina met me at the train station and whisked me off to the uni-versity's stylish restaurant for a buffet lunch of summer delicacies, including tiny bay shrimp, poached salmon, and dill-flavored crayfish.

After a quick stop at a nearby market to pick up a basket of strawberries, we entered the building where the home economics department was located. In con-trast to the building's nondescript concrete exterior, the entrance to the home eco-nomics wing was graced by *Martina*, a life-size Carl Larsson painting of a smiling young woman, dressed in white kerchief, ruffled apron, and red-and-white striped blouse, holding a tray laden with ham, cheese, rye bread, and beer. The painting had been commissioned at the turn of the century to illustrate the department's *Hemmets Kokbok* (The Home Cookbook), which is still being revised and reprinted. Unfortunately, the painting in front of me was only a copy; the original now hangs in Venice's Museo d'Arte Moderna.

This connection between Sweden and Italy reminded me of another early pastry. A cross between a waffle and a wafer, the round, honeycombed *brigidino* was sup-posedly brought to Italy by the Swedish saint Birgitta, a fourteenth-century noble-woman who moved to Rome. Although long gone in Sweden, this treat is still baked throughout Tuscany, where it is called a *brigidini*.

We stepped into one of the department's immaculate white and pine kitchens. Hanne was waiting for us with her mother's *rånjärn*, wafer iron, which looked vaguely like an old-fashioned waffle iron. The two circles of cast iron, smooth on the outside and incised on the inside with a pattern of swirling lines, were bolted together at one end, with two eighteen-inch-long handles at the other end. On an electric stove in the department's demonstration kitchen, Hanne first melted the butter in a small pan. She explained that she had once tried making the batter with oil instead of butter, but that "didn't work at all." She stirred the sugar, flour, and water into the butter, and then put the iron on the electric burner to heat.

When the pan was hot, Hanne spooned two tablespoons of batter onto the bottom plate and then closed the lid so that the batter spread. Each side needed only about forty-five seconds to bake. Just as she had expected, the first wafer stuck to the iron and had to be scraped off, but the others were easily lifted out with a fork. She then alternately rolled each cookie into a tube or shaped it into a basket by draping the wafer over a water glass, with a second glass on top to flatten the bottom. Hanne worked quickly, for as the wafers cooled, they changed from being soft and pliable to crisp and brittle.

She explained that today her family bakes *rån* only for Christmas but in the past, they served the cookies on other holidays and special occasions. Dusted with powdered sugar, the delicate wafers tasted like crisp butter cookies. Those shaped like baskets, filled now with freshly sliced strawberries, looked even more appealing. Several colleagues came by to sample the results and joked that they would all be scouring the city's antique stores looking for wafer irons.

Such lengths proved unnecessary. Not long after, I stopped at a housewares store in the small town of Lerum, where my husband's brother, Thomas, and his wife, Kerstin, live, to see if the proprietor might know where I could find a wafer iron—only to be led to a rack of new *rånjärn*. I bought one and tried it out that very afternoon. Although the first two wafers stuck to the pan, all of them disappeared quickly.

A few days later, I found a recipe for *rån* featured in the Swedish food magazine, *Allt om Mat* (All About Food)—a hopeful sign that this fancy cookie may be on the verge of a comeback.

Reindeer Land

Looking across the tarmac at the expanse of tree-covered mountains, I thought to myself, "So this is the *fjäll*." Although I had seen this highland wilderness on previous visits to northern Sweden, I had never before understood its vastness, had literally never seen the forest for the trees.

My seventeen-year-old son, Michael, and I had just landed at the Lapland airport outside the city of Gällivare, ninety kilometers north of the Arctic Circle. Lapland refers both to Sweden's northernmost province and to Sápmi, the homeland of the Lapps, or Saami (pronounced "Saw-me") as the indigenous Scandinavians call themselves.

A source of food, clothing, shelter, and tools, reindeer have stood at the center of Saami culture for more than eight thousand years, since the glaciers retreated at the end of the last Ice Age. In the beginning, "the people of the sun and the wind" hunted wild reindeer. Later, they herded semitame reindeer in an annual migration from summer pastures in the mountains to winter foraging grounds in the lowlands.

Through the Internet, I contacted Laila Spik, a Saami caterer and lecturer who graciously invited us to her home near the Gällivare airport. Raised in a nomadic, reindeer-herding family and later trained as a school teacher, Laila combines the traditional life of a reindeer herder with the modern lifestyle of a traveling businesswoman. A "consultant in native northern Scandinavian Saami culture," she travels within and outside of Sweden, lecturing and conducting culinary demonstrations promoting local foodstuffs, including Skaltjes Renprodukter, her husband Arild's line of reindeer charcuterie. She is also writing a book in Swedish on Saami culture, cooking, and art, complete with recipes, songs, and her own photographs.

As Michael and I settled ourselves around the pine dining table in Laila and Arild's modern Swedish-style wooden house, Laila apologized again for not having had time to really cook for us. She put water on for tea, then set out a basket of flatbread; a pitcher of *lingonsaft*, or sweetened lingonberry juice; a dish of moose sausage; and four plates of reindeer meat prepared in different ways. This was only the beginning.

She bustled about the kitchen while providing a running commentary in Swedish. The reindeer meat came from animals owned by Arild, Laila, or other herders, raised in the wild without antibiotics or hormones. To preserve the meat, Arild employs traditional methods of smoking, salting, and/or drying, without artificial coloring, flavoring agents, or chemical preservatives. Instead, he adds flavor by using certain woods in the smoking process, such as birch, aspen, and juniper, the last of which also imparts a red color to the meat.

Michael and I began by tasting slices of reindeer meat from the outer thigh and the even more tender inner thigh. Arild had first smoked the meat in juniper wood and then rubbed salt into the meat to let it continue curing a day or two longer. These succulent strips tasted somewhat like rare beef steak, but milder. We next tried moose sausage and smoked reindeer sausage, which Arild had spiced not only with garlic and black pepper but also with native thyme and *kvanne*, or angelica (Latin, *Angelica archangelica*).

Yet another way of preparing reindeer is to dry meat that has already been smoked and salted. At parties, *torkat renbog*, or dried reindeer shoulder, is served whole, with each guest carving off pieces for himself. Tasting a little like beef jerky, this dried meat was Michael's favorite.

With these cured meats, we ate a soft, thick flatbread with a pleasantly chewy texture, baked by a neighbor. Laila explained that this *matbröd*, literally "food bread," is well-suited to the nomadic life because it doesn't fall apart in a knapsack and, when warmed either in an oven or over an open fire, tastes almost as good as freshly baked bread.

Glöddkaka, or ember cake, is the name of another flatbread the Saami make from wheat flour, water, and salt, sometimes with the addition of baking powder or yeast. This campfire bread is usually baked outside on a hot stone that must come from the mountains, not from a beach or riverbed, as a rock long exposed to water will crack from the heat of the fire, she added.

We also tried crispbread with a tasty spread made from garlic, sour milk, and chopped salted reindeer meat; this creamy mixture can double as a filling for baked potatoes, with a sprinkling of diced leeks on top.

Seeing our enthusiasm for everything on the table, Laila brought out more delicacies for us to try, including cloudberry marmalade with the seeds removed, and a jar of cloudberry *mylta*. Not quite a jam, *mylta* is made from whole cloudberries briefly cooked with only a little sugar to thicken them. "There are two types of cloudberries, those from the mountains, which are sweeter, and those from the forests, which have a more bitter taste," explained Laila, as I took notes with one hand and tasted spoonfuls of the fabulous *mylta* and marmalade with the other. "The cloudberry jam that you buy in the stores is only sugar water and pits."

Rich in vitamins and minerals, wild berries are one of the key elements in the Saami diet. Fresh, dried, frozen, or preserved in the form of bottled jams or juice, berries are used to flavor meat and fish dishes as well as desserts. Cloudberries are perhaps the rarest and lingonberries the most common, but the Saami also pick cranberries, blueberries, juniper berries, bird cherries, ptarmigan berries, crowberries, rowanberries from the mountain ash tree—the list seemed endless.

Nonalcoholic drinks are made from nearly all of these, as well as from juniper twigs, rowanberry flowers, blueberry flowers and leaves, bird cherry flowers, and *älggräss*, or meadowsweet. Berries even have medicinal uses; for example, Laila keeps a small bowl filled with dried rowanberries handy for family members with sore throats to chew like lozenges.

Nowadays, the Saami consume the same cultivated vegetables as other Swedes, including *mandelpotatis*, the small, oval-shaped almond potato that thrives in the sandy soil of the far North. But there are also several wild vegetables that are staples in Saami cooking, including *kvanne*, or angelica. Every part of the angelica plant is edible, although not all at the same time. In the plant's first year, the green leaves are used as an herb in baking, while in the second year, the thick hollow stem, roots, and flowerbud can be eaten.

Laila peeled a tightly closed flower bud to show us the inside, which looked like a miniature yellow-green broccoli flower. Sautéed in butter, the *kvanne* flower tasted like broccoli crossed with fiddlehead ferns. Usually, it's eaten with bread, sour milk, or moose. Angelica has such a strong flavor that, when Laila fried a piece of reindeer meat in the same pan in which she had just cooked the flower, the meat tasted more of the plant than of the animal.

Another essential Saami herb is *fjällsyra*, or mountain sorrel (Latin, *Oxyrua digyna*). Containing oxalic acid as do rhubarb and spinach, *fjällsyra* is neutralized by chopping the leaves finely and then boiling them for several hours. The resulting bright green mass is used as a seasoning in sauces and salad dressings and as a stuffing for fish. Alone, *fjällsyra* is rather acidic but mixed with crème fraîche and a little sugar, the result was a refreshing, delicious, and undoubtedly nutritious dessert.

This dish seems to be a modern variation of the traditional Saami herb cheese, *grase-melke*, that I later read about in Phebe Fjellström's *Samernas samhälle i tradition och nutid* (The Saami Society Traditional and Modern). Each autumn, the nomads mixed chopped *fjällsyra*, *kvanne*, or other herbs with heated reindeer milk until the milk coagulated, forming a cheese. Stored in a barrel in a stone cleft in the mountains, this soft cheese provided the herders with needed sustenance when they returned in the spring after the long migration from their lowland winter homes.

In addition to foraging for berries and herbs, the Saami also catch freshwater fish and hunt for wild birds and moose. Bear are also hunted, but the meat is primarily sold to hotel restaurants that, Laila says, have created a market for it. "Bear doesn't taste good; bear meat is too sweet," she declared.

I was sorry that on this trip we would not be able to experience a *renkok*, or reindeer cookout, which I had read about. Held on festive occasions, when a reindeer has been freshly slaughtered, this elaborate meal is based almost entirely around this one animal. The Saami consume every edible part. First the marrow from the bones is eaten with the boiled tongue and the liver, which has been briefly cured in a salt solution and then fried. Then the brisket (breast) and the saddle (back), which have been simmered for several hours, are eaten, accompanied by *blodpalt*—dumplings made from previously dried or frozen reindeer blood. (Fresh blood would make the dumplings stick to the pan.) Hot reindeer bouillon is drunk throughout the meal and salt is the only seasoning used.

The *renkok* often ends with ice cream and cloudberries followed by coffee and coffee-cheese, reindeer-milk cheese that is baked, cut into small pieces, and dipped in the coffee to soften. Laila herself does not make reindeer cheese nor milk her cows, saying the calves need their mothers' milk, but she added that some people still make reindeer cheese "for memory's sake and for their children to taste." In the past, reindeer milk was preserved not only as cheese and butter but also by freezing. Sometimes a kind of reindeer-milk ice cream was made by mixing milk with black crowberries, orange cloudberries, or other local berries, then freezing it in a pouch made from a reindeer's stomach.

Both sides of Laila's family herded reindeer and she and her husband continue that tradition, each owning their own animals. She credits her parents with teaching her about the region's natural bounty. "We have our pantry outside. In the winter, I take the black lichen that hangs from the trees—lichen that the reindeer also eat—rinse, peel, and parboil it with mushrooms in reindeer soup." The lichen can also be sprinkled into dough to make a bread rich in fiber. Laila added that while she picks wild mushrooms, "the same mushrooms as the reindeer eat," many other Saami are skeptical about mushrooms. "They have lost the tradition," the knowledge of how to live from the land.

Laila is dedicated to preserving and sharing her people's traditional knowledge. "One has a big responsibility, if one has this knowledge, to spread it so that everyone can take away something." She is also eager to increase Swedes' and others' awareness and appreciation of Lapland's culture and food products, including reindeer meat. On average, Swedes consume only three hundred grams (about ten ounces) of reindeer meat per person per year; about twice as much as we ate at our tasting. Not only is reindeer meat low in fat, but it is high in selenium, iron, and the A, E, and B-complex vitamins.

"Not that everyone will eat like us every day but that they can taste it and know that there is an alternative to antibiotic- and hormone-injected meat. Instead of eating a hormone-injected pig, why not try our reindeer?" Laila asked rhetorically.

To that end, she has designed a "From the Mountains to the Sea" theme for her lectures and cooking demonstrations, which have included a banquet for a European Union meeting in Strasbourg, France, and a dinner for the Swedish king and queen. She sets the table from her collection of wooden bowls inlaid with pieces of ivory-color reindeer horn, spoons carved from antlers, and knives with engraved horn handles.

New visitors arrived to talk with Laila and it was time for us to continue our journey to the lodge where the Lapland Food Week was being held. Laila suggested that while we were at the hostel, we look for the nearby *kyrkkåta*, or Saami church, built by one of her ancestors.

As Michael and I climbed back into our rental car, the last thing Laila said to us was, "Watch out for puddles and animals in the road."

Lapland Food Week

Under darkening skies, Michael and I headed into Laponia, continental Europe's last great wilderness. This region of northern Sweden was recently declared a UNESCO World Heritage Site in an effort to preserve the landscape and to acknowledge its cultural importance as the homeland of the first Scandinavians, the Lapps, or Saami as they prefer to be called.

We would hopefully be spending the night at the lodge, Saltoluokta Fjällstation, in the Stora Sjöfallet (Great Falls Lake) national park. *Hopefully*, because I didn't know exactly how long the drive would take. We left Laila's at 3:20 P.M., and we had to arrive at the pier by five fifty to catch the second of the two daily ferries across the lake to the hotel.

Laila had warned me to "watch out for animals in the road." Moose have a tendency to dart into the road and, in a collision, the car and its occupants, tend to fare worse than the seven-foot-tall, thousand-pound animal. Friends had assured me that as long as I wasn't driving at night I'd be fine, but I was still nervous about the possibility of meeting a moose or even a reindeer in the road.

I was tempted to drive, say, 20 mph, but the speed limit was 110 kilometers per hour (kph), about 70 mph, and the few cars I saw were going even faster. The Inlandsbana, the road linking northern Sweden's main inland towns, was flat, the pavement in very good condition, and the trees and bushes alongside the road had been cleared about fifteen feet on each side, presumably the better to see any oncoming animals. Reassured that I would be able to spot trouble in advance, I began to relax my white-knuckled grip on the steering wheel a little and enjoy the scenery. Suddenly, the road banked and there, in the middle of the highway, stood a large animal with a full set of antlers.

I was unnerved by the sight of my first reindeer standing smack in the middle of the road, as unconcerned as a cow grazing in a pasture. Both male and female reindeer have antlers, so I couldn't tell which gender it was. Nor did I know why this herd animal was traveling alone. While Michael and I scrambled to find the camera, the reindeer meandered across the road and into the scrub, without ever once looking up at us. A retreating rear end was all I managed to capture on film.

The road worsened once we left the main highway, with potholes forcing us to drive slower than the posted 90 kph (about 60 mph) speed limit. As the rain began to fall steadily, my anxiety grew. Now I was worried not only about animals but also about where we were going and whether we would arrive on time. In the far North, road signs appear infrequently at best. Although we had a map and a cell phone, the former was only rudimentary and the latter was useless in this networkless wilderness. I didn't know how many miles we needed to travel, only that it should take about two hours. If we missed the boat, we might have to drive back to Gällivare in the gathering darkness.

Finally, we saw a small sign for Saltoluokta and pulled into the gravel parking lot near the pier, exactly two hours after leaving Laila's house and, fortunately, thirty minutes before the boat departed. The boat's schedule was synchronized with that of the regional bus, departing five minutes after the bus arrived. Watching the gray, choppy water I fervently hoped that I wouldn't get too seasick and that the Lapland Food Week dinner would be worth the journey.

Not having seen the menu, I could only guess at what we might be served. At Laila's, we had tasted some of the raw ingredients and basics of Saami cuisine; at the lodge, we would sample more complex dishes. I speculated that these would probably feature local fish, game, or reindeer meat; potatoes or other root vegetables; perhaps wild mushrooms since the recent rainy summer weather had produced a bumper crop; and some kind of berry dessert.

About ten travelers dressed in hiking clothes boarded the thirty-foot wooden boat, which proceeded to bob to and fro across the lake for twenty minutes. Sitting with the other passengers below deck, I tried to keep my eyes on the horizon to stave off nausea; thankfully, my stomach cooperated. Disembarking at the little wooden pier, we climbed up the hill to the lodge to check in.

As soon as I walked into the dining room, I felt the stress of the drive and the boat ride slip away. The room was cozy and serene. Simple white curtains framed the picture windows with their views of the nearby mountains, echoed by the landscape paintings that hung from the white stucco walls. The sturdy pine tables were decorated with woven linen runners, in serene shades of blue and green, and plain white candles in black iron holders that augmented the fading late summer daylight.

The hostel's young chef, Inger Broberg, came out of the kitchen to welcome us and describe the evening's meal. She began with an anecdote about her first visit to Saltoluokta as an eight-year-old on a family expedition to pick cloudberries. Her father had casually mentioned that the family would be driving toward the West— which Inger assumed meant the American Wild West she knew from imported television shows. She was terribly let down by the reality of endless forest and glittering lakes, which just couldn't compete with the cowboys and Indians her imagination had conjured—at least not then.

We had already sampled the self-serve buffet of tasty but rather ordinary salads: shredded carrots mixed with raisins, chickpeas garnished with parsley, white cabbage dressed with vinegar. However, the set three-course menu promised more exotic delights: saffron-scented soup with whitefish dumplings; reindeer joint and breast of ptarmigan (grouse); and cloudberry sorbet.

The meal was delicious and far more elegant than I had expected given the surrounding wilderness. The clear golden soup was infused with the delicate flavor of arctic char. The ptarmigan tasted a little like calves' liver, while the reindeer filet reminded me of a tender, juicy but lean steak. The meat was served with lingonberries, forest mushrooms, roasted potatoes and a gravy flavored with *messmör*, or caramelized whey. The whey imparted a sweet, milky taste to the gravy, the mildness modulated any gaminess the sauce might otherwise have had. A cloudberry aficionado, I reveled in the icy sorbet's concentrated flavor, enhanced by the whole berries spooned over the top and the lacy ginger cookie on the side.

For over a decade, the hostel has hosted a Lapland Food Week in late August. Formerly, a Saami woman came in to prepare these dinners but when she retired a couple of years ago, Broberg, the lodge's regular chef, took over. Rather than copy what her predecessor had done, the chef explained that she has developed her own blend of old and new, drawing on her knowledge of local ingredients and her training in game cooking. Defining her food philosophy, Broberg said, "Everything should be simple and the raw materials should not be handled too much. I spiced the grouse only with salt and pepper. I could never use thyme, for example, because it would taste like thyme and not grouse."

Twenty of the guests were staying for the entire week and I wished that we could extend our visit. Then we could have tasted such dishes as roast reindeer wrapped in birch leaves, juniper-scented char with *fjällsyra* sauce, ptarmigan pâté with mustard sauce, black currant cheesecake, and blueberry ice-cream bombe … not to mention the week's grand finale, the Lapland smorgasbord with thirty-seven dishes, including several Saami specialties that might be found at a *renkok*, such as boiled reindeer tongue, marrow bones, liver, blood dumplings, and, for dessert, coffee with coffee cheese. Another item on the menu was *tjälknöl*, slices of tender, brine-cured moose, which takes a long time to cook but requires little labor: the frozen meat is first baked in a slow oven for ten to twelve hours, then marinated in a salt solution for an additional five hours.

The camaraderie at our table rivaled the quality of the food. Seated family style, Michael and I chatted with our neighbors: two older, married couples and two single women. All of them had traveled to Stora Sjöfallet from southern Sweden for a week or more of hiking in the *fjäll*. Although the older couples spoke mostly Swedish, one woman at our table spoke English to include Michael.

Perhaps being on vacation had melted their reserve or perhaps this was another example of my friend Birgitta's theory that there are two Swedens—village Sweden and Stockholm—and that people living in the smaller towns are much friendlier than those in the capital. The next morning, when we were having some difficulty getting an early boat back to the mainland, our dinner companions thoughtfully inquired about how we were managing and offered their suggestions.

Missing that boat, however, gave us an opportunity to enjoy a waffle with cloudberry jam and whipped cream in the lodge's dining room. We also had time to explore the area around the hostel, including the *kyrkkåta*, Saami church, as Laila had suggested. From the outside, this *kåta* looked like a moss and wildflower-covered mound, topped with a wooden cross and fitted with pastel glass windows and a heavy wooden door. Inside, we could see the structure's triangular teepeelike frame. The room's only heat source was a firepit in the center; smoke escaped through a hole in the ceiling. Wallhangings with abstract designs in green, blue, red, and yellow wool felt, the traditional Saami colors and fabric, adorned the birch altar and pulpit. A few portable low wooden benches and a pile of reindeer hides were the only other furniture in the church. A copper plaque honored Laila's ancestor who built the church in the early twentieth century.

Sitting on one of the benches, looking at the trees through the lavender and yellow windowpanes, breathing in the scent of the birch boughs that covered the dirt floor, I felt a sense of peace that I have seldom found in the grand spaces of Europe's crowded cathedrals. Rather, the coziness and the closeness to nature recalled the serenity of a dappled forest clearing.

We also had time to stop in another moss-covered *kåta* where an old Saami man—who lived in an adjacent wood-framed modern house—had his showroom. Here he sold smoked mackerel; homemade *glöddkaka* flatbread; and his own carved and sewn handicrafts. Too full to sample the fish or the bread, we perused the craft tables for a suitable souvenir. While Michael chose a reindeer hide cushion, I wavered between a reindeer-skin leather bag made for carrying coffee, and a spoon carved from reindeer antler. Finally, I decided on the spoon, with a simple design engraved on the handle, as a reminder of our meeting with Laila, and as a memento of our visit to the land of the reindeer.

Bread and Butter Table

The meal begins with a creamy bite of sweet-and-sour pickled herring, marinated with diced leeks, apples, and dill pickle, dressed in mayonnaise and crème fraîche. A taste of cold seafood salad follows: bay shrimp, leek, and cucumber in a tomato vinaigrette. A sip of aquavit flavored with anise, caraway, and bitter orange. A slice of smoked reindeer meat. A tiny chocolate shell filled with cranberry parfait.

These are what come to mind when I hear the word," smorgasbord"—perhaps the only Swedish culinary term that most Americans are familiar with.

In Swedish, the word *smörgåsbord* literally means sandwich table—but that is a vast understatement. Take, for example, the smorgasbord at the Stockholm restaurant, Ulriksdals Värdshus, which features more than fifty dishes, half of which are fish.

The first time I went to Ulriksdals was in August, 1980, in the company of my husband, Carl, and his father, Arne. I remember being enchanted by the graceful, moss green clapboard building with white gingerbread trim, on the grounds of a castle just north of the city. On the front lawn, the Midsummer pole was still standing, although the birch branches entwined around it were dry and brown two months after the solstice holiday. In the photo on the menu cover, the pole was still green and the staff was holding hands, encircling this fertility symbol, men and women wearing flower crowns woven of daisies and red clover. Six months pregnant with my first child, I, too, looked like a fertility symbol.

The restaurant's interior continued the conservatory theme, with a green-and-white color scheme, floral china, and picture windows that let in plenty of sunlight and a view of the surrounding woods and lake. The tables were decorated with small flags from various countries, indicating the restaurant's popularity with foreigners.

Upon my return nearly twenty years later, the restaurant looks much the same as I remember it. But Ulriksdals has become a rarity—one of the few Stockholm restaurants that still offer a real smorgasbord.

Cookbook author Dale Brown uses "fire and ice" as a metaphor for the restaurant smorgasbord. Like all smorgasbords, the one at Ulriksdals begins with ice: chilled *sill*, or herring; *strömming*, or Baltic herring; shrimp, and other fish dishes. The fire comes from *brännvin*. Served ice-cold, each sip of this Swedish vodka goes down like fire. After the first course of fish, boiled potatoes, bread, and butter, I return to the buffet table, take a new plate, and continue down the line to the cold salads and cold cuts. Another clean plate and it's time for warm, comfort foods such as omelets, meatballs, and stewed mushrooms—tasty but uninspiring compared to the cold delicacies. As at most smorgasbords, dessert seems to be almost an afterthought, but I sample a mini square of Oscar II torte anyway. Named after the grandfather of the current king, this cake has layers of almond meringue, crushed almonds, and buttercream, garnished with a sprinkling of sliced almonds.

Brännvin is not only the traditional drink but also seems to be reason behind the smorgasbord, originally called a *brännvinsbord*, or aquavit table. Among the upper classes, from the early 1700s to the late 1800s, dinner parties began with a *brännvinsbord* featuring smoked meats, salted fish, cheeses, pickled vegetables, bread, butter, and as many as six different kinds of aquavit flavored with various combinations of herbs and berries.

At least one foreign visitor found the smorgasbord dismaying. "A great number of dishes are served, but there is no taste in their arrangement or disposition. Everything is put on the table at once and left to go cold during a ceremonial meal lasting at least two hours," wrote English author N. Wraxall in 1774, as quoted in Kestin Torngren's *Smörgåsbord*. Noting the importance of not only brännvin but also bread and butter, he added, "But worst of all is the prologue to this spectacle. Before the Swedes sit down to dinner, the company eat bread and butter, which they wash down with two glasses of aquavit, and this frightful custom is observed not merely by the gentlemen, but by the ladies as well."

A century later, another European travel writer, Paul B. Du Chaillu, described his first encounter with a predinner smorgasbord, "a series of strange dishes eaten as a relish." Invited to help himself first, Du Chaillu had no idea how to begin. The hostess rescued him by taking the lead, picking up a piece of bread, buttering it, and then putting a tidbit on it with a fork, standing all the while. Fortunately for us, smorgasbords are no longer eaten standing up.

At the end of the nineteenth century, the smorgasbord was transformed from a private to a public institution thanks to the development of canning techniques and the building of the railroads. In Scandinavia, where the growing season is so short, canned fish, meat, vegetables, and fruit offered restaurant chefs new opportunities for creativity. At the same time, more restaurants and hotels were built to accommodate the growing number of rail travelers. In the smorgasbord's glory years, railway station restaurants competed to serve the most elaborate spreads, which could be as large as 160 square feet, with dozens, if not hundreds, of dishes.

Rationing during World War II abruptly ended this opulence. Although the ban on restaurant smorgasbords was lifted in 1949, the institution nearly disappeared within the following decade, a victim of changing tastes and times. Determined to save the smorgasbord, Swedish chef Tore Wretman not only promoted the tradition on his radio and television appearances, but also created an elaborate smorgasbord in his restaurant, Operakällaren, which became the model for all others.

Today, Operakällaren, together with Ulriksdals Värdshus, is one of the few Stockholm restaurants that still offers a smorgasbord year-round. However, during the month of December, many restaurants prepare a special *julbord*, or Christmas smorgasbord, often booked by companies for their office parties. And of course, most Swedish families, including ours, celebrate Christmas Eve with their own *julbord*, with such quintessential holiday dishes as ham, pickled herring, potato sausage, braised red cabbage, and, for dessert, rice pudding and gingersnap cookies.

Many families also serve a smorgasbord on other major holidays, with seasonal foods such as eggs at Easter and *matjesill*, a special herring dish, at Midsummer.

While the lavish smorgasbords of yesteryear seem to have largely disappeared from restaurant culture, many visitors to Sweden have encountered another permutation at their hotel's breakfast table. Here, icy aquavit is replaced by hot coffee.

My favorite of these breakfast smorgasbords is at the Wisby Hotel on the island of Gotland. I appreciate the touches of luxury, such as the loose tea with individual strainers, the thermos of warm milk, and the bone china cups and saucers in the white-with-blue-hyacinths Blå Blom pattern. Although there are a few hot dishes—scrambled eggs, bacon, small *prinskorv* sausages—in warming trays to one side, the heart of this, and every other, smorgasbord is the array of cold foods. The center island is laden with platters of sliced ham, salami, and liver pâté; crocks of herring in mustard sauce and in sour cream; boiled eggs and cod roe *kaviar*; plates of sliced tomatoes, cucumbers, and bell peppers; and the local mild, yellow cheese (called *Blå Gotland* for its blue wax wrapping). On the side is a table with crispbread, slices of white bread, and *Gotlandslimpa*, the island rye bread flavored with Seville orange peel. In other words, all the fixings for a Swedish-style sandwich.

For here, the smorgasbord comes full circle, becoming a sandwich table extraordinaire.

In his book *The Land of the Midnight Sun* (published in 1882), European travel writer Paul B. Du Chaillu gave the following description of the smorgasbord:

> "I was led to a little table, called *smörgås-bord*, around which we all clustered, and upon which I saw a display of smoked rein-deer meat, cut into small thin slices; smoked salmon with poached eggs; fresh, raw, sliced salmon, called *graflax*, upon which salt had been put about an hour before; hard-boiled eggs; *caviare*; fried sausage; a sort of anchovy, caught on the western coast; raw salted Norwegian her-ring, exceedingly fat, cut into small pieces; *sillsallat*, made of pickled herring, small pieces of boiled meat, potatoes, eggs, red beets and raw onion, and seasoned with pepper, vinegar, and olive-oil; smoked

goose breast; cucumbers; soft brown and white bread, cut into small slices; *knäckebröd*, a sort of flat, hard bread, made of coarse rye flour and flavored with aniseseed; *siktadt* bread, very thin, and made of the finest bolted flour; butter; *gammal ost*, the strongest old cheese one can taste, and *kummin ost*, a cheese flavored with caraway; three crystal decanters, containing different kinds of *brännvin* (spirits); *renadt*, made from rye or potatoes; *pomerans*, made from *renadt*, with the addition of oil of bitter orange, and somewhat sweet; and *finkelbrännvin*, or unpurified spirit ... the dishes and the spirits were alike strange to me."

Epilogue

Pizza was one of my favorite foods when I was growing up. I was particularly fond of the thin, crisp pizza produced by Pizza Hut, a chain started by two brothers in my hometown of Wichita, Kansas. Every year on my birthday, I chose pizza for dinner. Later, when I was a high school student in Las Vegas, Nevada, my best friend, Jan, and I would spend hours sitting in a booth at the local franchise, sipping iced tea and talking about boys and parents, astrology and reincarnation, envisioning our future selves.

Part of the appeal of pizza was its foreignness. This proved to be as true in Stockholm in the late 1970s as it was in the western United States.

On my first trip to Sweden, I visited Michaelangelo's Italian restaurant in Stockholm's Old Town, Gamla Stan. That April night I was with Carl, Arne, and Carl's high school friends Gunilla and Lepich. We drank beer and ate calzone pizza under the arched whitewashed ceiling. Downstairs was a wine cellar and an aquarium filled with tropical fish. Outside, snow was softly falling. The tablecloths were blue and white checked, the oil lamps at each table were white porcelain, and the trilingual menu was in Italian, Swedish, and English. Instead of sharing one or two pizzas, we each ordered our own. Although they were as thin and crisp as the ones I had grown up eating, these pies were much larger, about the size of a serving platter. Some of the toppings, such as ham and

Located on the pedestrian street Västerlånggtan, Michelangelo's Italian restaurant is a fixture in Stockholm's Old Town, Gamla Stan.

pineapple or shrimp and tuna, seemed a little strange, as did the accompanying salad of shredded cabbage and red peppers in vinaigrette, served family style. But what really shocked me was the fact that everyone ate pizza not with their hands but with a knife and fork!

At that time, Italian pizzerias, along with Turkish kebab stands, were the height of exoticism. Twenty-five years later, Michaelangelo's is still in the same medieval building in Stockholm's touristy old quarter. The interior and the menu are nearly identical, even the prices are about the same thanks to a strong dollar. But Italian food is no longer unusual. In fact, according to one recent survey, pasta and pizza are two of the top ten weeknight supper choices for Swedish families. Italian food has become nearly as Swedish as *falukorv*, or Falun sausage, and fried herring; it has become part of *husmanskost*.

This increasing internationalization reflects the country's changing demographics. For centuries, the population was ethnically homogenous, with only a small minority of indigenous Saami, or Lapps, who now number about fifteen thousand. That homogeneity has dramatically changed in the last hundred years as people from around the world have immigrated to Sweden. Nearly 2 million Swedish residents, out of a total population of 9 million, are either immigrants or the children of immigrants, including the German-born Queen Silvia.

As Swedish chef and author of *Aquavit and the New Scandinavian Cooking* Marcus Samuelsson, himself adopted from war-torn Ethiopia said, "The great thing with food is that you can take a catastrophic situation in one part of the world and turn it into a beautiful experience in another part of the world. And Swedes are open to that."

Not only have immigrants brought their culinary traditions to their adopted homeland, but Swedes themselves have been traveling abroad in unprecedented numbers, returning with more adventurous palates. This globalization can be seen at fine restaurants like Bon Lloc, where our family has enjoyed Catalonian food, and at the proliferation of Thai takeout stands. Marked by only a weatherbeaten sign and housed in a tiny trailer, the one closest to us dishes out pad thai noodles and *tom kha gai*, chicken and coconut milk soup, to a long line of customers waiting patiently even in pouring rain. It can also be seen in the range of imported foodstuffs now available at even small grocery stores like Strömma Market.

On one of the final days of my summer sojourn, I stop at Strömma Market to pick up a few things to take back home. Because of U.S. agricultural import restrictions, my choices are limited to packaged items, like instant rosehip soup or vanilla sauce, jars of elderflower jam or rhubarb drink, or Marabou dark chocolate bars. Sometimes I buy a bag of soft flatbread and a package of smoked reindeer meat for the flight, although I have to consume the latter before landing. Although I stick to traditional Swedish items, I could bring back garam masala spice mixture from India or arborio rice from Italy or even purchase a Japanese-style chicken yakitori skewer or a Russian-style pirogi, or meat pie, to eat on the plane.

From Strömma Market, the four of us head into Stockholm. My children are now adults. Earlier this summer, Michael, now twenty-two, graduated from college and eighteen-year-old Tina is about to begin her undergraduate education. These two weeks with them have a precious intensity.

After lunch at Östermalms Saluhallen, the kids took off to visit friends while Carl headed for an Internet café. The streets of the city are full of people enjoying the warm August sunshine after several days of showers. I cross the downtown park, Kungsträdgården, and sit on the grass at one end, with a view of the royal palace directly in front of me, the Grand Hotel to my left, the parliament building to my right, the East Asian and Modern Art museums in the distance.

Watching the passersby, I think about how international Sweden has become in the last twenty-five years. Just walking here, I passed Asian fusion and Indian restaurants and several sushi bars. Throughout the city, a spate of new "coffeeshops" selling American-style flavored lattes, brownies, and carrot cake is vying for customers with old-fashioned *konditoris* still making *mazariner* and *prinsesstårtor*.

Just as Sweden has become more international, we have become more Swedish. For years, the children resisted learning Swedish, arguing that they would get confused when they returned to school and their required French classes. Now, for the first time, Michael has asked that we not speak to him in public in English, not translate when the maître d' asks if we want to sit inside or outside. "I understand more than you think," he adds. Of her own volition, Tina ordered a Swedish grammar book on-line and has started reading it.

Continuing my walk, I pass the herring stand and Gondolen, the first Swedish restaurant I visited. Crossing onto Söder, the island where my husband grew up, I come back to the beginning of my journey. Tonight, we'll all have dinner at a crêperie here and then Carl and I will head back to Fågelbro to pack while the kids stay in town a few more hours with friends. Early tomorrow morning, Carl will make a final run to Munkens Konditori to pick up a few *kokosbollar*, or coconut cocoa balls, and *kanelbullar*, or cinnamon buns, for the flight back home.

But where is home? For most of the year, I live with my husband in Silicon Valley, while my son resides in Chicago and my daughter in Los Angeles. But through all the changes of the past fifteen years, the constant has been our forest-green home on the granite island of Fågelbrolandet in the Stockholm archipelago. This is the place where we have lived the shortest number of days and the longest number of years. This is the place that holds most of our memories.

This summer, the kids announced that they intend to redecorate the place, including the kitchen. After an initial hesitation, I realized that I'm glad they feel invested enough to make the effort to update the early '90s decor. Even if they replace the table and wobbly chairs, the kitchen will still be the heart of our home away from home, the place we gather with family and friends to celebrate our connections with this land, its good food, and each other.

EPILOGUE

Recipe Index

RECIPE INDEX

Blueberry Oven Pancake

Blåbärspannkaka

Perfect for brunch, this easy dish is very different from an American pancake—it's more like a savory custard pie, with a soft-crust bottom layer and a custardlike top layer. To add sweetness, serve with blueberry jam or maple syrup.

3 eggs
2½ cups milk
1 cup all-purpose flour
⅓ cup sugar

½ teaspoon salt
1 cup fresh or frozen unsweetened
  blueberries

Preheat the oven to 400°F. Grease a 9½-inch glass pie plate.

In a large bowl, whisk the eggs lightly. Add 1½ cups of the milk, the flour, sugar, and salt. Whisk until well-combined; some lumps will remain. Stir in the remaining 1 cup milk and the blueberries.

Pour the batter into the prepared pan and set on the middle rack of the oven. Bake until the pancake begins to turn golden brown on top, its edges pull away from the pan, and a cake tester inserted in the center comes out clean, about 40 minutes. Cool on a rack.

Savory Oven Pancake with Bacon

Skånsk Äggkaka

4 to 6 servings

I learned to make this eggy pancake from Ingmarie, who remains the most enthusiastic cooking teacher I have ever met. Although her version did not call for any seasonings besides salt and pepper, I have added thyme, an herb traditionally used in Skåne, Sweden's southernmost province. In Skåne, *äggkaka* is eaten with lingonberry preserves but you can substitute red currant jelly. For a different, more savory note, try another regional product, mustard. To make this omelet without the bacon, grease the cast-iron pan with vegetable oil before pouring in the eggs.

6 slices bacon
5 eggs
¾ cup all-purpose flour
2 cups milk
½ teaspoon salt

⅛ teaspoon white pepper
1 teaspoon fresh thyme
Lingonberry or red currant preserves (optional)
Mustard (optional)

Preheat the oven to 450°F.

Fry the bacon until crisp in a cast-iron skillet about 9 to 10 inches in diameter. Set the bacon slices on a plate covered with a double thickness of paper towels and pat to remove excess grease; set aside and keep warm. Pour off the bacon fat and let the pan cool, then wipe out almost all of the remaining fat.

In a large bowl, whisk the eggs, add the flour, and then slowly whisk in the milk, stirring until all lumps have dissolved. Stir in the salt, pepper, and thyme. Pour the mixture into the cast-iron skillet and place on the middle rack of the preheated oven.

After 15 minutes, turn the oven temperature down to 425°F and continue baking until the top of the omelet has puffed up and turned golden brown, about 10 minutes. Serve immediately with the bacon and preserves or mustard.

Swedish Pancakes

Plättor

My brother-in-law Thomas gave me this recipe, that he received from his maternal aunt Ulla. I bake these silver-dollar-size pancakes in a special cast-iron *plättor* pan readily available from cookware or Scandinavian import shops. We serve these for Sunday brunch but, in Sweden, *plättor* were traditionally eaten on Thursday nights after a dinner of yellow split pea and ham soup. If you do not own a plättor pan, you can use this batter to make larger pancakes on a griddle or skillet. You can then create a kid-pleasing "layer cake" by stacking several pancakes with whipped cream, jam, and fresh berries between the layers.

To vary the flavor, add ½ teaspoon or more of ground cardamom to the batter.

2 cups all-purpose flour
1 tablespoon sugar
½ teaspoon salt
2 eggs

3½ cups milk
2 tablespoons butter, melted and cooled

In a medium-size bowl, combine the flour, sugar, and salt; mix with a fork until thoroughly blended. In a larger bowl, beat the eggs lightly. Add the milk and the melted butter. Stir in the dry ingredients. Whisk the batter until the ingredients are thoroughly blended and few lumps remain. This batter will be much more liquid than traditional American pancake batter. Let the batter rest in the refrigerator for at least one hour or, better yet, overnight.

Grease the *plättor* pan with a bit of butter or oil in each depression. Whisk the batter again and spoon in just enough to fill each depression. When the batter sets, flip the pancake and bake a minute or two longer, then remove. Add more butter to the pan as needed; if the butter immediately burns, remove the pan from the heat for a couple of minutes.

Serve immediately with jam or maple syrup.

Egg Waffles

Äggvåfflor   *About 6 waffles*

In Sweden, these waffles are served with jam and whipped cream, although my children prefer maple syrup.

1 cup all-purpose flour
1 teaspoon baking powder
2 eggs, separated

1 cup milk
2 tablespoons butter, melted and cooled

In a small bowl, stir the flour and baking powder together with a whisk until blended. In a larger bowl, whisk together the egg yolks, milk, and the melted butter. Stir in the dry ingredients and whisk until few lumps remain.

Whip the egg whites to stiff peaks and gently fold into the batter.

Bake in a waffle iron according to manufacturer's directions.

This Swedish waffle is served on blue-on-blue Östindia, or East India, dinnerware from the Gustavsberg porcelain factory in the Stockholm archipelago town by the same name.

Sour Cream Waffles

Gräddfilvåfflor

My son, Michael, prefers this tangier version of *frasvåfflor*, the traditional Swedish crisp waffles. These waffles are best eaten as soon as they come off the waffle iron, while still crisp. If you want to wait until the entire batch is ready, then don't stack the waffles but rather put them on a rack or on separate plates to maintain their crispness. This recipe can be halved or doubled.

1½ cups all-purpose flour
1 teaspoon baking powder
1½ cups ice-cold water

2 cups sour cream
½ cup butter, melted and cooled

In a medium-size bowl, whisk the flour and baking powder together. Then whisk in the water, sour cream, and melted butter.

Using a brush, lightly grease an electric waffle iron with additional melted butter or vegetable oil. For each waffle, pour a scant ½ cup of batter into the waffle iron. Bake according to the manufacturer's directions.

Serve immediately with jam and whipped cream. The waffles will soften as they cool.

Blueberry Soup

Blåbärssoppa   *4 servings*

In Sweden, hot blueberry soup is featured as a beverage at the annual Vasa cross-country ski race. But this versatile soup can also be served chilled in the summer as a refreshing first course or light dessert. My father-in-law, Arne, even recommended it as a hangover cure.

This recipe can be made from fresh or unsweetened frozen berries. Fresh or frozen, the berries should only be rinsed just before using.

5 teaspoons sugar   2 cups blueberries
1 tablespoon lemon juice

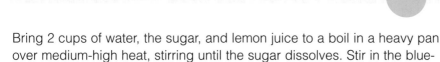

Bring 2 cups of water, the sugar, and lemon juice to a boil in a heavy pan over medium-high heat, stirring until the sugar dissolves. Stir in the blueberries. Cook the berries for about ten minutes, until soft. Remove from heat and cool.

Purée the soup in a blender or food processor, working in small batches if the soup is still warm. Strain the puréed soup through a sieve, pressing down on the pulp with the back of a spoon. Discard the pulp. Serve the soup warm or cold.

NOTE: To freeze berries at home, place them, unwashed, in a single layer on a cookie sheet for 24 hours, then put the frozen berries into freezer bags and store in the freezer for up to one year.

Raspberry Soup

Hallonsoppa

This soup can be cooled more quickly by pouring it into a stainless-steel bowl and then setting that bowl into a larger metal bowl filled with ice cubes. Stir until the ice cubes melt, then pour into a serving bowl and refrigerate until serving time.

4 cups raspberries	2 teaspoons cornstarch
2½ cups cranberry-raspberry juice	¼ cup cold water

Rinse the raspberries and drain. Mash 3 cups of the raspberries; set the remaining berries aside.

Pour the cranberry-raspberry juice into a 3-quart pot. Add the mashed berries and bring to a boil.

Dissolve the cornstarch in the cold water and add to the boiling juice. Bring to a boil again and then turn the heat to low. Continue cooking for several minutes, then remove from the heat.

Pour the soup through a sieve, pushing the purée through the mesh with the back of a spoon to separate the pulp from the juice. Add the remaining berries to the soup and pour into a heatproof serving bowl. Chill.

Rhubarb Soup

Although rhubarb soup is a traditional Swedish dish, the first time I tasted it was on a visit to Mathias Dahlgren's two-Michelin-starred Catalan restaurant, Bon Lloc, where the soup was served over a cinnamon-flavored rice pudding. On that warm summer night, the chilled rhubarb soup was so refreshing that I tried to replicate it the very next day.

Through trial and error, I eventually discovered that this recipe is much easier and quicker if you use a jelly bag to strain the rhubarb; the alternative is to let the soup rest overnight in the refrigerator so that the fine sediment settles in the bottom of the pitcher.

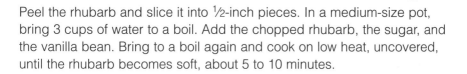

1 pound rhubarb, ends trimmed
½ cup sugar
1 (2-inch) piece of vanilla bean,
   sliced open lengthwise, or
   1 teaspoon vanilla extract

4½ teaspoons cornstarch
¼ cup cold water

Peel the rhubarb and slice it into ½-inch pieces. In a medium-size pot, bring 3 cups of water to a boil. Add the chopped rhubarb, the sugar, and the vanilla bean. Bring to a boil again and cook on low heat, uncovered, until the rhubarb becomes soft, about 5 to 10 minutes.

Dissolve the cornstarch in the cold water. Pour the cornstarch mixture into the rhubarb mixture and bring to a boil again, cooking for a couple of minutes. Remove from the heat and, if not using a vanilla bean, stir in the vanilla extract. Let cool.

Strain the stewed rhubarb through a jelly bag, gently squeezing the outside of the bag to release the liquid. If you don't have a jelly bag, strain the rhubarb using a fine sieve, repeating several times to remove most of the pulp.

Pour the strained soup into a nonreactive pitcher or bowl—preferably the same one you will be serving from—and refrigerate eight hours or overnight. The sediment will settle into the bottom of the container; do not stir before serving. Serve cold, alone, or as a sauce over rice pudding or vanilla ice cream.

Spring Salmon Soup

Laxsoppa

This classic fish soup can be prepared year-round, but its delicate flavor seems particularly appropriate for spring.

1 tablespoon butter
1 leek, white part only,
  about ¾ cup chopped
1 cup fresh or frozen fish stock
1 teaspoon salt
¼ teaspoon ground white pepper
3 tablespoons finely
  chopped fresh dill
2 medium carrots (about
  1 cup chopped)

2 celery stalks (about
  1 cup thinly sliced)
2 medium Yukon Gold potatoes
  (about 1 cup chopped)
1¼ pounds salmon or arctic char
  filet, pin bones and skin
  removed, cut into 2-inch pieces

In a heavy-bottomed 4-quart pot, melt the butter and sauté the leek over medium heat for several minutes, until it softens and begins to look translucent.

Pour in the stock, salt, pepper, dill, carrots, celery, potatoes, and 2 cups of water. Bring to a boil, turn the heat down to low, and simmer, uncovered, for about 15 minutes, until the carrots are tender and the potatoes can be pierced easily with a fork.

Add the salmon chunks. Bring to a boil, turn the heat down, and simmer, uncovered, about 5 minutes, until the fish becomes opaque. Serve immediately.

Yellow Split Pea Soup with Ham

Ärter med Fläsk   *4 to 6 servings*

The custom of eating pea soup with ham on Thursdays may date back to Sweden's Roman Catholic era in the Middle Ages, when Fridays (and often Wednesdays) were meatless days by church decree. Although meat was allowed on Thursdays, only the wealthy could afford to sit down to leg of lamb or pork chops; poorer people, however, might have been able to spare a bit of meat that day to add to their everyday soup of dried legumes. No longer limited to Thursdays, pea soup is still comfort food.

Despite the name, this soup is tasty without the ham. Try it with rye circles (see recipe, page 164) for a nutritious, filling supper or do as the Swedes do and end the meal with pancakes and lingonberry jam (see recipe, page 117).

1 tablespoon butter
¼ cup finely chopped yellow onion
½ cup chopped carrots
1 thick slice of ham (about 4 to 8 ounces), chopped into ½-inch pieces
1 pound yellow split peas

1 teaspoon salt
½ teaspoon ground white pepper
1 teaspoon fresh marjoram and 1 teaspoon fresh thyme, or 1 teaspoon fresh rosemary, finely chopped

Melt the butter in the bottom of a heavy-bottomed 3-quart saucepan. Add the onion, carrots, and ham. Sauté for a few minutes, until the onion softens and becomes translucent.

Add the split peas and enough water to cover two inches above the surface of the peas (about 6 cups). Add the salt, pepper, and your choice of herbs. Bring to a boil and skim any foam from the surface. Lower the heat and simmer at least 45 minutes, adding more water if necessary, until the peas are tender and the texture is to your liking. The longer you cook the soup, the more the peas will break down into mush.

Dill-Cured Salmon

Gravlax

4 servings

The "grav" in gravlax comes from the word for "buried," referring to the fact that, in the centuries before refrigeration, burying fish in the ground was a way to preserve it. Later, salting became more common but the older name was retained.

This dish is easier to prepare with one large filet rather than two smaller pieces. The U.S. Food and Drug Administration recommends using commercially frozen fish in all recipes for raw or cured fish dishes, including gravlax.

Gravlax is traditionally served with mustard dill sauce (see recipe, page 152).

FISH

1 pound previously frozen salmon filet, thawed	¼ cup salt
1½ teaspoons ground white pepper	3 tablespoons sugar
	1 bunch fresh dill

Remove any pin bones; wipe the fish clean. If using one large filet, cut it in half. Mix the pepper, salt, and sugar together. Rub the spice mixture thoroughly into the top and sides of the filets.

Lay one filet half, skin-side down, on a large sheet of plastic wrap. Top with the dill and then the second filet half, so that the flesh sides are together and the thin end is laid against the thick end. Wrap the filets together tightly with the plastic wrap, then again with aluminum foil. Place this package in a pie dish, place a second pie dish on top, and add weights, such as a couple of heavy cans, to compress the filets together.

If the filets are thin, they'll be ready in 24 hours, thicker filets (a little over 1 inch thick) take 36 hours, and the thickest filets (about 2 inches thick) take about 48 hours. Turn the wrapped fish over 3 or 4 times during the curing. To serve, pour off the brine, rinse off the dill and spices, and slice as thinly as possible. Gravlax will keep for several days in the refrigerator.

Salt-Cured Salmon

Lenrimmad Lax

A variation on the familiar gravlax but with quite a different taste, this summery salmon dish is often served chilled with a wedge of lemon and *stuvad potatis*, or potatoes cooked in milk (see recipe, page 150). Or make open-faced sandwiches, laying the salmon on rye crackers or on slices of toasted rye or French bread and topping it with *inlagd gurkar*, or pickled cucumbers (see recipe, page 154).

The U. S. Food and Drug Administration recommends using fish that has been commercially frozen, for all raw or cured fish dishes. If you have leftovers, use them to make *laxpudding*, salmon and potato pudding (see recipe, page 130).

---

1 pound previously frozen boneless   2 tablespoons granulated sugar
    salmon filet, thawed
2½ tablespoons salt

Wipe the fish clean; remove any remaining pin bones. Cut the filet in half crosswise. In a small bowl, combine the salt and sugar. Rub the mixture thoroughly into the sides and tops of the filets. Lay one filet half, skin-side down, on a large sheet of plastic wrap. Top with the second filet half, so that the flesh sides are together and the thin end is laid against the thick end. Wrap the filets together tightly with the plastic wrap, then again with aluminum foil.

Place this package in a pie dish, place a second pie dish on top, and add weights, such as a couple of heavy cans, to compress the filets together. Refrigerate.

Turn the fish package over several times during curing, which will take 24 to 48 hours, depending on the thickness of the fillets. Pour off the brine that seeps out of the package. Rinse the filets and then slice as thinly as possible. The cured salmon will keep several days in the refrigerator.

Jansson's Temptation

Janssons Frestelse

4 servings

FISH

For best results, use anchovy-style sprats fillets, which are packed in brine and imported from Sweden. This recipe can be made with light cream, half-and-half, or whole milk. The lower the fat content of the milk, the more likely it is that the heat will separate the milk solids from the liquid, so substituting low-fat or skim milk may give the dish a curdled appearance.

1 tablespoon butter
1 medium yellow onion, thinly sliced
4 medium-to-large peeled potatoes, preferably Yellow Finn or Yukon Gold, cut into ¼-inch wide matchsticks (about 5 to 6 cups total)
1 (3½-ounce) can anchovy-style sprats fillets in brine (If you can only find oil-packed anchovies, rinse well and soak in milk before using.)

¼ teaspoon salt
⅛ teaspoon white pepper
1½ cups half-and-half
2 tablespoons dry bread crumbs

Preheat the oven to 375°F. Grease a 2-quart baking dish. In a medium-size pan, melt the butter and sauté the onions on medium heat until soft and translucent, about 10 minutes.

Cover the bottom of the baking dish with half of the potatoes, then add the onions. Place the anchovies, along with a little of the brine, on top of the onions. Cover with the remaining potatoes.

Stir the salt and pepper into the half-and-half and pour over the potatoes. Sprinkle the bread crumbs on top.

Bake until the potatoes are tender and the top is beginning to brown, about 45 minutes. Serve immediately.

129

Salmon and Potato Pudding

Laxpudding   *4 to 6 servings*

This easy supper dish is a traditional Swedish favorite and works particularly well using leftover *rimmad lax*, salt-cured salmon (see recipe, page 128) Serve with asparagus, pickled cucumbers (see recipe, page 154), or a salad.

3 medium-to-large potatoes,
   preferably Yukon Gold, peeled
   and thinly sliced (about 4 cups)
½ pound smoked, salt-cured, or
   raw salmon, cut into small pieces
   or thin slices

3 eggs
1½ cups whole milk
½ teaspoon salt
⅛ teaspoon ground white pepper
1 tablespoon finely chopped dill

Preheat the oven to 375°F. Grease a 10-inch pie plate or 7 x 11-inch baking pan.

Cover the bottom of the baking dish with a layer of potatoes. Add half of the salmon, then cover it with another layer of potato slices, followed by a second layer of salmon and a final layer of potatoes.

In a bowl, beat the eggs, milk, salt, pepper, and dill with a fork. Pour the mixture over the potatoes and salmon. Place in preheated oven and bake about 45 minutes to an hour, or until a knife inserted into the center comes out clean, the top is lightly browned, and the potatoes are tender.

Every Wednesday and Saturday afternoon in the summer, Laxbåten, the Salmon Boat, docks at Strömma Canal. Here Anna Horngren displays a whole fish.

Salmon Quiche

Laxpaj   *4 servings*

Quiches are quite popular in contemporary Sweden, so for dinner parties, I often serve this make-ahead salmon quiche, along with pickled cucumber slices (see recipe, page 154) and a vegetable dish of stewed tomatoes, onions, and zucchini, followed by chocolate cake (see recipe, page 170) for dessert.

1 (10-inch) unbaked pie shell
1 large leek, white part only
1½ cups half-and-half or whole
  milk
4 ounces smoked salmon, cut into
  strips

4 eggs
½ teaspoon salt
¼ teaspoon white pepper
½ cup finely chopped dill

FISH

Preheat the oven to 350°F. Fill the pie shell with dried beans, raw rice, or pie weights, and prebake for approximately 10 minutes. Set aside to cool. Remove the weights.

Trim and rinse the leek and slice it into thin strips. Cook the leek in the half-and-half on medium-high heat for about 5 minutes. Strain the half-and-half and discard the leek. Set the half-and-half aside to cool.

Place the salmon in the bottom of the prebaked pie shell. In a medium-size bowl, beat the eggs, add the cooled half-and-half, and then pour through a sieve. Add the salt, pepper, and dill to the egg mixture and stir well. Pour the egg mixture into the pie shell.

Bake until the crust begins to brown and a knife inserted into the center of the pie comes out clean, about 30 minutes. Cool on a rack. Serve warm or cold.

Pasta with Smoked Salmon and Saffron Sauce

Pasta med Rökt Lax och Saffranssås   *4 servings*

This quick pasta dish reflects the modern Swedish love affair with all things Italian. Although saffron is expensive, I urge you to use it if at all possible as it provides not only a deep yellow color but also a unique subtle flavor to this dish.

12 ounces uncooked fusilli
  (corkscrew-shaped pasta)
2 teaspoons butter
1 small shallot, finely diced
2 teaspoons all-purpose flour
½ cup vegetable or fish stock
½ cup white wine

½ teaspoon saffron threads,
  ground to a powder
4 ounces smoked salmon, sliced
  into strips
¼ cup sour cream (light is OK)

Cook the pasta according to the package directions.

In a large skillet over low heat, melt the butter, then add the shallot and cook for several minutes, stirring continuously, until translucent. Sprinkle the flour over the shallot; cook 1 minute. Stir in the stock, wine, ground saffron, and salmon strips; bring to a boil.

Turn down the heat and simmer for several minutes, stirring constantly, until the sauce thickens. Stir in the sour cream and gently heat through; do not boil. Remove from the heat.

Drain the cooked pasta. Immediately pour the sauce over the drained pasta and stir to coat the noodles with the sauce. Season to taste with salt and pepper. Serve at once.

Pasta with Shrimp and Swedish Pesto

Pasta med Räkor och Svensk Pesto

Although once considered exotic, pasta has become an integral part of the contemporary Swedish kitchen. This easy supper dish is one of several ways to use Swedish pesto, another Italian dish the Swedes have adopted as their own.

1 (8-ounce) package fettuccine or
   egg noodles
2 teaspoons butter

½ pound deveined and peeled
   medium shrimp
1 cup Swedish Pesto
   (see recipe, page 156)

FISH

Boil the noodles according to the package directions. In a medium-size sauté pan, melt the butter and cook the shrimp over medium heat, stirring, until they turn pink and opaque, about 3 minutes. Add the pesto and shrimp to the hot noodles. Toss to coat. Serve immediately.

Shrimp Toast

Toast Skagen

This easy shrimp salad served on toasted bread is a popular appetizer in restaurants throughout Sweden. It also makes a great filling for baked potatoes.

1 pound bay (cocktail) shrimp
1/4 cup finely chopped dill
1/2 teaspoon salt
1/4 teaspoon white pepper

1/2 cup mayonnaise
4 slices white bread, toasted

Rinse the shrimp and drain well; pat dry with a towel. In a medium-size bowl, stir together the shrimp, dill, salt, pepper, and mayonnaise. (At this point, the mixture may be chilled until ready to serve.) Spoon the shrimp mixture onto the center of each slice of toast. Serve immediately.

Chicken in Dill Sauce

Dillkött   *4 servings*

Dillkött is traditionally made with veal or lamb, but here I've substituted chicken, which cooks more quickly while still absorbing the dill flavor. Serve this stew with French bread or over rice or barley.

1 pound chicken breasts	1 teaspoon salt
½ leek, white part only, diced (about ½ cup)	½ teaspoon white pepper
	½ cup finely chopped fresh dill
2 carrots, thinly sliced diagonally (about 1 cup)	2 teaspoons sugar
	1 tablespoon white vinegar
2 stalks celery, thinly sliced diagonally (about 1 cup)	½ tablespoon butter
	1½ teaspoons all-purpose flour
3 medium potatoes, preferably Yukon Gold, chopped into bite-size pieces (about 2 cups)	2 tablespoons sour cream

POULTRY and MEAT

Bring a large pot of water to a boil. Add the chicken. Bring to a boil again, turn down the heat, and simmer a few minutes. Drain the meat into a colander and rinse under running cold water. This removes proteins that can cloud the dill sauce.

In a clean medium-size pot, place the chicken, leek, carrots, celery, potatoes, salt, pepper, and ¼ cup of the dill. Cover with water. Bring to a boil, turn down the heat, and simmer for 20 minutes, until the meat is tender but not overcooked. Drain the vegetables and meat, reserving the broth. Remove and discard the skin and bones from the chicken, and chop the meat into 1-inch pieces. Place the chicken and vegetables in a serving dish and cover to keep warm.

TO MAKE THE SAUCE: Dissolve the sugar in the vinegar and set aside. In a small pan, melt the butter and stir in the flour, whisking constantly. As soon as the mixture starts to thicken, pour in ½ cup of the reserved broth, the sugar-vinegar solution, and the remaining ¼ cup dill. Bring to a boil and continue cooking until the sauce coats a spoon. Stir in the sour cream, cooking until heated through; do not boil. Pour the sauce over the meat and vegetables in the serving dish. Serve immediately.

Apple, Onion, and Pork Stir-Fry

Äppelfläsk   *4 servings*

At home, I like to prepare this quick supper dish in early fall when apples are harvested. Although any apple can be used, the McIntosh softens more readily than some other varieties and has a level of sweetness that marries well with the pork and onion. Try serving it with a salad of greens, sliced pears, and toasted walnuts.

2 tablespoons butter
1 pound smoked (cooked) pork
  chops, cut into strips, or
  Canadian bacon, thinly sliced
2 medium-size yellow onions
  (about 1 pound), peeled and
  sliced vertically

2 large apples, preferably
  McIntosh (about 1 pound), sliced
½ teaspoon salt
¼ teaspoon cracked black pepper
¼ teaspoon nutmeg

Melt the butter in a large skillet. Add the pork, then the onions, apples, salt, pepper, and nutmeg.

Sauté over medium-high heat until the onions turn golden, the apples become soft, and the meat is lightly browned, about 15 to 20 minutes. Serve immediately.

Christmas Ham

Julskinka

10 to 12 servings

In Sweden, Christmas hams are first cured in a brining solution, then either boiled on the stove or baked, and finally finished in the oven with a mustard and bread crumb crust. If you cannot find a brine-cured ham, look for a fresh (unsmoked and uncooked) ham. But even a fully cooked smoked ham, the kind most commonly available in American markets, can be given a Swedish flavor by decorating the top of the ham with whole cloves, coating the outside with the mustard and bread-crumb mixture and roasting it for fifteen to twenty minutes.

1 fresh (uncooked) bone-in ham
  (approximately 8–10 pounds)
20 whole cloves (optional garnish)
1 egg

3 tablespoons Dijon or Swedish
  mustard
3 tablespoons dry bread crumbs

Preheat the oven to 350°F. Rinse the ham and pat dry. Insert a meat thermometer into the thickest part of the ham, away from the bone. Wrap the ham in foil, with the thermometer sticking out so that the temperature can be read without unwrapping the meat. Place the ham in a roasting pan and bake on the oven's lowest rack until the meat's internal temperature reaches 175°F, approximately 4 to 5 hours (about 30 minutes per pound). Remove the ham from the oven and drain off the pan drippings.

Increase the oven temperature to 400°F. Remove the foil and insert the cloves into the top of the ham in a criss-cross pattern. In a small bowl, beat the egg and mustard together, then spread the mixture over the outside of the ham. Sprinkle the bread crumbs over the mustard mixture. Place the ham back into the oven, and roast until the outside of the ham is golden brown and the inside reaches a temperature of 180°F, about 15 to 20 minutes.

Ham and Potato Hash

Pytt i Panna

Literally translated as "bits in the pan," *pytt i panna* is the quintessential Swedish leftovers dish. Regarded today as comfort food, *pytt i panna* can be found in both homes and restaurants, particularly at lunch time.

Each summer on our first night in Sweden, my husband, Carl, usually makes *pytt i panna*. He uses *falukorvor*, or Falun sausage; raw potatoes; onions; and carrots—this last his own addition. We usually follow Swedish tradition and top each serving with a fried or poached egg, with pickled beets on the side.

1½ pounds red or russet potatoes, chopped into ½-inch pieces (about 3½ cups)

3 tablespoons butter

3 medium yellow onions, peeled and chopped into ½-inch pieces (about 3½ cups)

2 carrots, peeled and chopped into ½-inch pieces (about 1 cup)

1½ pounds ham with a smoky flavor, such as Black Forest, chopped into ½-inch pieces (about 3½ cups)

Salt and pepper

4 eggs (optional)

1 to 2 tablespoons finely chopped parsley (optional)

Rinse the potatoes and pat dry.

Melt the butter in a large frying pan over medium heat. Add the potatoes first and cook, stirring continually for about 5 minutes. Then add the onion, carrots, ham, salt, and pepper. Avoid crowding the ingredients in a small pan; if necessary, use two pans or cook in two batches.

Continue cooking over medium heat, until the carrots and potatoes are tender and the onions are golden. Serve immediately. If desired, place a fried or poached egg on top of each serving and sprinkle with parsley.

138   a SWEDISH kitchen

Honeyed Pork Ribs and Cabbage

Honungsglaserad Revbenspjäll och Vitkål

4 servings

A re-creation of a dish that we enjoyed at the medieval-themed restaurant Medeltidskrogen Clematis in Visby, this easy entrée goes well with barley, rice, or rye bread.

1 whole green cabbage (about 2 pounds)
1½ pounds boneless country-style pork ribs or pork tenderloin
1½ teaspoons salt
⅜ teaspoon finely ground black pepper

¾ teaspoon ground cinnamon
⅜ teaspoon ground nutmeg
¼ cup plus 1 tablespoon honey

Preheat the oven to 400°F. Remove and discard the outermost leaves from the cabbage, slice it in half lengthwise, and cut out the core. Shred the cabbage into ½-inch or thinner slices.

Grease the bottom of a 10 x 13-inch baking pan and cover with shredded cabbage. Place the pork on top of the cabbage. Mix the spices together in a small bowl and sprinkle evenly over the cabbage and pork. Drizzle the honey over the meat and cabbage. Put in the center of the oven to roast.

Halfway through the cooking time, turn the cabbage and the meat over, to prevent burning. Continue roasting until the pork is just slightly pink inside and the cabbage is tender and translucent, about 30 minutes for the tenderloin and 45 minutes for the ribs. Serve immediately.

Roast Pork Tenderloin with Root Vegetables

Fläsk med Rotsakspytt   *4 servings*

Particularly suited to autumn and winter evenings, this hearty dish can be served with applesauce and/or mustard. Because of the moisture in the meat, the vegetables partially steam, so expect them to be softer and not as dark as they would be if roasted alone.

½ large celery root (about 6 ounces), peeled and chopped into ½-inch cubes
4 large carrots, peeled and sliced
½ medium yellow onion, peeled and chopped
6 small potatoes, chopped
2 parsnips, peeled and sliced
1 teaspoon salt
½ teaspoon black pepper
2 tablespoons olive oil
1 teaspoon juniper berries, crushed (optional)
2 tablespoons Dijon or Swedish mustard
1½ pounds pork tenderloin

Preheat the oven to 425°F. Grease a 12 x 17-inch roasting pan. Place the vegetables in the bottom of the roasting pan and sprinkle with ½ teaspoon of the salt, ¼ teaspoon of the pepper, and 1 tablespoon of the olive oil.

In a small bowl, whisk together the remaining tablespoon oil, ½ teaspoon salt, ¼ teaspoon pepper, the crushed juniper berries, and the mustard. Coat the pork tenderloin on both sides with this mixture. Place the meat on top of the vegetables.

Roast for about 45 minutes, turning the tenderloin at least once so that both sides evenly brown. The meat should reach an internal temperature of 165°F or, if you don't have a meat thermometer, cut into the meat and check; the color should be pale pink. If the meat is done before the vegetables, remove the meat to a warm plate and continue roasting the vegetables until tender. Serve immediately.

Swedish Meatballs

Köttbullar 　　　　　　　*2 to 3 dozen small meatballs; 4 servings*

Unlike the large meatballs in sweet-and-sour sauce, which are often called "Swedish," genuine *köttbullar* are small meatballs served alone or with a thin pan gravy and traditionally accompanied by tart, red lingonberries or lingonberry preserves.

　Nearly every Swedish cook has his or her own recipe for this national dish. Renowned restaurateur Tore Wretman's recipe calls for a mixture of ground meats: half beef, one quarter veal, and one quarter pork, plus a pinch of sugar. My sister-in-law Kerstin makes her meatballs with ground beef alone and no sugar, which is also the way I prefer them. Altho[ugh]... recipe calls for broiling the meatballs, you can also fry them. Red c[urrant] preserves or whole-berry cranberry sauce can be substituted for th[e lin]gonberry preserves.

⅓ cup finely ground plain dry
　bread crumbs
⅓ cup milk
1 small yellow onion, peeled and
　quartered
1 egg

1⅓ pounds leanest ground [beef]
½ teaspoon salt
⅛ teaspoon pepper
¼ teaspoon allspice
Lingonberry preserves (optio[nal])

Soak the bread crumbs in the milk for 5 to 10 minutes, until the liquid [is] absorbed.

In a food processor, finely dice the onion. Add the egg, ground beef, soaked bread crumbs, salt, pepper, and allspice to the onion, and pu[lse] until thoroughly blended.

Preheat the broiler. Lightly grease a rimmed cookie sheet or broiler pan with oil and place the meatballs on the sheet. Shape the mixture into small balls, less than 1 inch in diameter. If the mixture sticks to your hands, wet them with cold water. Do not crowd the meatballs; if necessary, cook them in batches. Broil for several minutes, until browned, then drain the meatballs on paper towels. Serve immediately.

Filled Potato Dumplings

Kroppkakor

About 16 dumplings; 4 servings

This comfort food reminds me of my first visits to Stockholm. I recall sitting at the Formica kitchen table in Arne's apartment, looking out the window at the iron filigree church spire, listening to my future father-in-law's travel stories, and eating the kroppkakor that we bought earlier that afternoon at the food hall Östermalms Saluhallen.

To make these vegetarian, substitute an equal amount of chopped carrots or carrots and beets for the ham.

2 pounds potatoes, preferably Yukon Gold (about 6 medium)
1 teaspoon butter, plus additional for serving
1 small onion, peeled and diced (about ⅓ cup)

⅓ pound baked or boiled ham, finely diced (about ½ cup)
2 eggs, lightly beaten
1 teaspoon salt
1 cup all-purpose flour, plus additional

Preheat the oven to 375°F. Prick the potatoes all over with a fork. Place in a baking pan and bake in the center of the oven until tender, about 1 hour.

Meanwhile, melt the butter in a frying pan and sauté the onion and ham until the onion is translucent. Let cool.

Remove the potatoes from the oven and peel. Put the potatoes through a ricer or thoroughly mash. Beat in the eggs, salt, and 1 cup of flour to make a stiff dough, adding more flour if necessary.

Put a large pot of water on to boil. Shape the dough into balls slightly smaller than a tennis ball. Make a depression in the center of the dumpling and add a teaspoon of the ham mixture, then close up the opening by pinching the sides together. Roll the dumpling between your hands to form a ball.

Drop the dumplings into the boiling water; they will rise to the surface when done, in about 5 minutes. Remove the dumplings with a slotted spoon. Serve immediately with a pat of butter, salt, and cracked black pepper.

Beef à la Lindstrom

Biff à la Lindström   4 servings

A framed letter in the dining room of the Wisby Hotel in Gotland gives one version of the origins of *Biff à la Lindström*. One day in 1862, at the Hotel Witt in Kalmar, Sweden, Henrik Lindström, a Swede raised in St. Petersburg, wanted to introduce some friends to a Russian dish. Several items were ordered, including fine, well-aged beef, mixed at the table according to his directions, and then taken back to the kitchen to be fried in a cast iron pan. This dish became known as *Biff à la Lindström*, according to the letter, which was signed by Henrik's great-grandchild.

Note that this recipe calls for cooked beets. You could use pickled beets imported from Sweden or follow the directions for Pickled Beets. The beets can be boiled a day ahead of time and stored in the refrigerator.

⅓ cup finely ground plain dry
   bread crumbs
⅓ cup milk
1 small yellow onion, peeled and
   quartered
¼ cup cooked and sliced red beets
   or Pickled Beets (see recipe,
   page 153)

1 egg
1 pound lean ground beef
¼ teaspoon salt
⅛ teaspoon white pepper
1 tablespoon capers
1 tablespoon chopped parsley

Stir the bread crumbs and milk together with a fork. Let the mixture rest 5 to 10 minutes, until the liquid is absorbed.

Finely chop the onion and beets in a food processor. Add the bread crumb mixture, egg, meat, salt, pepper, capers, and parsley and pulse until thoroughly blended. Shape into patties about 3 inches in diameter. Broil or fry the patties in a small amount of oil, as you would a hamburger. Serve immediately.

Beef Rydberg

Biff Rydberg

Named for the Hotel Rydberg, Stockholm's first large modern hotel, built in 1857, this classic dish is a fancy version of the Swedish hash, *pytt i panna*. There are two ways to make this dish: in the more formal version given here, each ingredient is cooked individually and arranged in a row on a serving platter. In the more casual version, the potatoes and onions are sautéed together, while the meat is seared in a separate pan before being combined with the other ingredients.

Traditionally, *Biff Rydberg* was topped with a raw egg yolk, but today this is best avoided because of the risk of salmonella. A fried egg cooked sunny-side up can be substituted. For a condiment, try Dijon mustard.

3 tablespoons vegetable oil
1 tablespoon butter
1 pound potatoes, preferably Yellow Finn or Yukon Gold, cut into ½-inch cubes
1 pound beef tenderloin, cut into ½-inch cubes

½ cup finely chopped onion
Salt and pepper
Chopped parsley, to garnish

Heat 2 tablespoons of the oil and 1 teaspoon of the butter in a large heavy-bottomed frying pan. Add the potatoes and cook, stirring until tender and golden; remove from heat and set aside.

In another, preferably cast-iron, frying pan, heat the remaining 1 tablespoon of oil over high heat and sear the meat. Then, reduce the heat and continue cooking for a few minutes, until tender.

At the same time, in a third, smaller skillet, melt the remaining 2 teaspoons of butter and sauté the onion until translucent and soft; remove from the heat and set aside. Season the potatoes, meat, and onion to taste with salt and pepper.

Arrange the beef, onions, and potatoes side by side on a serving platter. Sprinkle with parsley. Serve immediately.

Veal Burgers Wallenberg

Wallenbergare   4 servings

My friend and colleague David Bartal is the author of a biography of the Wallenberg family, Sweden's equivalent to the Rockefeller and the Rothschild clans, entitled *The Empire*. One of the stories in his book has to do with the origin of the aristocratic dish that came to be known as *Wallenbergare*.

As a young woman, Amalia Hagdahl Wallenberg worked with her father, Charles Emil Hagdahl, on his pioneering cookbook, *Kok-konsten som vetenskap och konst* (*The Art and Science of Cooking*). Later, she invented this rich veal dish, still served in Swedish restaurants, named after the industrial dynasty into which she married.

These burgers go well with mashed potatoes, and peas or green beans splashed with lemon juice.

1 pound ground veal
2 egg yolks
½ teaspoon salt
⅛ teaspoon white pepper
½ cup dry bread crumbs

¼ cup plus 2 tablespoons half-and-half or heavy cream (do not substitute milk)
3 tablespoons olive oil

In a medium-size bowl, mix the veal, egg yolks, salt, and pepper with a fork. Gradually add the half-and-half. With wet hands, shape the mixture into 4 patties. Dip the patties into the bread crumbs.

Heat the oil in a skillet over medium heat and add the patties. Cook for at least 3 minutes on each side until golden brown. Serve immediately.

Braised Red Cabbage and Apples

Rödkål med Äpplen

Rich in vitamin C, this colorful and aromatic vegetable dish is especially good in the fall, and goes well with meatballs, roast chicken, pork, and game.

1 pound red cabbage (about ½ of a large cabbage)
1½ tablespoons butter or oil
2 apples, thinly sliced, preferably McIntosh or Cortland, (about 3 cups)
1 teaspoon ground cinnamon

½ teaspoon ground cloves
¼ teaspoon ground nutmeg
¼ teaspoon ground allspice
Dash of ground cumin
½ cup raisins
½ cup cider vinegar
1½ cups apple cider

Remove the outermost leaves of the cabbage. Slice the cabbage in half vertically, remove the core, then shred coarsely.

In a large shallow sauté pan, melt the butter (or heat the oil) and add the cabbage. Sauté uncovered over low-to-medium heat for 8 to 10 minutes, stirring frequently, until the cabbage is wilted and soft.

Add the sliced apples, spices, raisins, cider vinegar, and 1¼ cups of cider to the cabbage, and stir. Bring to a boil, turn down the heat, and simmer, covered, for 45 minutes to one hour, adding more cider as needed, until the cabbage and apples are soft and tender. Serve immediately.

SALADS, VEGETABLES, and SAUCES

147

Braised Winter Vegetables

Stuvad Rotfrukter

4 to 6 servings

I often make this vegetable dish during our summer visits to Sweden, using the newly harvested carrots, parsnips, leeks, potatoes, and cauliflower. Back home, I like to replace the cauliflower with broccoflower (green or purple cauliflower) for added color. This recipe can also be adjusted to whatever you have on hand, so that if you are out of parsnips, for example, just add more carrots.

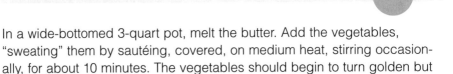

2 tablespoons butter
1 head broccoflower or cauliflower, cut into small florets
1 leek, white part only, chopped
3 to 4 small white or red potatoes, chopped
2 to 3 medium-to-large carrots, chopped
2 parsnips, chopped

1½ cups chicken or vegetable stock
½ teaspoon salt
¼ teaspoon ground white pepper
SEASONINGS: either ¼ teaspoon ground cumin and ½ teaspoon ground nutmeg, or 2 tablespoons fresh, chopped dill
½ cup milk

In a wide-bottomed 3-quart pot, melt the butter. Add the vegetables, "sweating" them by sautéing, covered, on medium heat, stirring occasionally, for about 10 minutes. The vegetables should begin to turn golden but not burn.

Pour in the stock, salt, pepper, and your choice of seasonings. Cover and simmer. After the first 15 minutes, add the milk and continue cooking for another 5 to 10 minutes, until the vegetables are quite soft. If a lot of liquid remains, turn the heat up to medium-high and cook until the liquid reduces. Serve immediately.

Chanterelle Toasts

Toast Kantareller   *4 servings*

Chanterelle mushrooms, with their golden color, trumpet shape, and distinctive apricot aroma, are one of the joys of a Swedish summer. And one of the consolations of a rainy summer is an abundance of this delicacy. This open-faced sandwich is a simple but elegant way to serve this seasonal specialty. The idea of adding a few drops of vinegar to balance the cream comes from chef Mathias Dahlgren.

1 pound chanterelle mushrooms
2 tablespoons butter
¼ cup heavy cream
¼ teaspoon salt

⅛ teaspoon white pepper
½ teaspoon distilled white vinegar
4 slices white bread, toasted

Gently rinse the mushrooms and dry them with paper towels. Melt the butter and add the mushrooms, cooking over medium-high heat for a few minutes. Add the cream, salt, and pepper, and continue cooking, stirring occasionally, until most of the liquid has been absorbed. Stir in the vinegar and cook for another minute or two. Place one slice of toasted bread on each of four plates. Top each slice of bread with one quarter of the mushrooms. Serve immediately.

SALADS, VEGETABLES, and SAUCES

Dill Creamed Potatoes

Stuvad Potatis   *4 servings*

One of Sweden's most popular summer meals is warm *stuvad potatis* and cool *lenrimmad lax*, salt-cured salmon (see recipe, page 128). Or serve this as a side dish with poached or baked salmon or arctic char.

½ tablespoon butter
12 to 16 small potatoes, preferably
    Yukon Gold or red bliss, peeled
    and quartered (about 4 cups)
2 cups 2% or whole milk
¼ teaspoon ground white pepper

½ teaspoon salt
2 sprigs fresh dill, stem and leaves
    intact
1 tablespoon fresh, finely chopped
    dill

Melt the butter in a medium-size pot, add the potatoes and sauté for a few minutes, stirring constantly to keep them from sticking to the pan. Then add the milk, pepper, salt, and dill sprigs.

Simmer, uncovered, on low heat, until the potatoes are soft and most of the liquid has been absorbed, about 30 minutes. Remove the sprigs of dill. Season again to taste. Stir in the chopped dill. Serve immediately.

Mashed Root Vegetables

Rotmos

This traditional vegetable dish goes particularly well with roasted meats. To obtain the best consistency, use a potato ricer to purée the vegetables.

1 large rutabaga, peeled and
  chopped (about 2½ cups)
3 medium carrots, peeled and
  chopped (about 1 cup)
½ teaspoon ground allspice

1 teaspoon salt
½ teaspoon cracked black pepper
4 medium potatoes, preferably
  Yukon Gold, peeled and
  chopped (about 2 cups)

Place the chopped rutabaga and carrots in a pot and add enough water to cover. Add the allspice, salt, and pepper. Bring to a boil, reduce the heat, and simmer for 20 to 30 minutes, until almost soft.

Add the potatoes and, if necessary, more water to cover the vegetables. Bring to a boil, turn the heat down, and simmer 20 additional minutes, until all of the vegetables are very soft, adding more water as necessary.

Reserving ½ cup of the cooking liquid, drain the vegetables. Put the vegetables through a potato ricer (or mash well with a potato masher or purée in a food processor) and stir to blend. If the mixture is too thick, dilute with the reserved liquid as needed. Adjust the seasonings to taste. Serve immediately.

SALADS, VEGETABLES, and SAUCES

Mustard Dill Sauce

Hovmästarsås   *¹/₃ cup*

Traditionally served with gravlax (see recipe, page 127), this sauce is also delicious with poached, broiled, or baked salmon or arctic char. The idea of adding coffee to "enhance the mustard flavor" comes from Marcus Samuelsson, executive chef at Manhattan's Aquavit restaurant.

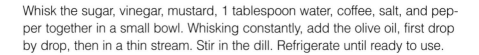

5 teaspoons sugar
1 tablespoon distilled white vinegar
2 tablespoons Dijon or Swedish mustard
¾ teaspoon coffee, brewed or prepared from instant

¼ teaspoon salt
⅛ teaspoon ground white pepper
2 tablespoons olive oil
2 tablespoons finely chopped dill

Whisk the sugar, vinegar, mustard, 1 tablespoon water, coffee, salt, and pepper together in a small bowl. Whisking constantly, add the olive oil, first drop by drop, then in a thin stream. Stir in the dill. Refrigerate until ready to use.

Pickled Beets

Inlagd Rödbetor

In Sweden, pickled beets are such an integral part of the cuisine that glass jars of them are readily available in even the smallest grocery store. For our family, this is the essential side dish to serve with *pytt i panna*, ham and potato hash (see recipe, page 138). It's also one of the ingredients in red beet and apple salad (see recipe, page 155) and beef à la Lindström (see recipe, page 143).

3 medium beets (about 1¼ pounds), with ½ inch of stalk remaining
2 tablespoons distilled white vinegar
2 tablespoons sugar
⅛ teaspoon salt
Pinch ground white pepper

Place the beets in a large pot and add enough water to cover. Bring to a boil over medium heat and continue cooking until the beets can be easily pierced with a fork, 20 to 30 minutes. Drain.

Peel the beets under cold running water. Set aside to cool. Thinly slice the beets.

Mix together ½ cup water, the vinegar, sugar, salt, and pepper in a small pan. Heat until the sugar dissolves. Place the sliced beets in a heatproof glass or ceramic bowl and pour the pickling mixture over them. Cover with plastic wrap and chill for several hours or overnight. The beets will keep several days in the refrigerator.

SALADS, VEGETABLES, and SAUCES

Pickled Cucumber Slices

These quick pickles go particularly well with Swedish meatballs (see recipe, page 141).

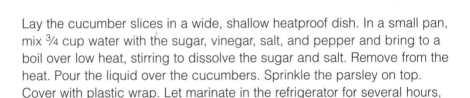

½ large seedless European
   cucumber, thinly sliced
   (about 2 cups)
2 tablespoons sugar
2 tablespoons distilled white or
   rice wine vinegar

⅛ teaspoon salt
Pinch ground white pepper
1 tablespoon finely chopped fresh
   parsley (optional)

Lay the cucumber slices in a wide, shallow heatproof dish. In a small pan, mix ¾ cup water with the sugar, vinegar, salt, and pepper and bring to a boil over low heat, stirring to dissolve the sugar and salt. Remove from the heat. Pour the liquid over the cucumbers. Sprinkle the parsley on top. Cover with plastic wrap. Let marinate in the refrigerator for several hours, until chilled. The pickles will keep for several days in the refrigerator.

Red Beet and Apple Salad

Rödbetssallad

4 to 6 servings

Serve this traditional salad with warm meatballs (see recipe, page 141). Leftovers can be transformed into *köttbullarsmörgås*, or meatball sand-wiches. Butter a large white roll, top with a Boston lettuce leaf, red beet salad, and cold meatballs sliced in half.

1¼ pounds raw red beets, or 2 cups cooked or pickled	⅔ to ¾ cup sour cream (light is OK)
⅓ cup diced cornichons	1½ teaspoons sugar
1 cup peeled and grated apple (about 1–2 large apples)	1 tablespoon distilled white vinegar
	Salt and pepper

Begin by cooking the raw beets. Trim the stalks, leaving about 1 inch attached. Place the beets in a medium-size pot and cover with cold water. Bring to a boil, lower the heat, and simmer until the beets are tender, about 20 to 30 minutes, depending on the size. Remove the beets and place in a colander; slip the skins off under cold running water.

Finely dice the cooked beets and place them in a medium-size bowl. Stir in all of the other ingredients and refrigerate for several hours or preferably overnight. This salad will keep for a couple of days in the refrigerator.

SALADS, VEGETABLES, and SAUCES

155

Swedish Pesto

Svensk Pesto

3/4 to 1 cup

Instead of the basil, pine nuts, and olive oil traditionally used in Italian pesto, this variation substitutes native Swedish ingredients. While the hazelnut oil is optional, it adds a depth of flavor. This sauce goes well with mild-flavored fish, baked or boiled potatoes, or pasta.

2 ounces Västerbotten or Parmesan cheese, grated (scant ½ cup)
⅓ cup hazelnuts
¼ cup finely chopped dill
¼ cup finely chopped flat-leaf parsley

½ teaspoon salt
¼ teaspoon white pepper
⅓ to ½ cup canola oil
1 tablespoon hazelnut oil (optional)

Process the cheese, nuts, herbs, and salt and pepper in a food processor until finely chopped. While running the processor, slowly pour in ⅓ cup canola oil and 1 tablespoon hazelnut oil, first one drop at a time, then in a thin stream until the dry ingredients are thoroughly moistened. If the pesto is too thick, add more canola oil. Store in the refrigerator.

Lucia Muffins

Lussemuffinar

10 to 12 muffins

Inspired by Maud Onnermark's recipe in the Swedish food magazine *Allt om Mat*, these saffron muffins are an easy alternative to Lucia buns. The batter can be prepared the night before and the muffins baked in the morning; the recipe can also be doubled.

3 tablespoons butter
1 teaspoon saffron threads
   (one .25-gram vial)
3 tablespoons sugar
1 cup buttermilk
2 egg whites
1¾ cups flour

1 teaspoon baking powder
½ teaspoon baking soda
½ teaspoon salt
2 tablespoons finely chopped
   almonds
½ cup raisins

BREADS and BUNS

Preheat the oven to 400°F. Grease a 12-muffin pan. Melt the butter over low heat; set aside to cool slightly.

Briefly toast the saffron in a skillet over low heat, shaking the pan continually to prevent burning. Remove from the heat when the threads begin to smell like saffron, but before threads change color. It's better to undercook than overcook.

Using a mortar and pestle, grind the threads with 1 teaspoon of the sugar, until finely ground. Pour the buttermilk into a medium-size bowl. Add the saffron mixture and stir to dissolve. Add the egg whites, 2 tablespoons water, and the melted butter; stir well.

In a larger bowl, whisk together the flour, baking powder, baking soda, salt, and the remaining sugar; add the almonds and whisk again. Form a well in the center of the dry ingredients and pour in the wet ingredients and the raisins. Using a rubber spatula or wooden spoon, stir until just barely incorporated. (Overmixing results in tough muffins.) The batter will be very thick. Spoon the batter into the muffin cups until about three-quarters full.

Bake 15 to 20 minutes, or until a toothpick inserted in the center of a muffin comes out clean and the muffin tops are just beginning to turn golden brown. Cool on a rack.

157

Lucia Buns

Lussekatter

About 24 buns

This recipe can be doubled but that works best if you have two ovens and multiple cookie sheets so that the rising time is consistent for the whole batch. Of the many traditional Lucia bun shapes, my two favorites are the figure-eight "cat" with a raisin in the center of each loop and the "bridal crown," a strip of dough topped with three or four smaller rings of dough, each loop embedded with a raisin like stones in a tiara.

1 teaspoon saffron threads
  (one .25-gram vial)
½ cup sugar
7 tablespoons butter
1¼ cups milk
3 packages (1 tablespoon each)
  active dry yeast

⅛ teaspoon salt
1 egg, lightly beaten
3¼ cups all-purpose flour, plus
  additional flour for kneading
Raisins, for decorating
1 egg
3 tablespoons milk

Grease a baking sheet or line it with parchment paper.

With a mortar and pestle, grind the saffron and one teaspoon of the sugar together until blended; set aside.

Melt the butter in a small saucepan over low heat. Remove from the heat and immediately add the milk and the saffron mixture. The butter mixture should be "finger warm," or about 98°F on an instant-read thermometer; gently warm on the lowest heat or stir to cool until the proper temperature is reached. Err on the cooler side; if the liquid is too hot, the yeast will die.

158   a SWEDISH kitchen

Place the yeast in a large bowl and pour about ¼ cup of the warm saffron mixture over the yeast; stir gently. Sprinkle the salt and 1 tablespoon of the sugar over the moistened yeast and let rest five minutes. Stir in the remainder of the sugar, the saffron mixture, the beaten egg, and 3 cups of flour. Sprinkle ¼ cup of flour on top and knead the dough in the bowl for several minutes, adding more flour if the dough is too sticky to handle. Shape into a ball. Dust the top of the dough with flour, cover with a clean, dry dish towel, and let rise in a warm, draftfree place until doubled in size, about 1 to 1½ hours.

Turn the dough out onto a floured board and knead for 5 to 10 minutes, adding flour as needed to keep the dough from sticking. Divide the dough into small pieces about the size of a golf ball and, using your hands, roll each piece of dough into a figure-eight or other traditional Lucia shapes and decorate with raisins. The raisins will be less likely to fall out if you first snip the dough in the desired spot with a pair of kitchen scissors and then push the raisin firmly into the dough.

Place the buns on the prepared baking sheet. Re-cover the buns with the dish towel and let rise again in a warm, draftfree place until doubled in size, about 30 minutes.

Meanwhile, preheat the oven to 425°F. Beat the egg with the milk. Brush the tops of the buns with this glaze just before baking. Bake in the middle of the oven for 5 to 10 minutes, until shiny and golden brown on top and just beginning to brown on the bottom. Cool on a wire rack.

Cinnamon Buns

Kanelbullar

This recipe calls for pearl sugar, a type of baking sugar that does not melt under high heat. It is available at specialty food stores, Scandinavian import shops, and by mail order. Pearl sugar gives Swedish cinnamon buns their characteristic crunchy topping. If you can't find it, don't worry—the buns will still be delicious.

For a variation, try using cardamom in the filling, instead of cinnamon. Or make half a batch of both kinds of buns, by dividing the sugar in the filling evenly into two small bowls, one flavored with half of the amount of cinnamon called for and the other with an equal amount of cardamom. Spread each of the two rectangles of dough with a different spice mixture.

DOUGH:

3 (.06-ounce) cubes fresh yeast, or
   3 packages (1 tablespoon each)
   active dry yeast
1 teaspoon sugar
7 tablespoons butter
2¼ cups milk
½ teaspoon salt
⅓ cup sugar
5 to 6 cups unbleached all-purpose
   flour

FILLING:

2 tablespoons butter, softened
¼ cup sugar
1 tablespoon ground cinnamon or
   cardamom
1 egg, lightly beaten

Pearl sugar (optional)

Grease a baking sheet or line it with parchment paper.

In a large bowl, stir together the yeast and 1 teaspoon of sugar; set aside. In a small pot, melt the butter over low heat. Remove from heat and immediately add the milk. The butter mixture should be "finger warm," or about 98°F on an instant-read thermometer; gently warm on the lowest heat or stir to cool until the proper temperature is reached. Err on the cooler side; if the liquid is too hot, the yeast will die. Pour about ¼ cup of the liquid over the yeast, stir once, and let the yeast rest for 5 minutes.

Stir in the rest of the warm liquid, the remaining sugar, the salt, and nearly all of the flour. Gather the dough into a ball and knead until smooth and shiny, about 5 to 10 minutes. Place the dough in the bottom of the bowl, cover with a clean dry dishtowel, and set in a warm, draftfree place to rise 30 minutes, until nearly doubled in size.

Turn the dough out onto a floured surface and knead again until supple, smooth, and shiny. Divide the dough into two parts. Roll out each part into a rectangle about ¼ inch thick.

Spread 1 tablespoon butter over each rectangle. In a small bowl, stir together the ¼ cup sugar and the cinnamon and spread half of the mixture on each rectangle. Roll up the rectangle and cut it into ½-inch-thick slices. Place the slices on the prepared cookie sheet, cover with a clean, dry dish towel, and let rise in a warm, draftfree place for about 30 minutes.

Preheat the oven to 425°F. Brush the tops of the buns with the beaten egg and sprinkle with the pearl sugar. Bake the buns in the center of the oven until golden brown, about 5 to 10 minutes. Cool on a rack.

A *kanelbulle*, or cinnamon bun and tea service at Tant Brun cafe in Sigtuna, Sweden's oldest town.

Fat Tuesday Buns

Semlor   *8 to 10 buns*

Sweden hasn't been Catholic since the 1500s, but the custom of feasting on Fat Tuesday, the day before the Lenten fast began, has been preserved in a single bun. Called *fettisdagsbulle*, Fat Tuesday bun, this pastry is also known as *semla* (plural, *semlor*), after the Latin word for wheat bun, *simila*. These buns came from Germany to southern Sweden's upper-class households in the 1600s. Originally, *semlor* were unfilled caraway buns baked from finely ground wheat flour, a luxury reserved for the well-to-do.

In 1771, the buns became infamous when the Swedish King Adolf Frederick died after a meal of oysters, lobster, meat with turnips, caviar, smoked Baltic herring, champagne—and *semlor*. Blamed for the royal death, the buns were immediately banned. But by the early 1800s, wealthy Swedes were buying the buns from bakeries and distributing them, along with alcohol, coffee, and other treats, to their serving folk on Fat Tuesday.

First limited to Fat Tuesday, then to Tuesdays during Lent, *semlor* can now be purchased in some Swedish bakeries from the week after Christmas until Easter, and in a few places, even year-round.

DOUGH:
5 tablespoons butter
1 cup milk
3 packages (1 tablespoon each)
    active dry yeast
3 tablespoons sugar
1 egg, lightly beaten
¼ teaspoon salt
2 teaspoons cardamom
3 cups all-purpose flour

GLAZE:
1 egg, or 1 egg white, lightly beaten

FILLING:
7 ounces almond paste, grated
⅓ cup milk, approximately, plus
    additional (optional)
Whipping cream
Powdered sugar

Grease a baking sheet or line it with parchment paper. Melt the butter in a small saucepan over low heat. Remove from the heat and immediately add the milk. The butter mixture should be "finger warm," or about 98°F on an instant-read thermometer; gently warm on the lowest heat or stir to cool until the proper temperature is reached. Err on the cooler side; if the liquid is too hot, the yeast will die. Put the yeast into a large bowl. Pour about one quarter of the warm butter mixture over the yeast and stir once. Sprinkle one teaspoon of the sugar on top of the yeast. Allow the yeast to proof for about five minutes in a warm, draftfree place.

When the yeast has formed little bubbles in the liquid, add the rest of the butter mixture, the sugar, the egg, the salt, the cardamom, and the flour. Mix well with a fork. Form the dough into a ball and knead the dough in the bowl for a couple of minutes. Cover the bowl with a clean, dry dish towel, and let the dough rise for 30 minutes in a warm, draftfree place.

Remove the dough from the bowl and knead on a lightly floured surface for 5 to 10 minutes. Divide the dough into two halves. Then divide each half into four or five smaller pieces and roll into balls that are slightly smaller than a tennis ball. Place these balls of dough on the prepared baking sheet, re-cover with the dish towel, and let rise in a warm, draftfree place for about 20 minutes.

Meanwhile, preheat the oven to 375°F. Brush the top of each bun with the beaten egg. Bake 15 to 20 minutes, until the tops of the buns are a light golden brown. Remove from the baking sheet and let cool on a rack.

FILLING:

When cool, cut a small slice off the top of each bun and set aside. Using a fork, scrape out the center of each bun and put in a medium-size bowl. Add the grated almond paste and a little milk, a tablespoon or two at a time, mashing and stirring the mixture with a fork until a paste forms.

Spoon this paste back into the buns.

Whip the cream until stiff peaks form. Using a spoon or a pastry tube, put the whipped cream on top of the filling. Place the lid back on each bun and, using a sieve or tea strainer, sprinkle the buns with powdered sugar.

The buns can be served at room temperature on a plate or, more traditionally, in a bowl with hot milk.

Rye Circles

Warm from the oven, this tangy rye bread is the perfect foil for butter or a slice of mild cheese—or both. You might also serve this with soup, such as yellow split pea soup with ham (see recipe, page 125) or spring salmon soup (see recipe, page 124). If you have any left over, toast it the next morning.

2 to 3 tablespoons butter
2 cups buttermilk (regular milk can be substituted)
3 packages (1 tablespoon each) active dry yeast
2 tablespoons sugar

2 teaspoons salt
2 cups rye flour
2 to 2¼ cups all-purpose flour, plus additional for kneading

Grease 2 baking sheets or line them with parchment paper.

Melt the butter in a small saucepan over low heat. Remove from the heat and immediately add the buttermilk. The butter mixture should be "finger warm," or about 98°F on an instant-read thermometer; gently warm on the lowest heat or stir to cool until the proper temperature is reached. Err on the cooler side; if the liquid is too hot, the yeast will die.

Place the yeast in a large bowl. Pour about ⅓ cup of the butter mixture over the yeast, stir, and sprinkle the sugar on top. Let it rest for a couple of minutes. Add the remaining liquid, the salt, the rye flour and 1¾ cups of the all-purpose flour. Stir with a wooden spoon until the dough pulls away from the sides of the bowl.

Gather the sticky dough into a ball and knead for a couple of minutes in the bowl, adding more all-purpose flour as needed, until smooth and pliant. The dough may still be slightly sticky. Place the kneaded ball of dough into a clean large bowl, cover with a clean, dry dish towel, and set in a warm, draftfree place. Let the dough rise at least 30 minutes, until doubled in size.

Punch down the dough and remove from the bowl. On a floured surface, knead the dough for about five to ten minutes, adding more flour as needed. The dough should be smooth and pliant but not sticky.

Divide the dough into four pieces and form each into a circle about ½ inch thick. Poke holes into each disk, using a fork. Place two discs on each prepared baking sheet, cover with clean, dry dish towels, and let rise at least another 30 minutes in a warm, draftfree place.

Meanwhile, preheat the oven to 375°F. Bake the bread for about 15 minutes, until lightly browned on top and bottom. Let cool on a rack, covered with a clean, dry dish towel.

Soft Flatbread

Mjuk Tunnbröd

About a dozen 7-inch discs

Baking *tunnbröd* was traditionally a group activity, with several women meeting at the village baking hut. One woman would roll out the dough until it was as thin as paper, another would lift the sheet of dough onto a special paddle and transfer it to the peel to be placed in the oven, a third would do the actual baking. Although the recipe below can be easily made by a single person, the process is more fun and faster if there are two of you, one to roll while the other bakes.

A staple of the province of Dalarna and of northern Sweden, *tunnbröd* comes in two versions: soft and hard. Both are made from the same dough; the difference is primarily in the cooling. As soon as the bread begins to cool, it also begins to harden. To stop that process, cool the bread only slightly between thick dish towels on top of a rack. Then place the still-warm bread in a plastic bag and slip the plastic bag into a paper one. The softer bread does not keep long, so any bread that you will not be eating within a couple of days should be wrapped in plastic and frozen.

This flatbread can be made with a regular rolling pin, but if you can find a die-cut wooden rolling pin with stripes or points, you will get a more authentic outcome. For best results, bake the bread on a pizza or baking stone, as this provides more even heat than a cookie sheet. If you don't have a baking stone, the *tunnbröd* can alternatively be cooked in an ungreased cast-iron pan on top of the stove.

7 tablespoons butter
4¼ cups milk
3 packages (1 tablespoon each) active dry yeast
⅓ cup plus 1 tablespoon honey

1 teaspoon salt
1½ cups rye flour
1½ cups white bread flour
4 to 6 cups unbleached all-purpose flour

In a heavy-bottomed medium-size pot, melt the butter over low heat. Remove from the heat and immediately add the milk. The butter mixture should be "finger warm," or about 98°F on an instant-read thermometer; gently warm on the lowest heat or stir to cool until the proper temperature is reached. Err on the cooler side; if the liquid is too hot, the yeast will die.

166   a SWEDISH kitchen

Place the yeast in a large bowl, then add the butter mixture and the honey. Stir until the honey is dissolved. In a separate bowl, mix the salt and flours. Add the dry ingredients to the wet ingredients and stir with a wooden spoon until well blended. The dough will be very soft, loose, and sticky. Cover the bowl with a clean, dry dish towel and let rise in a warm, draftfree place for one hour.

Prepare the cooling rack by placing a thick dish towel on top of the rack, with another towel ready to cover the bread. Preheat the oven to 450°F with the baking stone in the oven (if using).

Turn the dough out onto a well-floured surface. Knead the dough until smooth and no longer sticky, about 10 minutes. Form the dough into a foot-long log. Slice off one piece at a time, about ½ to 1 inch thick, and shape into a disk. Keep the rest of the dough covered with a dish towel. On a very well-floured surface using a die-cut rolling pin, roll out the disks one at a time, as thinly as possible, no more than ⅛ inch thick and about 7 inches in diameter.

Place the disks one at a time on the hot baking stone in the preheated oven or in a hot pan on the stove. Bake on one side for a couple of minutes, until bubbles form on the top. Flip and bake the other side until it is just beginning to brown. The longer the bread bakes, the crisper it becomes.

Remove to the cooling rack and let cool slightly between the two thick dish towels. To keep the bread soft, store the still warm bread in a plastic bag, then put the plastic bag into a paper bag. Or better yet, serve immediately, spread with regular butter, herb or garlic butter, or a slice of mild cheese.

Blueberry and Lemon Cake

Blåbärcitronkaka

This moist cake is a particularly good choice for parties because it's easy to serve on a napkin and doesn't leave too many crumbs.

1¼ cups sifted cake flour
2 teaspoons baking powder
4 eggs
1 cup sugar
1 teaspoon lemon zest, grated
½ cup milk

7 tablespoons butter, melted and cooled
1 cup blueberries, fresh or frozen (no need to thaw)

Preheat the oven to 350°F. Grease and lightly flour a 10 x 13-inch pan.

In a small bowl, stir the flour and baking powder together and set aside. In a large bowl, whisk together the eggs and the sugar for several minutes, until foamy. Add the lemon zest to the eggs. Stir the milk into the butter.

Beat the butter mixture into the eggs, then stir in the flour. Beat by hand for one to two minutes, until the batter is smooth. The batter will be rather thin. Pour the batter into the prepared pan. Drop the blueberries into the batter, spacing them evenly across the entire pan.

Bake until top turns a light golden color and a cake tester inserted into the center of the cake comes out clean, about 30 minutes. Cool in the pan on a rack.

CAKES, TARTS, COOKIES, and CANDIES

Chocolate Cake

Chokladtårta

This moist, relatively low-fat chocolate cake has become our family's birthday cake. Cinnamon is frequently used in Swedish baking although it's seldom combined with chocolate as it is here. Because of the small quantity of flour, the cake will rise only slightly.

½ cup all-purpose flour
⅓ cup unsweetened cocoa powder
½ teaspoon baking powder
¼ teaspoon salt
1 teaspoon cinnamon
3 eggs

1 cup sugar
1 teaspoon vanilla extract
1 tablespoon cold coffee (optional)
8 ounces plain, nonfat yogurt
2 tablespoons butter, melted and
    cooled

Preheat the oven to 375°F. Grease and lightly flour a 9 x 12- or 10 x 13-inch cake pan.

In a medium-size bowl, mix the flour, cocoa, baking powder, salt, and cinnamon. In a large bowl, whisk the eggs lightly. Stir in the sugar and continue whisking until the mixture forms a ribbon when the whisk is lifted. Add the vanilla extract, coffee, yogurt, and butter to the egg and sugar mixture. Then add the flour mixture. Beat by hand for a couple of minutes, until thoroughly mixed.

Pour the batter into the prepared pan and bake on the lower oven rack for 20 to 25 minutes, until the center looks set. A toothpick or cake tester inserted in center should come out a little sticky, otherwise the cake will be too dry. Serve at room temperature or chilled, alone or with whipped cream or vanilla ice cream.

Nut Cake

Nötkaka

The first time I tasted a Swedish nut cake was at the party celebrating my nephew Carl's graduation from *gymnasium*, the European equivalent of high school. My sister-in-law Kerstin used ground almonds in the batter, and, after baking, covered the cake with a layer of sweetened whipped cream and decorated it with strawberries.

During Kerstin's 1950s childhood, her mother baked nut cakes but, instead of imported almonds, she used hazelnuts gathered from the local woods.

⅔ cup sliced almonds
  (about 3 ounces)
½ cup cake flour

1 teaspoon baking powder
3 eggs
1¼ cups sugar

Preheat the oven to 325°F. Cut a circle of parchment paper to fit the inside of a 9-inch springform pan and press into the bottom of the pan. Grease and lightly flour the bottom (over the parchment paper) and sides of the pan.

Grind the nuts in a food processor until finely chopped. In a small bowl, mix the nuts with the flour and baking powder. In a separate, medium-size bowl, whisk the eggs and sugar together until they form a ribbon when you lift up the whisk. Add the nut mixture to the egg mixture and beat with a wooden spoon for several minutes until smooth.

Pour the batter into the prepared pan. Bake until a cake tester inserted in the center comes out clean and the top is a light golden brown color, about 40 minutes. Cool completely in the pan. Run a knife dipped in hot water around the edge of the pan to make the cake easier to remove. Peel away and discard the parchment paper.

Kerstin and Carl Rosenberg at the latter's graduation party. Carl wears the student cap worn by all who graduate from gymnasium, the Swedish equivalent to high school.

Princess Cake

Prinsesstårta   *8 servings*

Often tinted pale green, the popular *prinsesstårta* appears at baptisms, graduations, confirmations, birthdays, weddings, and even funerals. This cake is usually bought from a bakery, but the simplified version that follows can be made at home. (The sponge cake and the vanilla pastry cream can be made ahead of time.)

1 Sponge Cake, cooled
  (see recipe, page 175)
½ cup heavy cream
¾ cup Vanilla Pastry Cream,
  chilled (see recipe, page 201)

⅓ cup jam, preferably raspberry
2 packages (7-ounce) marzipan
Green food coloring (optional)

With a bread knife, slice the cake in half horizontally. Whip the heavy cream and stir half of it into the pastry cream.

TO ASSEMBLE THE CAKE: place the bottom cake layer on a serving platter. Spread the jam on top of the bottom layer, then cover with half of the pastry cream mixture. Lay the second cake layer on top. Spread the remaining pastry cream mixture over the top of the second cake layer, then spread the remaining whipped cream on the top and sides.

Knead a few drops of green food coloring into the marzipan until it is as evenly colored as possible. Between two sheets of plastic wrap or waxed paper, roll out the marzipan as thinly as possible, a little larger in diameter than the cake. Carefully lay the marzipan sheet on top of the cake. With flattened palms, gently stretch the marzipan to cover the top and sides of the cake.

If not serving immediately, wrap well in plastic wrap and refrigerate.

Saffron Cake

Saffranskaka

Maria Ohlsson gave me this recipe for saffron cake, which she baked for her family's summer café near the Strömma Canal bridge. As with all cake recipes, for best results, spoon the flour into the measuring cup and then level it off with the blunt edge of a knife.

½ teaspoon saffron
1¼ cups sugar
3 eggs
1 cup all-purpose flour
1 cup cake flour

2 teaspoons baking powder
½ cup milk
13 tablespoons butter
Confectioners' sugar (optional)

Preheat the oven to 350°F. Grease and flour a 9-inch cake pan, preferably a springform pan.

With a mortar and pestle, grind the saffron threads with 1 teaspoon of the sugar. In a large bowl, whisk the eggs together with the remaining sugar until they form a ribbon when you lift up the whisk. Add the saffron to the egg mixture.

In a medium-size bowl, whisk the flours and baking powder together. Stir the milk and butter into the egg mixture, then add the flour mixture. Pour the batter into the prepared pan.

Bake on the oven's bottom rack until a cake tester inserted in the center comes out clean, about 45 to 50 minutes. Cool in the pan. If you like, you can decorate the top by sprinkling on confectioners' sugar through a sieve.

CAKES, TARTS, COOKIES, and CANDIES

Spice Cake

Mjuk Pepparkaka

A Christmas specialty, this Swedish-style gingerbread reminds me of the spice cakes my mother baked when I was growing up in Kansas. For a gingerbread flavor, use ginger; for a more exotic but still Swedish taste, try substituting an equal amount of cardamom.

1 egg	1 teaspoon ground cloves
2 egg yolks	1½ teaspoon ground ginger
1 cup light brown sugar	or cardamom
¾ cup cake flour	¾ cup sour cream or buttermilk
½ cup all-purpose flour	¼ cup orange marmalade
1 teaspoon baking soda	6 tablespoons butter, melted and
2 teaspoons ground cinnamon	cooled

Preheat the oven to 350°F. Grease and lightly flour a 9-inch round pan.

In a large bowl, whisk the egg, egg yolks, and sugar together until they form a ribbon when you lift up the whisk. In a medium-size bowl, whisk the flours, baking soda, and spices together until well blended.

Add the sour cream, marmalade, and butter to the egg mixture, and stir until thoroughly blended. Add the flour mixture and stir to combine the ingredients. Do not overbeat. Pour the batter into the prepared pan and bake until a cake tester or toothpick inserted into the center of the cake comes out clean, about 30 minutes. Cool completely before removing the cake from the pan.

174   a SWEDISH kitchen

Sponge Cake

Sockerkaka

One 9-inch cake; 8 servings

This simple yellow cake is particularly suited for layer cakes, such as *prins-esstårta* (see recipe, page 172) and *jordgubbstårta* (see recipe, page 176), because it absorbs the filling without becoming soggy. For a subtle citrus flavor, substitute the grated zest of one lemon for the vanilla extract. Sifting the flour gives the cake a lighter texture and a more even rise.

1½ cups sifted cake flour	½ cup milk
1½ teaspoons baking powder	1 teaspoon vanilla extract
3 eggs	¼ cup butter
1 cup sugar	

Preheat the oven to 350°F. Cut a circle of parchment paper to fit the inside of a 9-inch springform pan and press into the bottom of the pan. Grease and lightly flour the bottom (over the parchment paper) and sides of the cake pan.

Mix the flour and baking powder together and set aside. In a large bowl, whisk together the eggs and the sugar for several minutes, until foamy. Whisk the milk, vanilla extract, and butter into the egg mixture, until thoroughly mixed.

Stir the dry ingredients into the wet ingredients. Beat by hand with a wooden spoon for a couple of minutes, until the batter is smooth. Pour the batter into the prepared pan.

Bake until a cake tester inserted into the center of the cake comes out clean, about 30 minutes. Cool on a rack. Remove from the pan and gently peel off the parchment paper.

CAKES, TARTS, COOKIES, and CANDIES

175

Strawberry Torte

If the strawberries available are not as sweet or juicy as you would like, try adding a teaspoon of sugar to half of the sliced berries and leave them in the refrigerator for a few hours to extract the juice, then drain.

1 Sponge Cake (see recipe, page 175)
1 cup heavy cream

1 pint fresh or frozen (thawed and drained) strawberries
⅓ cup strawberry jam

With a bread knife, slice the sponge cake into two horizontal layers. Whip the cream until soft peaks form; do not overwhip, or the cream will turn into butter. Hull and slice the strawberries. Mix half of the sliced berries with half of the whipped cream.

Lift off the top cake layer. Spread the bottom layer with the jam and then the whipped cream and strawberry mixture. Replace the top layer and cover with the remaining whipped cream.
Decorate the top with the rest of the strawberries.

Cover lightly with plastic wrap and refrigerate until ready to serve.

Apple Crisp

Äppelkaka

4 to 6 servings

Every Swedish cook has his or her own recipe for this national dessert, which is nearly always served with vanilla sauce (see recipe, page 202). This dish tends to fall into one of three categories: a batter cake topped with apples; a pudding made with layers of applesauce alternating with bread crumbs, similar to the colonial American apple betty; and sliced apples with a crumbly topping, sometimes called *smulpaj*. When I'm hungry for Swedish *äppelkaka*, I think of this last version, soft apples bubbling under a buttery, slightly crisp oatmeal topping. I add my own American touch by including maple syrup.

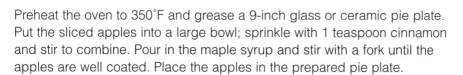

5 to 6 medium apples, sliced (about 5 cups)	2 tablespoons brown sugar
2 teaspoons cinnamon	1 cup old-fashioned oats
2 tablespoons maple syrup	2 to 3 tablespoons butter, softened

Preheat the oven to 350°F and grease a 9-inch glass or ceramic pie plate. Put the sliced apples into a large bowl; sprinkle with 1 teaspoon cinnamon and stir to combine. Pour in the maple syrup and stir with a fork until the apples are well coated. Place the apples in the prepared pie plate.

To make the crumb topping, stir together the sugar, oats, and remaining teaspoon of cinnamon in a medium-size bowl. Using your fingertips, rub the softened butter into the sugar and oat mixture until well combined and crumbly. Evenly sprinkle this mixture over the sliced apples.

Bake until the crumb topping begins to turn golden brown and the apples soften, about 30 to 40 minutes. Serve warm or cold.

CAKES, TARTS, COOKIES, and CANDIES

Swedish Cheesecake

Ostkaka

Although literally "cheese cake," *ostkaka* might be more accurately translated as "curd cake," since this dessert has a light, dry crumbly texture rather than the heavy smoothness of American cheesecake.

Ostkaka is a specialty of Småland, the southern Swedish province immortalized in the Lasse Hallström movie, *My Life as a Dog*. As late as the 1950s, the residents of small villages such as Kosta, Boda, and Orrefors in the region's "Glass Kingdom," would gather at the glassworks in the evenings, to hear the tales of traveling vagabonds over a simple meal of salted herring and potatoes baked in the cooling oven.

In recent years, the area's tourist associations have revived this tradition for summer tourists. I visited two such events, one at the famous Orrefors, the other at the smaller Bergdala glassworks.

Catered by two different companies, the Orrefors event was more polished, the Bergdala one more home-grown. Each featured a singer–guitar player who led us through a medley of Swedish drinking songs. Each offered its own blend of spiced aquavit. Each featured the same main dish that gave the event its name: *hyttsill*, or glassworks herring, salted herring and sliced onions in individual paper packets baked in the glassworks' cooling ovens at 250 degrees Centigrade (482 degrees Fahrenheit). Also baked in this same oven were potatoes, *isterband* (a Småland sausage), and, for dessert, *ostkaka*, or Swedish cheesecake, which we ate topped with whipped cream and jam.

2 eggs
3 tablespoons sugar
1 tablespoon plus 2 teaspoons all-
   purpose flour
½ cup milk
¼ cup half-and-half or heavy
   cream

1 cup part-skim ricotta cheese
¼ cup blanched almonds, finely
   chopped
Lingonberry jam (optional)
Whipped cream (optional)

Preheat the oven to 350°F. Grease an ovenproof glass or ceramic 9 x 12-inch baking dish.

Whisk together the eggs and sugar. Stir in the flour, milk, half-and-half, ricotta cheese, and almonds. Pour the batter into the prepared pan.

Bake on the middle rack of the oven until a toothpick or cake tester inserted into the center of the cake comes out clean and the top turns golden, approximately 40 minutes. Serve at room temperature with a dollop of jam and whipped cream.

Swedish Cheesecake with Pineapple

Ostkaka med Ananas   *8 servings*

A modern variation on the traditional cheesecake, this recipe reflects the Swedes' love of travel and interest in the new and exotic.

6 eggs
1 (15-ounce) container part-skim
  ricotta cheese
½ cup sugar
3 tablespoons cornstarch

2 teaspoons vanilla extract
1 (8-ounce) can pineapple chunks,
  drained

Preheat the oven to 350°F. Grease a 9 x 5-inch loaf pan or a 10-inch pie plate.

Lightly whisk the eggs, then add the ricotta, sugar, cornstarch, and vanilla extract and beat until smooth. Stir in the pineapple. Pour the batter into the prepared pan.

Bake on the middle rack of the oven until a toothpick or cake tester inserted into the center of the cake comes out clean, the sides of the cake are pulling away from the sides of the pan, and the top is just beginning to turn golden, approximately 80 minutes for a loaf pan; about 40 minutes for a pie plate. Cool before serving.

Almond Tarts

Mazariner

About 10 tarts

This pastry is said to have been named after Jules Mazarin, a French states-men of Italian descent, or perhaps the name comes from an early French word, *mazarine*, a type of deep plate with the same characteristic oval shape as the pastry. In Sweden, potatoes were added to "stretch" the expensive, imported almonds; the potatoes also produced a moister filling than ground almonds alone. Although the Swedish version is usually topped with a slick of white icing, I think these are sweet enough as is.

SHELL:
1 recipe Short-Crust Pie Shell
   dough (see recipe, page 193)

FILLING:
⅓ cup blanched almonds
   (about 1⅓ ounces)
6 tablespoons butter, softened
¾ cup sugar
2 eggs

½ cup mashed potato (about 1
   medium potato), preferably
   Yukon Gold, cold
⅓ cup all-purpose flour
1½ teaspoons baking powder

ICING (optional):
½ cup plus 1 tablespoon
   confectioners' sugar
2 tablespoons boiling water

Preheat the oven to 350°F. Grease and flour a 12-muffin tin. Press the chilled short-crust pie dough into the cups, creating a thin shell.

TO PREPARE THE FILLING: In a food processor, grind the almonds; set aside. In a large bowl, cream the butter and the sugar together. Beat in one egg at a time, then add the mashed potato and the ground almonds. In a separate smaller bowl, whisk the flour and baking powder together, then add them to the batter. Spoon the batter into the pie dough–lined muffin tins until about three-quarters full.

Bake in the middle of the oven until a cake tester inserted in the middle comes out clean and the tops are just beginning to turn golden, about 20 minutes. Remove the pan from the oven and let the tarts cool in the pan. Meanwhile, PREPARE THE ICING by whisking together the sugar and boiling water. When cool, remove the tarts from the pan and top with a thin layer of icing

CAKES, TARTS, COOKIES, and CANDIES

181

Cranberry Pie

Tranbärpaj

One 9½-inch pie; 6 to 8 servings

Swedes love berry pies, many of which are made without a top crust. Since I like to preserve some of the cranberries' tart character, I use the smaller quantity of sugar given below, but you may prefer a sweeter pie. This recipe can also be made with other berries, such as blueberries or blackberries, and the smaller quantity of sugar.

If you are using an eight-inch pie shell, reduce the berries to two and a half cups, the sugar to between a third and a half cup, the cornstarch to two teaspoons, and the spices to a half teaspoon each.

1 Short-Crust Pie Shell
  (see page 193)
4 cups cranberries, fresh or frozen
  (no need to thaw)
⅔ to ¾ cup sugar, depending on
  desired sweetness

1 tablespoon cornstarch
1 teaspoon ground cinnamon
1 teaspoon ground dried orange
  peel

Preheat the oven to 375°F. Rinse and dry the cranberries. In a bowl, mix the sugar, cornstarch, cinnamon, and orange peel together. Add the cranberries and stir so that the berries are thoroughly coated. Let sit 5 to 10 minutes.

Pour the coated cranberries into the piecrust shell and place on the middle rack of the oven. Bake until the berries are soft and the crust is golden brown, about 30 minutes. If the edges of the crust brown too quickly, cover them with aluminum foil or a pie shield. Cool the baked pie on a rack.

Serve warm or cold, alone or with vanilla ice cream or vanilla sauce (see recipe, page 202).

Meringue Tart

Marängtårta   *6 servings*

This meringue tart, filled with vanilla ice cream or frozen lingonberry parfait and garnished with fresh raspberries or red currants, makes a simple and elegant dessert.

4 egg whites   1 tablespoon cornstarch
¾ cup sugar   1 teaspoon vanilla extract
½ teaspoon cream of tartar

Preheat the oven to 350°F. Grease a baking sheet or line it with parchment paper.

Whip the egg whites until they begin to form stiff peaks. Add half of the sugar and all of the cream of tartar. Continue whipping. Stir the cornstarch into the remaining sugar and add to the egg whites. Add the vanilla extract. Continue whipping until the egg whites are very stiff.

Pile the whipped egg whites onto the center of the baking sheet, shaping the meringue into a circle about 8-inches in diameter with a depression in the center. Bake at 350° for 6 or 7 minutes, then turn the oven down to 225°F and continue baking for another 1½ hours, until the top of the meringue is beginning to turn golden and a toothpick or cake tester inserted into the meringue comes out clean.

Let cool on the baking sheet. To serve, fill the center depression with ice cream and berries.

Red Currant Meringue Pie

Rödvinbärsmarängpaj

For those who don't have access to a red currant bush, this recipe stretches a small quantity of berries into a full-scale dessert. In case you don't have quite enough currants, you can substitute blueberries, but decrease the sugar proportionately. This recipe can also be made with other berries and less sugar.

1 Short-Crust Pie Shell (see recipe, page 193), fitted to a 9¹/₂-inch pie plate
2 egg whites
²/₃ cup sugar
2 cups red currants, stems removed

Preheat the oven to 350°F. Line the pie shell with aluminum foil and add pie weights or dried beans and prebake the shell for about 10 minutes. Remove the pie shell from the oven and cool.

Whip the egg whites until foamy; add the sugar and continue whipping until stiff peaks form. Fold in the red currants and spoon the mixture into the cooled pie shell. Return the pie to the center of the oven and bake until the top begins to turn golden brown, about 30 minutes more. Remove from the oven and cool before serving.

Almond Shells

Mandelmusslor   *About 20 tarts*

I first tasted these cookies, filled with whipped cream and topped with cloudberry or lingonberry preserves, on Christmas Eve at the home of my husband-to-be's grandmother. Although Ingrid gave me her recipe, I eventually developed my own, which works better with American ingredients. You will need small tart tins—I prefer the oval ones with scalloped edges—which can be purchased at cookware stores.

½ cup almonds, sliced thinly
   (about 2 ounces)
⅓ cup plus 1 tablespoon sugar
12 tablespoons butter, softened

1 egg yolk
1½ cups all-purpose flour

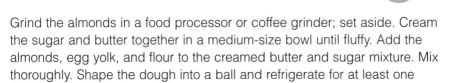

Grind the almonds in a food processor or coffee grinder; set aside. Cream the sugar and butter together in a medium-size bowl until fluffy. Add the almonds, egg yolk, and flour to the creamed butter and sugar mixture. Mix thoroughly. Shape the dough into a ball and refrigerate for at least one hour.

Preheat the oven to 325°F. Generously butter and lightly flour small, fluted tart tins. Break off pieces of the dough and line the greased baking tins with the dough, gently depressing the center with a floured thumb. Don't use too much dough as it will rise slightly while baking. Place the tins on a cookie sheet and bake for about 10 minutes, until light brown.

Cool the tarts in the tins on a rack. Turn the cooled tins upside down over a plate and gently tap the bottom with a butter knife to unmold. Serve alone or with whipped cream and jam.

Dream Cookies

Drömmar

About 4 dozen cookies

These delicate cookies get their tender texture from *hjorthornssalt* (hartshorn)—ammonium bicarbonate, also known as baker's ammonium—which was commonly used in the days before double-acting baking powder and was originally made from deer antlers. Today, it is artificially constituted and can be found in the U.S. at specialty grocers, including Greek markets as well as Scandinavian import stores.

Because this ingredient has strong fumes, be careful not to hold it too close to your nose. I'll never forget the time when I was cleaning out my spice cabinet and made the mistake of taking a deep whiff of this stuff. Yeow! The burning sensation reminded me of why this leavener is an ingredient in smelling salts. Fortunately, all of the fumes vanish in the oven, leaving behind only a tingly lightness. In a pinch, you can substitute an equal amount of baking powder, but the texture and taste will not be the same.

To ensure a light texture, I suggest that, when measuring the flour, you spoon it into the measuring cup, then level it with a knife.

7 tablespoons butter, cut into pieces
1¼ cups sugar
⅓ cup plus 1 tablespoon vegetable oil (mild olive oil works well)
1 teaspoon vanilla extract
1 teaspoon ammonium bicarbonate
¼ cup all-purpose flour
1⅔ cups cake flour

Cream the butter and sugar, preferably with an electric mixer. Slowly pour the oil into the mixture and continue beating. Stir in the vanilla extract.

In a separate bowl, mix together the ammonium bicarbonate and one tablespoon of the all-purpose flour, rubbing through a sifter or a fine-mesh strainer to ensure that no lumps remain. Sift this together with the remaining all-purpose and cake flours. Add the sifted flour and leavening mixture to the butter and sugar mixture, one half at a time, and continue beating until the ingredients are thoroughly incorporated. Wrap the dough in plastic and refrigerate for 30 minutes.

186   a SWEDISH kitchen

Preheat the oven to 300°F. Grease a cookie sheet or line it with parchment paper.

Form the dough into two rolls, each about a foot long, and cut into ½-inch pieces. Using the palms of your hands, shape each piece into a slightly flattened circle about the size of a teaspoon. Bake the cookies until they are just beginning to turn golden on the bottom, about 20 to 30 minutes. Cool on the baking sheet for a few minutes, then remove the cookies to a rack to continue cooling.

Gingersnaps

Pepparkakor

Start these cookies a day ahead as the dough needs to chill for eight hours or overnight.

The Swedish word *pepparkakor* literally translates to mean "pepper cakes." The first *pepparkakor* were honey cakes, flavored with pepper and other spices such as cloves, cardamom, cinnamon, and anise, and were imported from German monasteries beginning in the 1300s. Over time, the pepper was eliminated from most but not all Swedish *pepparkakor* recipes, and the honey was replaced by beet sugar syrup. Today, Swedes buy gingersnaps year-round from bakeries and grocery stores. But for many families, baking *pepparkakor* at home, using cookie cutters shaped like Christmas goats, pigs, angels, hearts, stars, men, and women, remains an essential part of the Christmas festivities.

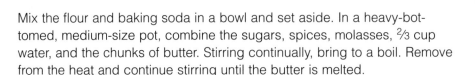

4½ cups all-purpose flour
2 teaspoons baking soda
¼ cup white sugar
¾ cup brown sugar
4½ teaspoons cinnamon

4½ teaspoons ginger
½ teaspoon cloves
½ cup molasses
13 tablespoons butter,
   cut into pieces

Mix the flour and baking soda in a bowl and set aside. In a heavy-bottomed, medium-size pot, combine the sugars, spices, molasses, ⅔ cup water, and the chunks of butter. Stirring continually, bring to a boil. Remove from the heat and continue stirring until the butter is melted.

Pour the hot liquid into a large metal bowl and stir in the flour mixture. Shape the dough into a loaf, wrap in plastic wrap, then foil, and chill overnight.

If you don't intend to bake all of the dough at once, cut off only as much as you need from the loaf, then rewrap it in plastic and foil and return it to the refrigerator. You may have to let the dough sit at room temperature for 30 minutes or more, until it warms up enough to roll out.

Preheat the oven to 375°F. Lightly grease a sheet pan. Roll out the dough on a lightly floured surface with a lightly floured rolling pin. The thinner you roll the dough, the crisper the cookies will be. Cut into shapes and place on the baking sheet.

Bake about 10 minutes, or until the cookies are lightly browned. Remove the baking sheet from the oven and transfer the cookies to a wire rack. They will crisp as they cool. When completely cool, the cookies can be stored in airtight plastic bags or metal tins, and will keep several weeks.

Oatmeal Lace Cookies

Havreflarn

About 2 dozen cookies

This recipe comes from Marta Malmborg, my father-in-law Arne's maternal cousin. I first met Marta during my second visit to Sweden. Arne, Carl, and I spent New Year's Eve, 1978 with Marta and her family at their vacation home two hours north of Stockholm. Like many older Swedish summer cottages, the house lacked both indoor plumbing and heating. Although it was the coldest New Year's Eve in sixty years, what I remember most is the warmth of the company.

Many years passed before our next meeting, but I felt that same warmth when Marta invited us to her elegant apartment in downtown Västerås for a summer lunch. She baked these cookies specially for our children.

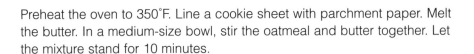

5 tablespoons butter	1 teaspoon baking powder
1 cup old-fashioned oats	½ cup sugar
1 tablespoon flour	1 egg

Preheat the oven to 350°F. Line a cookie sheet with parchment paper. Melt the butter. In a medium-size bowl, stir the oatmeal and butter together. Let the mixture stand for 10 minutes.

In a small bowl, blend the flour and baking powder together. In another, larger bowl, whisk the sugar and egg together until foamy. Add the oatmeal mixture and the flour mixture to the sugar and eggs, and stir just until blended; the dough will be quite liquid.

Drop the batter onto the cookie sheet by the scant teaspoonful, leaving several inches between each cookie. The batter will spread in the oven so expect to fit only 8 or 9 cookies on a standard baking sheet.

Bake 6 to 8 minutes, until the edges are just beginning to turn golden. Lift the entire sheet of parchment paper onto the cooling rack; let the cookies cool completely before attempting to remove them or they will crumble. Keep the dough in the refrigerator, if baking in batches. The cookies will be crisp on the bottom and around the edges, becoming chewier as they cool. Store in a plastic bag.

Chocolate-Covered Raisin Marzipan

Fruktmarsipanrulle   *One 8-inch roll, about 16 servings*

For years, I've made this candy at Christmastime, but I only recently discovered baking raisins, ordinary raisins packaged with filtered water, which produce a moister candy, even without the cognac marinade.

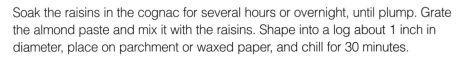

½ cup raisins, preferably baking raisins

2 tablespoons cognac (or 2 tablespoons warm water)

7 ounces almond paste, at room temperature

2 ounces dark chocolate

Soak the raisins in the cognac for several hours or overnight, until plump. Grate the almond paste and mix it with the raisins. Shape into a log about 1 inch in diameter, place on parchment or waxed paper, and chill for 30 minutes.

Melt the chocolate and brush over the log. Chill until the chocolate sets, then cover tightly with plastic wrap. Slice into ½-inch-thick pieces to serve.

Coconut Cocoa Balls

Kokosbollar

12 to 36 balls, depending on size

This is a perfect recipe for a child to help make, since there is no heat or chopping involved and the best way to mix the ingredients is with your hands. For best results, do not substitute regular oats unless you first run them through a food processor until finely ground.

1 tablespoon lukewarm coffee
  (or water)
6 tablespoons butter, softened
1 teaspoon vanilla extract
1¼ cups quick-cooking oats

2 tablespoons unsweetened cocoa
  powder
⅓ cup plus 2 tablespoons sugar
¼ cup shredded coconut, preferably unsweetened

Mix together all of the ingredients except the coconut. Shape into balls. Roll the balls in the coconut. Keep covered in the refrigerator.

Short-Crust Pie Shell

Mördeg Pajskal   *One 9½-inch pie shell or ten muffin-tin tart shells*

This shell is a perfect base for cranberry (see recipe, page 182) and other berry pies as well as for *mazariner*, filled almond tarts (see recipe, page 181). For savory pies, such as salmon quiche (see recipe, page 131) omit the sugar.

1¼ cups all-purpose flour   1 egg, lightly beaten
3 tablespoons sugar
½ cup butter, cold,
    sliced into ½-inch pieces

In a large bowl, mix the flour and the sugar together. Cut the butter into the flour mixture, using the paddle attachment of a heavy mixer or by hand with a pastry blender, two knives, or your fingertips, until the mixture resembles small peas.

Add the beaten egg and mix just enough to incorporate the egg into the dough. Gather the dough into a ball. Wrap in plastic and chill for 30 minutes before rolling out. Lay the dough into a greased pie plate or the cups of a muffin pan.

Cloudberry Frozen Dessert

Hjortronparfait

Instead of fresh cloudberries, which are difficult to find in most parts of the U.S., this light and easy dessert calls for the more readily available cloudberry jam. Red currant, black currant, elderberry, gooseberry, or other exotic fruit preserves may be substituted. Since the egg whites are not cooked in this recipe, I suggest using pasteurized egg whites such as No Yolk or Second Nature. Be sure to check the label of the product you intend to use, to make sure that it can be whipped; while these two brands can be whipped to stiff peaks, that is *not* the case with Egg Beaters.

1¼ cups cloudberry preserves	2 tablespoons sugar
½ cup pasteurized egg whites	

Push the preserves through a strainer into a small pot; discard the pulp and seeds. Bring the strained preserves and ¾ cup water to a boil over medium heat. Pour the hot liquid into a medium-size metal bowl set into a larger metal bowl half filled with ice cubes. Stir until cool. Place the bowl with the cooled liquid in the freezer until half frozen, about 1 to 1½ hours.

In a separate bowl, beat the egg whites until frothy, add the sugar, and continue beating until the mixture forms stiff peaks. Fold the whipped egg whites into the partially frozen purée until completely incorporated with no visible white streaks.

Freeze until solid, about two hours, stirring the mixture once or twice. This parfait can be made ahead of time and stored in the freezer until serving time.

Frozen Lingonberry Parfait

Lingonparfait

About 3 cups; 4 to 6 servings

This is a version of the lingonberry parfait we had at the wedding dinner of our friends Peter and Ingeborg. The vodka lowers the freezing point and keeps the ice cream a little softer than it would be otherwise.

3 eggs
5 tablespoons sugar
¾ cup lingonberry jam

1 teaspoon lemon juice
1 tablespoon vodka (optional)
1 cup heavy cream

Fill a large metal bowl halfway with ice cubes.

In a double boiler over simmering water, whisk the eggs and sugar together, stirring constantly until the mixture begins to thicken. Do not let the mixture become too hot or the eggs will curdle. Add the lingonberry jam and continue stirring over low heat until the mixture thickens again; the custard should coat the back of a spoon.

Pour the hot custard into a medium-size metal bowl set the into the larger metal bowl filled with the ice cubes. Stir until the custard cools. Mix in the vodka.

In another medium-size bowl, whip the cream until soft peaks begin to form. Gently fold the whipped cream into the lingonberry mixture. Freeze in an ice cream maker, following the manufacturer's instructions, or cover with plastic wrap and chill in the freezer for at least 6 hours. Can be stored in the freezer until serving time.

6   a SWEDISH kitchen

Queen's Parfait

Dröttningsparfait   *4 servings*

Raspberries and blueberries used in equal proportions are known as the queen's blend in Sweden, hence the name of this easy, low-fat dessert. You can drain the yogurt for as little as ten minutes, but the final product will be a little more watery.

1½ cups (12 ounces) plain, nonfat
   yogurt
Scant ⅓ cup sugar
1 cup unsweetened, frozen
   blueberries (do not thaw)

1 cup unsweetened, frozen
   raspberries (do not thaw)
1½ teaspoons lemon juice

Spoon the yogurt into a coffee filter basket with a paper liner and allow the excess liquid to drain for at least 10 minutes or, preferably, overnight.

A few minutes before serving, pour the sugar into the food processor and pulse briefly. Add the other ingredients and process until thoroughly mixed, stopping to scrape down the sides if needed. Spoon the parfait into individual wide-mouthed wine glasses or small cups, and serve immediately.

A sign advertising Sia brand ice cream. On the first warm spring day, ice cream stands all over Stockholm open for business as the city's population heads outdoors to enjoy the change in the weather.

ICE CREAMS, PUDDINGS, and SWEET SAUCES

Christmas Rice Pudding

Risgrynsgröt

Eaten warm or cold, this rice pudding goes particularly well with blueberry soup (see recipe, page 121); the slightly acidic but still sweet flavor of the blueberries cuts the richness of the pudding. Or follow the lead of Mathias Dahlgren, chef-owner of Michelin star–winner Bon Lloc, and serve a chilled, cinnamon-flavored rice pudding with cold rhubarb soup (see recipe, page 123) on a warm August night.

Pinch of salt
1½ cups arborio or other short-grained rice
1 cinnamon stick
2½ cups whole milk
½ cup heavy cream or half-and-half

1 teaspoon ground cinnamon (optional)
1 tablespoon brown or raw sugar

Bring 3 cups of water and the salt to a boil in a heavy-bottomed, medium saucepan over medium-high heat. Add the rice and the cinnamon stick. Stir once, turn the heat down to the lowest setting, and cover. Simmer 20 minutes without removing the cover.

When the rice has absorbed all of the water, stir in the milk and cream over low heat, adding more liquid if necessary to obtain a creamy consistency. Bring to a boil, stirring frequently. Remove from the heat.

Let the pudding rest for about an hour, covered, preferably on a thick wooden cutting board, so that the rice can absorb any remaining liquid. Remove the cinnamon stick. Pour into a serving bowl. Combine the cinnamon and brown sugar and sprinkle over the pudding in a cross-hatch pattern on top. Serve warm or cold.

Saffron Rice Pudding

Saffranspannkaka   *8 servings*

Found in nearly every restaurant and café on the island of Gotland, *saffranspannkaka* has a pronounced saffron taste. Be sure to buy saffron threads, rather than ground saffron. Sometimes the latter is not actually saffron at all but a cheaper substitute, such as safflower or turmeric. In Sweden, this dish is served with *salmbär*, or blue raspberry jam; in the States, blackberry jam is the closest substitute.

½ teaspoon salt
1 tablespoon butter
⅔ cup arborio rice
2 cups milk
1 teaspoon saffron threads
    (one .25-gram vial)
1 teaspoon sugar
2 cups half-and-half

¼ cup honey
3 eggs
2 tablespoons finely chopped
    blanched almonds (optional)
Blackberry jam (optional)
Whipped cream (optional)

Bring 1¼ cups water to a boil with the salt and butter, then add the rice and bring to a boil again. Cover and let the rice cook slowly on low heat for about 10 minutes.

Add the milk and cover again. Simmer on the lowest setting; do not lift the lid at all for at least the first 15 minutes. Cook until the rice is soft, 30 to 40 minutes. There may still be a lot of liquid. (The rice can be refrigerated and stored for several hours at this point.)

Preheat the oven to 350°F. Grind the saffron with the sugar in a mortar and pestle. Pour the rice and any milk not yet absorbed into a large bowl. Stir the saffron mixture, the half-and-half, and the honey into the cooked rice. With a whisk, beat in the three eggs, one at a time. Add the chopped almonds. Mix thoroughly. The batter will be quite thin.

Grease a 9 x 12-inch baking pan. Pour the batter into the pan and bake until a knife inserted in the center comes out clean, about 30 to 45 minutes. Cool on a rack and cut into squares. Serve warm or cold with blackberry jam and/or whipped cream.

Rhubarb Pudding

Rabarberkräm

My sister-in-law Kerstin introduced me to rhubarb and to *rabarberkräm*. From her large kitchen garden, Kerstin harvested a few stalks of rhubarb, chopped them, and stewed the fruit with sugar and water until the fibrous stems broke down, then thickened the purée with potato starch. After supper, she served the chilled rhubarb pudding with a pitcher of cold milk, for a light dessert. Here, I've substituted cornstarch for the more difficult-to-find potato starch.

1 pound rhubarb stalks (about 4 cups chopped)	2 tablespoons cornstarch
1 to 1¼ cups sugar plus 2 teaspoons	¼ cup cold water
	½ teaspoon vanilla extract

Trim the ends and peel the rhubarb stalks, then cut crosswise into slices; set aside. Bring 1½ cups of water to a boil in a medium saucepan, add the sugar, then the rhubarb, and cook on medium heat for about 10 minutes, stirring occasionally, until the rhubarb breaks down.

Meanwhile, dissolve the cornstarch in the cold water and stir into the cooked rhubarb. Stirring constantly, bring the rhubarb to a boil again and cook for about 1 minute, until the pudding begins to thicken. Remove from heat and stir in the vanilla extract.

Pour into a serving dish and sprinkle the surface lightly with the 2 teaspoons of sugar, to prevent a skin from forming. The rhubarb pudding will continue to thicken as it cools. Serve lukewarm or cold, alone or with a splash of milk or cream.

Vanilla Pastry Cream

Vaniljkräm

One of the key ingredients in *prinsesstårta*, princess cake (see recipe, page 172), this stirred custard can be made a day ahead and stored in the refrigerator. Or serve a dollop of vanilla cream with a slice of *appelkaka*, apple cake (see recipe, page 180).

¹/₃ cup whipping cream
¹/₃ cup whole milk
2 tablespoons cornstarch
2 tablespoons sugar

Pinch of salt
2 egg yolks
1 teaspoon vanilla extract

Fill a large metal bowl with ice cubes. In a small pan, blend the cream, milk, cornstarch, sugar, and salt, adding the egg yolks last. Cook over low heat, stirring constantly with a whisk, until the custard thickens. Do not allow the custard to boil, as it may curdle. Remove the pan from the heat and stir in the vanilla extract. Immediately place the pan in the bowl of ice cubes. Continue whisking; the custard will continue to thicken as it cools. Chill in the refrigerator until ready to use.

.

Vanilla Sauce

Gammaldagsvaniljsås

About 1 cup

Similar to the French crème anglaise, this stirred custard sauce is the classic Swedish dessert sauce. Traditionally paired with apple crisp (see recipe, page 180), vanilla sauce works well with a variety of other desserts including blueberry pie or spice cake (see recipe, page 174).

For the deepest vanilla flavor, this recipe calls not only for a whole vanilla bean but also for vanilla sugar. To make your own vanilla sugar, slice open a vanilla bean and store it in a glass or ceramic jar of sugar for a couple of weeks. If necessary, one teaspoon of pure vanilla extract and three tablespoons granulated sugar can be substituted for the vanilla sugar.

1 whole vanilla bean	1 egg, lightly beaten
1 cup milk	3 tablespoons vanilla sugar
2 teaspoons cornstarch	

Slice open the vanilla bean and scrape the seeds into a small pan with ¾ cup of the milk. Add the bean pod. Bring the milk to a boil over low heat. Remove from the heat and let the bean steep in the milk for about 15 minutes. Strain the milk, discarding the bean and seeds.

Fill a large metal bowl halfway with ice cubes. In a small bowl, dissolve the cornstarch in the remaining ¼ cup of cold milk. In a small pan over medium low heat, whisk together the vanilla milk, the cornstarch dissolved in milk, the egg, and the vanilla sugar. (If vanilla sugar is not available, add 3 tablespoons sugar at this point, then add the vanilla extract after the custard has thickened.) Continue whisking constantly on low heat until the custard begins to thicken. Do not let the custard boil, or it will curdle.

Remove the pan from the heat and immediately place it in the bowl of ice cubes. Continue whisking; the custard will continue to thicken as it cools. Chill in the refrigerator until ready to serve.

Blueberry Cordial

Blåbärslikör

For centuries, Swedes have flavored aquavit with fruit or herbs. In this recipe, I have diluted the vodka with an equal amount of water to keep the alcohol from overpowering the berries' delicate taste and aroma. You can substitute raspberries or blackberries (omitting the cinnamon) for the blueberries.

1 cup whole, fresh blueberries,
  preferably organic
¾ cup vodka

½ cup sugar
1 (3-inch) cinnamon stick (optional)

Put the berries into a clean, clear glass bottle. Pour ¾ cup water, the vodka, and the sugar over the berries. Close the bottle with a cork and gently shake a couple of times. If the sugar settles to the bottom, stir with a straw or skewer.

Store in cool, dark place, shaking now and then, for about two months. Strain off the berries and cinnamon stick and funnel the liqueur back into the bottle. The cordial will keep at least a year.

Reproduction glassware for sale in the market during Visby's annual Medieval Week.

BEVERAGES

Raspberry Drink Concentrate

Hallonsaft

About 4 cups syrup

For best results, you really do need a cloth jelly bag strainer. I tried making the recipe with a nylon bag that I bought in a wine-making supply house but found that even the finest mesh let too much of the pulp through. If this is your only option, pour the unsweetened juice through the strainer once or twice again after the overnight straining, to remove any remaining pulp. Otherwise, when the sugar is added, the syrup may resemble jelly that hasn't quite set.

8 cups raspberries
About 3 cups sugar

Rinse and drain the raspberries. Put the berries in a heavy-bottomed pot, and mash with a potato masher. Stir in 2 cups of water. Bring to a boil on medium-high heat and continue cooking for 15 minutes.

Place a jelly bag strainer into a large ceramic, glass, or stainless steel bowl or pan and pour the syrup through the strainer. Let the liquid drain through the jelly bag strainer overnight. Resist the temptation to speed up the process by pressing down on the raspberry mash, but rather allow gravity to do the work.

The next day, measure the amount of juice. For every 4 cups of juice, you will need approximately 3 cups of sugar. Measure the sugar and set it aside. Pour the unsweetened juice back in the pot and bring to a boil over low heat. Stir in the sugar. Bring to a boil again and cook for 10 minutes over low heat, skimming the surface as necessary to remove any foam or cloudiness. Do not overcook or the syrup may become too thick and jellylike.

Using a funnel, pour the syrup into a glass bottle, cork, and store in the refrigerator. The syrup will keep for a few weeks.

To dilute, add the syrup to cold water and stir. I like 1 to 2 tablespoons of syrup per 8-ounce glass, but you may prefer more or less.

Rhubarb Drink Concentrate

Rabarbersaft   *2½ cups; about 40 servings*

This pale pink, slightly tart syrup captures the flavor of rhubarb, which I always associate with early summer. Choose tender, firm red stalks. You will also need either a jelly bag strainer or a fine strainer lined with cheesecloth.

1½ pounds rhubarb stalks, ends   1½ cups sugar
   trimmed

Cut the rhubarb into ½-inch slices; do not peel. In a medium saucepan, bring 2 cups of water and the rhubarb to a boil over medium heat. Cook for 5 to 10 minutes, until the rhubarb softens.

Using a potato masher, press down on the fruit to release as much juice as possible. Strain the cooked rhubarb through a jelly bag or a strainer lined with cheesecloth. Discard the pulp. You should have about 2 cups of liquid; if you have more or less liquid, increase or decrease the amount of sugar accordingly. Bring the sugar and rhubarb juice to a boil and cook for a couple of minutes, until the sugar dissolves. Skim the surface to remove any cloudiness. Remove from heat and cool slightly.

Using a funnel, pour the syrup into a glass bottle, cork, and store in the refrigerator. The rhubarb syrup will keep a few weeks. To serve, pour 1 tablespoon of syrup into a glass and add ¾ cup water; adjust to taste by adding either more syrup or water.

Mulled Wine for a Crowd

Glögg för en fest   *About 1 quart; 8 to 12 servings*

If you're serving mulled wine for a larger group, this recipe is an easy one to multiply. Serve with gingersnaps, alone, or topped with blue cheese.

1 bottle (750 milliliters) red wine, such as Beaujolais
1 cup Madeira wine
1 or 2 cinnamon sticks
6 whole cloves
1 tablespoon white cardamom pods, cracked
1 tablespoon dried orange peel
⅓ cup light or dark brown sugar
24 to 36 raisins (optional)
12 to 24 blanched almonds (optional)

Place the wine, spices, and sugar in a stainless-steel pot and slowly heat, but do not boil. The mulled wine can be strained and served immediately but, for a stronger flavor, let the spices steep in the wine for several hours. Strain and gently reheat.

When ready to serve, drop several raisins and a couple almonds in the bottom of each cup, as a traditional garnish.

Mulled Wine for Two

Glögg för Två

There are dozens of recipes for *glögg*, some calling for Madeira or sherry, others for aquavit or brandy, still others for red wine or even white wine. Spices, too, vary, so if you are short of one, add a little more of the others. The name *glögg* is a shortened form of *glödgat*, mulled wine.

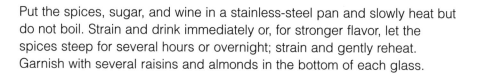

5 whole white cardamom pods, cracked
2 whole cloves
1 (1-inch) piece of cinnamon stick
1 teaspoon dried orange peel
2 tablespoons brown sugar

⅓ cup Madeira wine
1 cup good-quality red wine, such as Burgundy or Beaujolais
4 to 6 raisins (optional)
4 blanched almonds (optional)

BEVERAGES

Put the spices, sugar, and wine in a stainless-steel pan and slowly heat but do not boil. Strain and drink immediately or, for stronger flavor, let the spices steep for several hours or overnight; strain and gently reheat. Garnish with several raisins and almonds in the bottom of each glass.

Mail Order Sources

Anderson Butik
P.O. Box 151
Lindsborg, KS 67456
Tel: 1-800-782-4132
Fax: 1-785-227-3268
imports@andersonbutik.com
www.andersonbutik.com

Hemslöjd
P.O. Box 152
Lindsborg, KS 67456
Tel: 1-800-779-3344
Fax: 1-785-227-4234
order@hemslojd.com
www.hemslojd.com

Nordic House
3421 Telegraph Avenue
Oakland, CA 94609
Tel: 1-800-854-6435
Fax: 1-510-653-1936
pia@nordichouse.com
www.nordichouse.com

Polarica
P.O. Box 880204
San Francisco, CA 94188
Tel: 1-800-GAMEUSA
Fax: 1-415-647-6826
info@polarica.com
www.polarica.com

ScanSelect
6719 15th Avenue NW
Seattle, WA 98117
Tel: 1-206-784-7020
Fax: 1-206-783-6218
foods@scanselect.com
www.mindspring.com/~scanfoods

Sweden's Best
Tel/Fax: 1-877-864-8503
nyborgnelson@yahoo.com
www.swedensbest.com

Sweet Celebrations
P.O. Box 39426
Edina, MN 55439
Tel: 1-800-328-6722
Fax: 1-952-943-1688
sweetcel@maidofscandinavia.com
www.sweetc.com

Wikstrom's Gourmet Foods, Inc.
5247 N. Clark Street
Chicago, IL 60640
Tel: 1-773-275-6100
Fax: 1-773-275-7234
sales@wikstromsgourmet.com
www.wikstromsgourmet.com

Glossary

aquavit: See *brännvin*.

åkerbär: arctic raspberry (Latin, *Rubus arcticus*).

älg: moose (Latin, *Alces alces*). The name of Sweden's largest land animal is often mistranslated into English as "elk," which actually refers to a smaller member of the deer family called *kronhjort* in Swedish or *Cervus elephanus* in Latin.

bakstuga: community baking hut with wall oven and tables for preparing bread dough.

brännvin: distilled alcohol made from grain or potatoes and often flavored with berries or such herbs as caraway, dill, or fennel. Also called aquavit.

bulle (plural: *bullar*): yeast bun, usually sweet.

filmjölk: a sour milk thicker than American buttermilk and less acidic than yogurt.

fjäll: tree-covered highland wilderness landscape of northern Scandinavia.

fläder: elderflower (Latin, *Sambucus nigra*). Both the flowers and the berries of this plant are used in making jam and beverages.

fäbod: cabin-*cum*-dairy. A summer farmstead where the *valkullor*, or milkmaids, made butter and cheese for the coming winter.

glögg: mulled wine served at Christmastime.

gräddtårta: sponge cake topped with whipped cream and, often, decorated with berries or other fruit. *Jordgubbstårta*, strawberry torte, is a variation.

hjortron: cloudberry or bake apple (Latin, *Rubus chamaemorus*). Found mostly in northern Sweden, this berry with large drupelets looks similar to an orange raspberry, and is so fragile that it must be picked by hand.

jordgubbe (plural: *jordgubbar*): strawberry.

jordgubbstårta (plural, *jordgubbstårtor*): strawberry torte; most often a sponge cake layered and covered with whipped cream and sliced berries.

jul: Christmas. In Sweden, this is officially a three-day holiday spanning December 24 to 26.

julbord: Christmas smorgasbord.

julkorv: Christmas potato and barley sausage.

jultomte: the Swedish Santa Claus who delivers presents on Christmas Eve.

Jämtland: province in northwestern Sweden, bordering Norway.

kanelbulle: cinnamon bun. Usually smaller and less fluffy than its American counterpart, this bun is topped not with icing but with pearl sugar.

kaviar: cod roe cured in a sugar and salt solution for four to six months, then mixed with oil and spices; often packaged in a tube.

knäckebröd: crispbread that was traditionally hung from the rafters to keep through the winter.

konditori (plural: *konditorier*): bakery-café.

korvkiosk: hotdog stand. Found in virtually every Swedish town, these kiosks serve a variety of hotdogs as well as hamburgers, fries, and sodas.

kroppkakor: potato dumplings filled with salt pork and onion, boiled and served with butter and black pepper.

krukmakeri: ceramics studio.

kräftor: crayfish, also known in English as crawdads.

kräftskiva (plural: *kräftskivor*): party dedicated to eating crayfish, usually held in mid-August.

kräm: fruit stewed with sugar.

lingon: lingonberry (Latin, *Vaccinium vitis-idaea*). A small, tart red berry found throughout Sweden. Similar to a cranberry but with a softer skin, the lingonberry can be eaten raw or cooked into pies, cakes, breads, and jam.

Linneaus, Carolus: (1707–78) Also known as Carl von Linné, this botanist originated the modern taxonomic classification system for flora and fauna.

Lucia Day: holiday celebrated on December 13, primarily by processions of children dressed as Saint Lucia and her attendants.

lutfisk: A traditional Christmas Eve dish made from cod or stockfish, which is first dried; then soaked in an alkaline solution of water, slaked lime (calcium hydroxide), and birch ashes (which contain potassium hydroxide or lye); then soaked in changes of fresh water. This weeks-long process breaks down all of the proteins in the fish, resulting in a gelatinous texture.

löjrom: fine-grained orange roe of the *siklöja* (Latin, *Coregonus albula*), a freshwater European fish commonly called vendace or sometimes whitefish in English.

majstång: maypole. A large wooden cross with two rings, decorated with birch leaves and flowers, the maypole is erected in nearly every village and town on Midsummer's Eve, the Friday closest to June 24.

matjessill: special type of pickled herring that is particularly popular at Midsummer.

mazarin: small oval pastry with a buttery crust and almond-paste filling, topped with white icing.

messmör: caramelized whey butter.

Midsummer: summer solstice. Although officially a three-day holiday, most of the celebrating occurs on Midsummer's Eve, the Friday closest to June 24.

mjukpepparkaka: ginger cake often served at Christmas.

Nobel, Alfred: (1833–96) The Swedish inventor, most famously of dynamite, who established the Nobel Prizes, which are given out each year on the anniversary of his death, December 10, now known as Nobel Day.

pepparkaka (plural: *pepparkakor*): thin, crisp ginger cookie.

prinsesstårta (plural: *prinsesstårtor*): princess cake. A sponge cake layered with vanilla pastry cream and whipped cream, covered in a thin, often pale green layer of marzipan.

prinskorv: small, mild precooked pork sausages often served on holidays.

pärlsocker: pearl sugar; hard white sugar crystals that don't melt in the oven.

ren: reindeer (Latin, *Rangifer tarandus*). Related to the caribou, these semitame animals migrate across the far north with their herders, the indigenous Saami, who use virtually every part of the animal for food, clothing, shelter, and tools.

risgrynsgröt: rice porridge made with milk, served on Christmas Eve.

rån: wafer cookie baked in a *rånjärn*, a special engraved iron.

Saami: the indigenous Scandinavians, also called Lapps. The Saami are a nomadic people who have followed the reindeer herds across northern Norway, Sweden, Finland, and Russia for thousands of years.

Sankt, Birgitta: (1303–73) noblewoman and mother of eight who founded an order of nuns. She is Sweden's only canonized saint.

salmbär: blue raspberries (Latin, *Rubus caesius*). Indigenous to the Baltic island of Gotland but also found elsewhere in Sweden, these berries are usually commercially available only as a purplish jam that tastes more like blackberry than raspberry or blueberry.

semla (plural: *semlor*): yeast bun flavored with cardamom and filled with almond paste and whipped cream, often served in a bowl of hot milk. Traditionally *semlor* were eaten only on Tuesdays during Lent, the forty-day period before Easter.

sill: herring.

sirap: sugar syrup made from beets and used primarily to provide sweetness and color to rye breads. There are two kinds: *ljussirap*, light syrup, and *mörksirap*, dark syrup.

Skansen: The world's first open-air folk museum, this Stockholm attraction was built to preserve Sweden's preindustrial peasant culture.

smultron: wild strawberries (Latin, *Fragaria vesca*).

smultronställe: wild strawberry patch. Also means "a special place."

smörgåstårta: savory sandwich cake usually ordered from a bakery for parties and other special occasions.

spettekaka (plural: *spettekakor*): A specialty of the southernmost province of Skåne, this cake is baked on a rotating spit.

spettekaksgummor: women who specialized in baking *spettekakor*.

starboys: Part of the Lucia Day procession, these boys or young men wear long white robes and pointed white paper hats decorated with stars and carry a star-tipped wand.

strömming: Baltic herring. A smaller variety of herring found in the northern Baltic and the Bay of Bothnia.

tunnbröd: thin, flatbread. There are two types of these: a crispbread called *hardbröd* or *knäckebröd*, and a soft type similar to Armenian lavash.

vallkulor: milkmaids. These were usually unmarried or widowed farm women who led cows into the highland pastures for the summer.

vinbär: currants. The *röd vinbär*, red currant, (Latin, *Ribes rubrum*) is considerably sweeter than the *svart vinbär*, black currant (*Ribes nigrum*), from which the

French liqueur, cassis is made.

Västerbotten: province in northern Sweden. Also the name of an aged cheese similar to Parmesan.

vörtlimpa: Christmas rye bread made with *vört*, an infusion of malt used in beer brewing.

Warg, Cajsa: (1703–69) One of Sweden's earliest and most beloved cookbook authors. She is said to have coined the phrase "*Man tager vad man haver*" ("One takes what one has"), which epitomized her practical approach to cooking.

Bibliography

Andersson, Ingvar and Wiebull, Jörgen, *Swedish History in Brief*, 2nd revised edition, Stockholm: The Swedish Institute.

Andersson, Lars and Olsheden, Jan, *Hirkum Pirkum och Andra Brännvinskryddningar*, Orkelljunga: Bokförlaget Settern, 1996.

Arndt, Alice, *Seasoning Savvy: How to Cook with Herbs, Spices, and Other Flavorings*, Binghamton, NY: The Haworth Press, 1999.

Arnö-Berg, Inga, *Jul på Skansen*, Stockholm: Natur och Kultur, 1997.

Åberg, Alf, *Sveriges Historia i Fickformat*, Stockholm: LTs Förlag, 1985.

Åhman, Birgitta, e-mail message to author, February 16, 1999.

Åkerström, Jenny, *The Princesses Cookbook* (from the original Swedish *Prinsessornas Kokbok*), New York: Albert Bonnier, 1936 (translated and edited by Gudrun Carlson).

Backelin, Maria, *försäljningschef*, Stadshus Källaren, fax message to author, January 15, 1999.

Bartal, David, *The Empire: The Rise of the House of Wallenberg*, Stockholm: Dagens Industri, 1996.

Beach, Hugh, *A Year in Lapland: Guest of the Reindeer Herders*, Washington and London: Smithsonian Institution Press, 1993.

Beach, Hugh, "Perceptions of Risk, Dilemmas of Policy: Nuclear Fallout in Swedish Lapland," from *Social Science Medicine*, vol. 30, no. 6, pp. 729–38, 1990.

Bennetoft, Catarina, "Där Sverige Börjar Kakfesten," *Allt om Mat*, no. 11, 1999.

Berg, Gösta, "Det Svenska Smörgåsbordet," *Mat: Nordiska Museets och Skansens Årsbok*, Fataburen 1989, Stockholm: Nordiska Museet Förlag, 1989.

Bergenström, Anna and Bergenström, Fanny, *Vinterns Goda Ting*, Stockholm: Bonnier Alba AB, 1995.

Black, Maggie, *Den Medeltida Kokbok*, Stockholm: Alfabeta Bokförlag AB, 1993 (originally, *The Medieval Cookbook*, London: British Museum Press, 1992).

Blomquist, Torsten and Vögeli, Werner, *A Gastronomic Tour of the Scandinavian Arctic*, Stockholm: Timbro, 1987.

Bodin, Hélène, *Nobelfesten: Moderna Recept från Klassika Menyer*, Stockholm: Mixoft AB, 1998.

Braker, Flo, "Waffles," Internet article, Sally's Place.com, 1998.

Bringéus, Nils Arvid, *Matkultur i Skåne*, Stockholm: LTs Förlag, 1981.

Britton, Claes, "Sápmi—Europe's Last Wilderness," from *Stockholm New*, no. 6.

Brorson, Kerstin, *Sing the Cows Home: The Remarkable Herdswomen of Sweden*, Seattle: Welcome Press, 1985.

Brown, Dale, *The Cooking of Scandinavia*, New York: Time-Life Books, 1968.

Carr, Josephine, *Ö Hallen*, Stockholm: Informationsförlaget, 1997.

Chandonnet, Ann, *The Complete Fruit Cookbook*, San Francisco: 101 Productions, 1972.

Conradson, Birgitta och Conradson, Cia, *Änglar och Andra Pepparkakor*, Stockholm: Nordiska Museets Förlag, 1992.

Dahlgren, Mathias, *Kokbok*, Stockholm: Prisma Bokförlag, 2003.

Danielson, Anita, "Exklusiv bärodling i Norr," *ICA Kuriren*.

Danielson, Anita, *Ta Vara på Frukt & Bär: Allt Du Kan Göra av Sommarens Skörd*, Västerås: ICA Bokförlag, 1997.

DeMoor, Janny, e-mail message to author, March 22, 1999.

DeMoor, Janny, "The Wafer and Its Roots," *Proceedings of the Oxford Symposium on Food and Cookery, 1993 (Look and Feel: Studies in Texture, Appearance and Incidental Characteristics of Food)*, Totnes, Devon, UK: Prospect Books, 1994.

Du Chaillu, Paul B., *The Land of the Midnight Sun: Summer and Winter Journeys through Sweden, Norway, Lapland and Northern Finland*, vol. 1, New York: Harper & Brothers, 1882.

Dumas, Alexandre, *Dumas on Food: Selections from Le Grand Dictionnaire de Cuisine*, trans. Alan and Jane Davidson, Oxford: Oxford University Press, 1978.

Edenheim, Ralph; Larsson, Lars-Erik; and Westberg, Christina, *Skansen*, Stockholm: Informationsgruppet Hans Christiansen AB, 1991.

Editors, *The Organic Gardener's Complete Guide to Vegetables and Fruits*, New York: Rodale Press, 1982.

Elgklou, Lars, *Helan & Halvan: En Bok om Nordiskt Brännvin*, Stockholm: Natur och Kultur, 1995.

Elgklou, Lars, *Kaffebok*, Höganäs: Förlags AB Wiken, 1993.

Eriksson, Leif, ed., *IKEA's Real Swedish Food Book*, Delft, Netherlands: Inter IKEA Systems B.V., 2000.

Fackskolan för Huslig Ekonomi i Uppsala, *Hemmets Kokbok*, Stockholm: P. A. Norstedt & Söner Förlag, 1926.

Fant, Michaël and Lundgren, Roger, *Vikingars Gästabud*, Malmö: Egmont Richter AB, 1998.

Field, Carol, "Celebrating Italy," program notes, Culinary Historians of Boston newsletter, volume, XXII, number 2, November, 2001.

Fjellström, Phebe, *Samernas Samhälle i Tradition och Nutid*, Stockholm: P. A. Norstedt & Söner Förlag, 1985.

Fredlund, Jane, *Stora Boken om Livet Förr: Bilder och Minnen från Svenska Folkets Liv i Vardag och Fest*, Västerås: ICA-förlaget AB, 1981.

Frykman, Jonas and Löfgren, Orvar, ed, *Svenska Vanor och Ovanor*, Stockholm: Natur och Kultur, 1991.

Garnert, Jan and Wretman, Tore, *Svensk Allmogekost*, Stockholm: Carlssons Bokförlag, 1989; reprint of 1919 original by Keyland, Nils.

Garrett, Blanche Pownall, *A Taste of the Wild*, Toronto: James Lorimer & Co., 1975.

Gastronomisk Akademien, *Gastronomisk Kalender 1994*, Höganäs: Förlags AB Wiken, 1994.

Genrup, Kurt, *Mat och Måltidsseder på Gotland*, Visby: Guteböcker AB, 1992.

Grimlund, Inger and Halling, Björn, *Det Goda Sverige*, Stockholm: Page One Publishing AB, 1998.

Görman Gruppen, *Kräftans Lov: En Kulinarisk och Historisk Resa i Kräftans Värld*, Stockholm: Rabén Prisma, 1994.

Hansson, Ann-Marie, e-mail message to author, January 12, 1999.

Herbst, Sharon Tyler, *The New Food Lover's Companion*, New York: Barron's, 1995.

Hibler, Janie, *Wild About Game: 150 Recipes for Cooking Farm-Raised and Wild Game: from Alligator and Antelope to Venison and Wild Turkey*, New York: Broadway Books, 1998.

Holmblad, Lars, e-mail message to author, December 18, 1998.

Huey, John, "Crayfish Madness Sweeps Sweden," from the *Wall Street Journal*, September 5, 1984.

Hällberg, Stefan, *Matspråket: En Lättsmält Bok om Ord och Uttryck i Matens Värld*, Uppsala: Hällberg Publishing, 1996.

Höök, Lena Kättström, *God Jul!*, Stockholm: Nordiska Museets Förlag, 1995.

ICA Provkök, *Julens Kokbok*, Västerås: ICA-förlaget AB, 1996.

ICA Prokök, *Mat: En Faktabok om Matvarorna i Din Butik*, Västerås: ICA-förlaget AB, 1989.

ICA Provkök, *Sju Sorters Kakor*, Västerås: ICA-förlaget AB, 1985.

Israelsson, Isse, *Mat på Forntida Vis: Idé och Receptsamling*, Malmö: Stadsantikvariska avdelningen, Malmö museer, 1990.

Jonsson-Ekegårdh, Edith and Hallman-Haggren, Britta, *Stora Kokboken; Hushållets Uppslagsbok i Alla Matfrågor*, Göteborg: Esseltes Göteborgsindustrier AB, 1946.

Jönsson, Thomas, *Glasriket Runt*, Stockholm: Utbildningsförlaget Brevskolan, 1999.

KFs Provkök, *Vår Kokbok*, Stockholm: Rabén & Sjögren, 1989.

Kindblom, Maria and Kindblom, Johan, *Kondisboken: Klassika Svenska Kaféer och Konditorier*, Stockholm: Albert Bonniers Förlag, 1996.

Kramer, Jane, *Unsettling Europe*, New York: Vintage Books, 1981.

Kummer, Corby, "Currant Affairs," *The Atlantic Monthly*, December 1996.

Kvant, Christel, "Vinbär åt Barnen," *Femina*, August 1993.

Källberg, Sture, *Off the Middle Way: Report from a Swedish Village*, New York: Random House, 1972.

Källman, Stefan, *Vilda Växter Som Mat och Medicin*, Västerås: ICA Bokförlag, 1997.

Lagerqvist, Lars O. and Åberg, Nils, *Mat och Dryck i Forntid och Medeltid: Om den Ärbara Vällusten*, Stockholm: Vincent Förlag and Statens Historiska Museum, 1994.

Latour, Almar, "Even at the Dinner for the Nobel Prizes, They Steal the Spoons," *The Wall Street Journal*, December 7, 2000.

Lilla Sällskåpet, *Svensk Matglädje från Fyra Århundraden*, Stockholm: Lilla Sällskåpet, 1988.

Liman, Ingemar, *Högtid och Fest Året Runt*, Stockholm: Svensk Turistföreningen, 1995.

Liman, Ingemar, *Traditional Festivities in Sweden*, Stockholm: The Swedish Institute.

Lindvall, Gunvor and Törnblom, Marie, *Bär Vilda och Odlade*, Helsingborg: LTs Förlag, 1984.

Lingegård, Ingeborg, *Gotländska Mattraditioner: Seder och Bruk i Helg och Vardag*, Stockholm: LTs Förlag, 1978.

Liungman, Waldemar, *Luciafirandet och Dess Ursprung: Något om En Svensk-Tysk Folktro*, Lund: Carl Bloms Boktryckeri, 1944.

Lundgren, Birger and Schnitzer, Werner, *Tårtor, Bakelser & Desserter*, Partille: Warne Förlag AB, 1997.

Lyle, Katie Letcher, *The Wild Berry Book: Romance, Recipes and Remedies*, Minocqua, Wisconsin:: North Word Press Inc., 1994.

Lönnqvist, Bo, *En Studie i Lyxens Kulturella Formspråk*, Esbo, Finland: Schildts, 1997.

Maxén, Maria & Lindroth, Helena Waldetoft, *Glad Påsk!*, Stockholm: Nordiska Museets Förlag, 1995.

Montagné, Prosper, *Larousse Gastronomique*, New York: Crown, 1961.

Mulk, Inga-Maria, *Sámi Cultural Heritage in the Laponian World Heritage Area*; Jokkmokk: Ájtte, Swedish Mountain and Sámi Museum, 1997.

Nash, E. Gee, *The Hansa*, New York: Barnes & Noble Books, 1995.

Nilson, Siv and Key L., *Skördepraktikan*, Stockholm: Natur och Kultur, 1992.

Nordiska Museet, ed. *Mat: Nordiska Museets och Skansens Årsbok*, Fataburen 1989, Stockholm: Nordiska Museet Förlag, 1989.

Nydahl, Eva, *Medeltida Jul Mat och Dryck: Julseder och Traditioner Kring Advent*, Visby: Fornsalens Konferensarrangemang, 1991.

Olsson, Brita and Hemmingsson, Elisabeth Ekstrand, ed., *Julboken*, Västerås: ICA-förlaget AB, 1986.

Östman, Elisabeth, *Iduns Kokbok*, Stockholm: Aktiebolaget Ljus, 1911.

Petersen, Bengt, *Svensk Mat: Recept på Husmanskost Samlade och Förklarade*, Göteborg: Wezäta Förlag, 1980.

Pihl, Ove, *Hovmästar'n Får Jag Beställa: Klassika Krogar och Klassika Recept från Ett Svunnet Stockholm*, Stockholm: Page One Publishing AB, 1996.

Rask, Lars, *Samerna: Ett Gränslöst Folk*, Stockholm: Utbildningsförlaget Brevskolan, 1991.

Rensund, Lars, *Renen i Mitten*, Luleå: Norrbottens Museum, 1984.

Ramano, Rose, "In Praise of Santa Lucia: Lady of Light," *The SageWoman Cauldron: A Collection of Our First Five Years*, ed. Lunea Weatherstone, Point Arena, California: SageWoman Magazine, 1993.

Root, Waverley, Food: *An Authoritative and Visual History and Dictionary of the Foods of the World*, New York: Konecky & Konecky, 1980.

Salomonsson, Anders, "Till Bords," from *I Glädje och Sorg, Nordiska Museets och Skansens Årsbok*, Fataburen, 1995, Stockholm: Nordiska Museet Förlag, 1995.

Samuelsson, Marcus, with Robbins, Maria, *Aquavit and the New Scandinavian Cuisine*, New York: Houghton Mifflin Company, 2003.

Samuelsson, Marcus, interview with the author, February, 2002.

Sandberg, Marianne, *Våra Svenska Matrötter: Mat & Kultur i Skansenmiljö*, Stockholm: Svenska Dagbladets Förlags AB, 1990.

Schildt, Margareta, ed., *Trevlig Helg*, Stockholm: Bonniers Juniorförlag, 1984.

Schneider, Elizabeth, *Uncommon Fruits & Vegetables: A Commonsense Guide*, New York: William Morrow and Company, Inc., 1986.

Schotte-Lindsten, Ann-Sofi, "Rån och Våfflor," *Gastronomisk Kalender*, Stockholm: Gastronomiska Akademien, 1964.

Schön, Ebbe, *Folktrons År: Gammalt Skrock Kring Årsfester, Märkesdagar och Fruktbarhet*, Stockholm: Prisma Magnum, 1989.

Schön, Ebbe, ed., *I Glädje och Sorg: Nordiska Museets och Skansens Årsbok*, Fataburen, 1995, Stockholm: Nordiska Museet Förlag, 1995.

Schön, Ebbe, *Julen Förr i Tiden*, Stockholm: Natur och Kultur, 1980.

Scully, Terence, *The Art of Cookery in the Middle Ages*, Woodbridge, United Kingdom: The Boydell Press, 1995.

Skagegård, Lars-Åke, *Stadshuskällaren: Stockholms Stadshus*, Uppsala: Uppsala Publishing House AB, 1997.

Skagegård, Lars-Åke, *The Remarkable Story of Alfred Nobel and the Nobel Prize*, Uppsala: Konsultförlaget AB, 1994.

Spiller, Gene and Hubbard, Rowena, *Nutrition Secrets of the Ancients: Foods and Recipes for Optimum Health in the New Millennium*, Rocklin, California: Prima Publishing, 1996.

Stålbom, Göran, *Vintersolståndet: Om Jul, Jord och Äring i Folklig Tradition*, Stockholm: Prisma Bokförlag, 1994.

Svenska Kocklandslaget and Wretman, Tore, *Det Svenska Matåret*, Höganäs: Bokförlaget Bra Böcker, 1992.

Swahn, Jan-Öjvind, *Den Svenska Julboken*, Höganäs: Förlags AB Wiken, 1993.

Swahn, Jan-Öjvind, *Fil, Fläsk och Falukorv: Svenska Mattradtioner Genom Tiderna*, Lund: Historiska Media, 2000.

Swahn, Jan-Öjvind, *Mathistorisk Uppslagsbok: Mat och Dryck från Antikens Kök till Absolut Vodka*, Bromma: Ordalaget Bokförlag AB, 1999.

Swahn, Jan-Öjvind, *Maypoles, Crayfish and Lucia: Swedish Holidays and Traditions*, Stockholm: Svenska Institutet, 1997.

Swanberg, Lena Katarinam, *Till Bords Under 100 År: Recept från Tio Decennier*, Stockholm: Albert Bonniers Förlag, 1999.

Telegin, Marie Louise, ed., *Östermalms Hallen: Mattemplet Under Ett Sekel*, Stockholm: Consiluum Förlag AB/Informationsförlaget, 1988.

Tham, Ulla, *Den Nya Landskapsmaten*, Stockholm: Tidens Förlag, 1992.

Tham, Ulla, *Fjällkrögarnas Bästa Recept*, Stockholm: Tidens Förlag, 1989, 1995.

Tham, Elizabeth, *Husmoderns Köksalmanack 1966*, Stockholm: Åhlén & Åkerlunds Förlags AB, 1966.

Tham, Ulla, *Matpraktikan: Jämtland och Härjedalen*, Stockholm: Tidens Förlag, 1993.

Thorne, John and Thorne, Matt Lewis, *Serious Pig: An American Cook in Search of His Roots*, New York: North Point Press, Farrar, Strauss & Giroux, 1996.

Thyselius, Thorborg Tryggvesdotter, *Fäbodvall*, Stockholm: Rabén & Sjögren, 1963.

Toussaint-Samat, Maguelonne, *A History of Food*, trans. Anthea Bell, Oxford: Blackwell Publishers.

Töringe, Sanna and Åberg, Anette, *Sannas Likörbok: Smaker från Ortagård, Vildmark och Trädgårdsland*, Stockholm: Rabén Prisma, 1994.

Törngren, Kerstin, *Smörgåsbord: A Swedish Classic*, Stockholm: Svenska Institutet, 1996.

Uddman, Susanne, ed., *Brud & Bröllopsboken*, Stockholm: Ungförlaget, 1992.

Warg, Cajsa, *Cajsa Wargs Kokbok*, Stockholm: Klassikerförlaget, 1993 (reprint of 1755 original *Hjelpreda i Hushållningen för Unga Fruentimber*).

Wickman, Mats, *Stadshuset i Stockholm*, Stockholm: Sellin & Partner Förlag AB, 1993.

Widell, Carl-Bertil, *En Sockerbagare Här Bor i Staden*, Malmö: Edition Erikson, 1995.

Wiklund, Eva; Malmfors, Gunnar and Åhman, Birgitta, "Fakta om renkött," www.algonet.se.

Wikström, Kersti, e-mail message to author, Feb. 2, 1999.

Wägner, Ria, *Läsebok för Bröd Älskare*, Stockholm: LTs Förlag, 1988.

Index

NOTE: Page numbers in **bold** distinguish recipes from other discussions of particular foods.

INDEX

INDEX

233

Other Scandinavian Cookbooks from Hippocrene Books...

THE BEST OF FINNISH COOKING
Taimi Previdi

The Finnish-born author has compiled a delicious array of authentic Finnish recipes, adapted for the American kitchen. In addition to traditional recipes ranging from soups to desserts, menus for special holidays, such as Easter, Midsummer and Christmas are included.

242 PAGES • 5$\frac{1}{2}$ x 8$\frac{1}{2}$ • 0-7818-0493-0 • $12.95PB • (601)

THE BEST OF SCANDINAVIAN COOKING
Shirley Sarvis & Barbara Scott O'Neil

This exciting collection of 100 recipes includes such tempting dishes as Norwegian Blueberry Omelet, Danish Butter Cake, Swedish Pancakes with Ligonberries, as well as a section entitled "A Smørrebrød Sampling," devoted to those open faced Danish sandwiches.

142 PAGES • 5$\frac{1}{2}$ x 8$\frac{1}{4}$ • 0-7818-0547-3 • $9.95PB • (643)

THE BEST OF SMORGASBORD COOKING
Gerda Simonson

150 PAGES • 5$\frac{1}{2}$ x 8$\frac{1}{2}$ • 0-7818-0407-8 • $14.95PB • (207)

GOOD FOOD FROM SWEDEN
Inga Norberg

This classic of Swedish cookery includes recipes for fish and meat dishes, vegetables, breads and sweets. A large section is dedicated to the savory tidbits included in the traditional Swedish smorgasbord.

186 PAGES • 5$\frac{1}{2}$ x 8$\frac{1}{2}$ • 0-7818-0486-8 • $10.95PB • (544)

ICELANDIC FOOD & COOKERY
Nanna Rögnvaldardóttir

More than just 165 recipes for classic Icelandic dishes, this cookbook explores the evolution of Icelandic cuisine over the last two centuries. Sample such delicacies as Iceland Moss Soup, Grilled Rosemary-Flavored Char, Braised Wild Goose with Fruit Stuffing, and Bilberry Ice Cream.
158 PAGES • 5½ x 8½ • 0-7818-0878-2 • $24.95HC • (12)

TASTES AND TALES OF NORWAY
Siri Lisi Doub

This cookbook offers more than 100 recipes, as well as historical accounts, local customs, and excerpts from Norwegian folk songs, traditional blessings, poetry, and mythology.
280 PAGES • 6 x 9 • 0-7818-0877-4 • $24.95 • (341)

All prices are subject to change without prior notice. To order Hippocrene Books, contact your local bookstore, call (718) 454-2366, visit www.hippocrenebooks.com, or write to: **HIPPOCRENE BOOKS**, 171 Madison Avenue, New York, NY 10016. Please enclose check or money order adding $5.00 shipping (UPS) for the first book and $.50 for each additional title.